LINCOLN'S
COMMANDO

LINCOLN'S COMMANDO

The Biography of

COMMANDER W. B. CUSHING, U.S.N.

By

RALPH J. ROSKE *and* CHARLES VAN DOREN

HARPER & BROTHERS

New York

LINCOLN'S COMMANDO

CONTENTS

~~~~~~~~~~~~~~~~~~~~~~~~~~

ILLUSTRATIONS

ACKNOWLEDGMENTS

THE authors wish to express their gratitude to the following persons, without whose freely given assistance, both severally and collectively, the book could never have been written: the late Professor J. G. Randall, of the University of Illinois; Mrs. C. E. Krebs, of the reference department of the Buffalo Public Library, who made several valuable suggestions as to where Cushing material might be found; Dr. Josephine L. Harper, manuscript librarian of the State Historical Society of Wisconsin, who aided in obtaining microfilms of the Cushing manuscripts in the possession of the society; Miss Elizabeth L. Crocker, Historian, Town of Pomfret, Fredonia, New York; Miss Geraldine Bernstein; Mr. William P. Macaskill, of the St. Mary's College Library; the staffs of the Library of the University of California at Berkeley, the National Archives, the Manuscripts Division of the Library of Congress, the Columbia University Library, the Naval Academy Museum, the West Point Library, the Humboldt State College Library, and the New York Public Library; and Dr. John Blemer of Danville, California, who aided Mr. Roske in a discussion of the symptoms leading to Cushing's death. The authors wish also to express a special debt to Rosemary Roske and Dorothy Van Doren for services far beyond the call of duty.

A word as to the use of the title *Lincoln's Commando*. The word "commando" was not in use during the time of the Civil War, and yet no term seemed so aptly to describe Cushing

ix

and his small-boat raids deep in enemy territory. The authors
hope that the reader will pardon this relatively innocent
anachronism.

RALPH J. ROSKE
CHARLES VAN DOREN

PROLOGUE

"THANK you for your agreeable congratulations on the last hit off Wilmington," wrote Acting Rear Admiral Samuel Phillips Lee to Gustavus Vasa Fox, Assistant Secretary of the Navy, from the flagship *Minnesota*, off Hampton Roads, on February 20, 1864, ". . . which makes the number of blockade runners captured or destroyed since July 12th, twenty-six, and since the blockade was strengthened last fall the number is 23, twenty-three steamers lost to the trade.

"Can the history of blockade beat this?"

It was a singular record considering the difficulties the blockade had had to start with. Declaring it on April 19, 1861 from South Carolina to Texas and extending it April 27 to Virginia and North Carolina, the United States began with a force of only forty-two vessels of all types including obsolete ships, most of which were scattered over the seven seas. It was many months before the most distant vessels were informed of the outbreak of the war and recalled to home waters. This meager force, which included only one efficient warship, the *Brooklyn*, was to blockade 3,549 statute miles of Southern coast as well as 189 inlets. What was more, a "paper blockade" unenforced by squadrons of ships would not be honored by the European nations which traded with the Confederacy. The *Trent* affair, when an American warship, the *San Jacinto*, stopped an English vessel and removed two Confederate commissioners bound for England and France as diplomatic agents, almost provided the occasion for British intervention to break the blockade. In the end war was avoided by some adroit managing by President Lincoln and the blockade was allowed to go its way.

To overcome the lack of ships the Federal government began a huge building program—203 vessels had been built or were being built when the war ended—but for immediate needs bought every kind of craft that would float and carry a gun— liners, fishing boats, yachts, ferryboats, tugs. In August the first of a group of "ninety-day gunboats," built in that time from green wood, arrived off Southern ports; before the end of the year the first deliveries of "double-enders," with paddle wheels that could work in either direction so they would not have to turn around in rivers, were received. From the force of 42 vessels in March, 1861, the Union navy grew to 264 ships in December, 1861, 427 a year later, 588 a year after that, and 671 in December, 1864. The ships purchased, refitted, and built were said to include every type of vessel "from Captain Noah to Captain Cook." Many of the new ships were unsea- worthy, shoddily built, hard to manage even in the calm waters they were intended for, but the sheer numbers of them, and the wonderful skill with which they were used, were hampering Southern commerce by the end of 1861.

In the fall of that year luxuries were already scarce in the Confederacy. Newspapers were cut to half size. Between the Confederate cotton embargo and the blockade, most of the cotton could not be shipped abroad; thus, with little going out, little could come in. "Butter was made of persimmon seeds; tea of berry leaves; coffee of a variety of parched seeds; envelopes and writing-paper of scraps of wallpaper; shoes of wood and canvas." There was no bacon, starch, soap, or glue, and the earth beneath old smokehouses was tried out for its salt content, because salt was about as scarce as diamonds. There were no matches, and housewives resorted, clumsily, to flint and steel. There were no postage stamps, which was extremely inconvenient. The currency was so badly printed on such poor paper that counterfeits were often better than the original, and were sometimes preferred. There was a terrible shortage of iron, so that it was almost impossible even to find scrap for guns and railroad rails. In the end hardly anything was more important than cotton—and the things cotton would buy.

The blockade was by no means child's play, and for those who were engaged in it it was work of the most serious character. "Their task was the more arduous," wrote the Comte de Paris, "on account of its extreme monotony. To the watches and fatigues of every kind which the duties of the blockade involved, there were added difficulties of another sort. It was necessary to instruct the newly recruited crews, to train officers who had been taken from the merchant navy, and to ascertain, under the worst possible circumstances, the good and bad qualities of merchant vessels too quickly converted into men of war." The monotony was broken by the chasing and occasional capture of blockade runners. Profits almost beyond belief were made by the owners of these ships. The profits were not only in money—a successful blockade runner was entertained like a king in any port he managed to reach. And though the more important part of the cargo was always the food, guns, ammunition, and clothing that he carried, he usually brought with him what lace, perfume, and spices he could, for which he was paid fabulous prices.

The blockage runners had the odds in their favor on any particular voyage until late in the war. The best authorities believe the rate of capture was one in ten in 1861, one in eight in 1862, one in four in 1863, one in three in 1864, and in 1865, one in two. The number of vessels captured or destroyed by the Union was at least fifteen hundred. The value of blockade runners captured was about thirty-one million dollars. Their value ranged from the English steamer *Memphis*, which brought, with its cargo, over half a million dollars, to the *Alligator*, which was worth, as a prize, only fifty.

Still, many blockade runners did extremely well at it. The Robert E. Lee, under the command of Captain John Wilkinson, C.S.N., ran the blockade no less than twenty-one times, and carried out from six to seven thousand bales of cotton worth two millions in gold, at the same time bringing back cargoes of equal value. She was finally caught, however, trying to run in from Bermuda under another captain, and was captured off Cape Lookout Shoals by the *James Adger* and taken to Boston as a prize. Many of the captured blockade runners were added to the squadrons along the coast, the hare becoming the hound, and not a few of them, like the *Bat*, the *A. D. Vance*, and others, helped chase their sisters to death. Over three hundred ships piled their bones along the shore, and in the end every Southern harbor mouth was dotted with them.

On board the faster vessels which acted as scouts on the outer line of the blockading squadrons, the appearance of low-lying, black lines of smoke against the horizon late in the afternoon was the sure precursor of the dash of a runner, either to make port or to reach shoal waters along the beach—anyhow, to get through if possible. And since rewards were not only for the runners if they got through but also for the blockaders if they caught their prey, since they received prize money, often in large amounts, there were instances of chases lasting fixty-six hours or longer before the runner either escaped or was brought to with a shot across her bows. In 1863, one runner loaded with cotton to the gunwales brought as prize money to the captain of the Federal ship that captured her more than twenty thousand dollars, and even the cabin boys received large sums. Other ships in a certain radius or attached to the same station had a share in the prize money.

The Confederates tried various methods of breaking the blockade, the most dramatic of them being the C.S.S. *Hundley* (or *Hunley*). It was a completely submersible craft—a genuine submarine, as distinguished from another type the Confederates pioneered, the semi-submerged *Davids*. The "mechanical whale" or "peripatetic coffin," as its detractors called it, was propelled by seven men sitting in a row and working their feet against paddles; in its tail it carried a keg of powder and a detonator. On her first trial trip in Mobile Bay the mechanical whale got stuck in the mud and the seven men were suffocated, since no provision had been made for storing air. The vessel was raised and sent to Charleston, South Carolina, by rail. On the next trial the hatch combings were left open for air, the water dashed in, and another crew was drowned. Three times more all or most of her crew perished when the *Hundley* sank in experimental dives. Still seven other brave men were found to drive the peripatetic coffin down Charleston Harbor by night to blow up the U.S. sloop of war *Housatonic.* The powder exploded and the *Housatonic* sank to the bottom, but the *Hundley* was sucked down with her, the seven men not seen again. That was the end of submarines until the twentieth century.

The blockade would not be broken. In the spring of 1861 in a New York paper a cartoon appeared of General Winfield Scott, who had suggested the blockade in the first place, at least until the Union had a well-drilled, well-commanded army —a cartoon of old General Scott as a side-show snake charmer, with the caption, "Scott's Anaconda." The cartoon was not intended as a compliment, but the image was a good one, and the coils drew tighter and tighter as the war went on. Cape Hatteras on the North Carolina coast was taken in the first summer of the war; in November Port Royal and Beaufort in South Carolina fell. The next February Roanoke Island was taken, leaving the way open for the seizure of New Bern and other coastal North Carolina towns the next month. March, April, and May saw Fernandina, Apalachicola, and Pensacola, in Florida, captured. Almost simultaneously Fort Pulaski, at the mouth of the Savannah River, fell to the Union, as did Biloxi and Pass Christian on the Mississippi coast. The biggest blow of all that spring was the capture of the port of New Orleans. In the summer of 1862 Charleston passed under a siege which greatly reduced its effectiveness as a port, a siege which was not lifted until the city's fall as a mere incident of

Sherman's northward march. Galveston, Texas, was taken in August, 1862, only to be lost the next winter, but shortly thereafter the Mississippi was captured by the Union and the Texas ports became unimportant to the Confederacy. With every fort taken the South lost a seaport, a vital link with the outside world. The rebel doctors, snowed under by Union wounded at Fredericksburg, could not take care of them: "Tell your master Lincoln," they said, "to raise the blockade and we will tend to you. We have not enough medicaments for our own wounds."

The Prince de Joinville suggested that the task of the Union Administration in 1861 divided itself into three separate yet correlated problems. The first of them was to establish and maintain an effective blockade of the Southern coast; the second, to divide the Confederacy in two by seizing and holding the Mississippi River; the third, to defeat the Confederate armies in the field. Without making an assessment of the relative importance of the three tasks, it is certainly true that the third, and perhaps the second, have received more attention than the first. This is the story of one of the most celebrated of the young men who maintained the blockade.

I

Cape Fear River

~~~~~~~~~~~~~~~~~~~~~~~~~~~~~~~~~~~~~~~

ON THE 29th of February, 1864, the U.S.S. *Monticello*, Lieutenant William Barker Cushing, U.S.N., commanding, lay off the mouth of the Cape Fear River. Wilmington, North Carolina, is situated twenty-eight miles up the river, which has two outlets to the ocean, one to the eastward, New Inlet, the other to the southward, Western Bar Channel, at the river mouth. The outlets are not six miles apart in a straight line; but between the two lies Smith's Island, a long strip of sand and shoal, with the headland of Cape Fear projecting far out to the south. Continuing the line of the cape, the dangerous Frying Pan Shoals extend out into the ocean ten miles farther, making the distance between the two inlets little less than forty miles.

Each of the channels was protected by strong fortifications, and each required a separate blockading force. Smithville, a small town on the Cape Fear River about equidistant from the two inlets, was the point of departure of the blockade runners. Dropping down from Wilmington, they could wait for their opportunity and take the choice between the main channel and New Inlet, whichever seemed at the moment more favorable. Neither was difficult to navigate, though vessels entering from the south were occasionally caught on a round shoal in the channel called "the Lump." To the north of New Inlet, on Federal Point (called Confederate Point during the war), was Fort Fisher. Fort Caswell guarded the mouth of the river. The blockading squadrons were stationed in two semicircles, the extremities near the shore; if one of the Union ships ventured in too far it quickly learned about it. The Confederates had raised batteries of guns to different elevations and would fire a volley which blanketed a section of the water. It was better to stay out of range.

The blockade runners, sighting the land toward evening, would wait outside until it was dark and then, making a dash at full speed through the fleet, would be under the guns of the forts almost immediately, and safe from capture. Such a port, with such protection, was hard to close, and so it was at Wilmington that blockade running maintained itself longest and most actively, after it had nearly ceased elsewhere.

The *Monticello* had arrived off Wilmington on February 17, and Lieutenant Cushing, having waited ashore for several months for repairs on his ship, was anxious to get into action. On the 21st he anchored his ship in close, hoping to celebrate Washington's Birthday with a small-boat expedition into the river to cut out a prize, but the lookouts at Fort Caswell spied him and drove him off. Later that night he returned in his gig with about forty men in two other boats and got in past the silent guns of the fort and searched for a prize in the river, but saw no shipping. There was a battery on Smith's Island, however, and Cushing and his crew in the gig ran in close to it to investigate—capturing it would be sufficient celebration. He ran in a little too close and his oars grated on the rocks. The crew in the boat waited nervously for the Confederates to hail the gig and blast it out of the water, but the defenders had grown overconfident and were not keeping a sharp lookout. Cushing decided a raid would be a waste of a golden opportunity, pulled quickly back to his ship, and reported to the senior officer that if he were given two hundred men he could seize Smith's Island and hold it until a garrison could be moved in by the army. The risks were great but the advantage to the blockading force would be greater still, since control of Smith's Island would prohibit the Western Bar Channel to Confederate ships. Captain Sands was not at all sure the plan would work and declined permission on the grounds that he could not take responsibility. Cushing fumed. He vowed that he would get the Confederate general in charge of the area for breakfast one morning.

The next night, toward dawn, Cushing set out again with his small boats and attempted to capture the battery on Oak Island, a small island north of Smith's Island, to show the captain that such expeditions were worth the risk. They were not lucky; they were seen by rebel pickets and had to retire. Captain Sands was not convinced.

On the 29th, at 8:40 P.M., Cushing set out once more, again, as at Oak Island, without permission, this time with the gig and one cutter and about twenty men including Acting Ensign J. E. Jones and Acting Master's Mate W. L. Howorth. They rowed with muffled oars between Fort Caswell and Bald Head, were not seen, and continued up the channel until they were north of Smithville, then turned and approached it from the direction of Wilmington so that if they were observed it would appear that they were Confederates. They neared the wharves of the town and then veered quickly out again when they saw on one of the docks a sentry sitting on a chair, his rifle between his knees, his head resting on one arm. They waited, hardly moving, but he was asleep and did not give the alarm. They crept slowly toward the shore, the only sounds the lapping of the water against the piles, the occasional barking of a dog somewhere in the town.

They beached the boats without being discovered and filed up the sloping shore until they met a bluff which ran down to the water, below which Cushing left twelve or fourteen of his men. Lights shone in the windows of the building directly in front of them—the hotel. Thirty yards away down the town's one street was a large building with suspicious-looking narrow windows—probably the fort. They would steer clear of it. They seemed to be in the very center of town. Their attack would have the advantage, at least, of surprise. The Confederate report of the night's doings later stated that Cushing must have been to Smithville before, possibly in the coast survey before the war, and thus knew how to get in and out of the surrounding waters without being seen.

Cushing and Howorth and four or five men started up the street, walking in single file at about ten-foot intervals, keeping to the sides of walls and away from lighted windows. Cushing, in the lead, drew back suddenly against the wall of a house and signaled to the column to stop. Ahead was a large dark building with a fire blazing near it, beside which two Negroes were huddled. The sailors waited ten minutes but there did not seem to be anyone about except the Negroes. Cushing drew his pistol and crept across the intervening space on his hands and knees, unseen by the Negroes since their eyes were blinded by the light of the fire. When he was three feet from them he stood up and pointed his pistol at them, whispering that they must be quiet. They were. They were both quite willing to be captured, it seemed, and gave Cushing all the information he desired. He had planned to capture General Hébert and take him out of town by means of a captured steamer, but it turned out there were no steamers then at anchor in the harbor. Cushing decided to go ahead anyway.

He went back to where his other men were waiting and planted them so as to guard the boats, then, with Howorth, Jones, a single seaman and one of the Negroes as a guide, proceeded down the street to the general's residence. It was the largest house in town, painted white and sporting a "southern veranda." Directly opposite it, the Negro said, about fifty feet away, were the barracks, in which a thousand Confederate soldiers slept peacefully, dreaming of Yankees being many miles away.

Cushing deployed his troops carefully, "surrounding" the house with his three followers. The Negro was allowed to rejoin his companion by the fire. Cushing himself crept up the steps of the porch and slid to the door. The windows were dark, but one was open, and the curtains blew in the wind.

The door was open, and Cushing entered softly and closed the door behind him.

He found himself in a large hall with a high ceiling and black splotches on the walls which were probably pictures. He stood by the door for a minute, the only sounds the ticking of a clock somewhere in the house and the beating of his heart. With his hand on his pistol butt he moved slowly away from the wall. A door was open; in the room beyond was a large table with six or eight chairs around it, on which a silver cruet stand gleamed in the faint light from a window—evidently the dining room. On his left were the stairs—he found them when his foot struck a step. He crept up them, thankful that the house was solidly built and no boards creaked. At the top he was in darkness—it must be a hall with no windows. He struck a match cautiously. The sound was thunderous in the silence, and the light leaped all about him. In front of him were several doors. After hesitating a moment he chose the middle one, opened it and was about to peer in, when he heard a loud noise from below and then Howorth calling, "Captain! Captain!" He raced down the stairs and pushed open a door which seemed to lead toward the sound. Striking another match he saw a tall man standing in a night gown with a night cap on his head, holding a chair above his head with the evident intention of striking the first enemy to enter the room. Cushing rushed toward him. "Dashing in at once I had him on his back in an instant with the muzzle of a revolver at his temple and my hand on his throat."

Cushing assumed that he had captured General Hébert, and lightheartedly struck another match and lit a candle. But he was chagrined to learn that the general was not in the building, having gone to Wilmington for the night. He usually spent Monday night in the house, so Cushing was particularly unfortunate to have missed him. As he was swallowing his disappointment Howorth rushed into the room and shouted that he had seen someone running away from the house toward the barracks, and that it would be best to leave, since the alarm would surely be given. The escaped officer, as it turned out, was the Adjutant General, W. D. Hardman. He had been sleeping close to a window and awoke at a noise and looked out the window to see, two or three inches from his face, the large butt of a heavy naval pistol carried by Howorth. He was duly astonished at the sight and threw down the window, catching his arm in the process and making the noise that Cushing had heard upstairs. Wrenching his arm free and injuring himself painfully, he succeeded in escaping from the house in his night-clothes, certain, as he said later, that a mutiny had broken out among the troops. When he discovered that this was not the case, the only other explanation was Yankee maurauders, and he gave the alarm.

Not in time to catch Cushing and his men, however. They pocketed all the loose papers lying about the room, got their prisoner, a Captain Kelly, chief engineer of the defenses of the port, into a pair of pants, and started for the boats. The alarm had been given by this time and the streets were full of running men—"like the old gent with the spectacles on his forehead," Cushing said, "looking everywhere but in the right place." Cushing and his three sailors and Captain Kelly walked sedately back the way they had come, picking up the Negroes, who were anxious to be liberated, on the way. Nobody paid any attention to them, though once a party of searchers almost knocked them down when they ran around a corner. Captain Kelly was as silent as a pistol buried in his side could make him. When they reached the rest of the men Cushing hurried them down the hill to the boats, which were shoved off before the first rifle shots began to splash in the water. The Negroes cowered in the bottom of the boat and the sailors pulled for all they were worth down the channel, oars no longer muffled. As they neared Fort Caswell they heard the long drum roll sending the Confederate artillerymen to their stations. The sailors pulled harder than ever and were through the narrow neck of the channel before a shot was fired. It was 3:25 in the morning when the cutter and gig reached the *Monticello*.

Lieutenant Cushing was a good host, though he had a laugh at his guest's expense. He gave Kelly dry socks and a glass of sherry, and saw that he was comfortably put up for the night. Kelly was awakened from what was not a very sound sleep at seven o'clock to be rowed to the commanding officer's ship for breakfast, as Cushing had promised a week before.

The papers turned out to be unimportant—they were mostly records of General Hébert's mess. But in the afternoon Cushing sent Ensign Jones to Fort Caswell under a flag of truce, ostensibly so that Captain Kelly might obtain clothes and money to make his stay in a Northern prison more comfortable. Jones was conducted to the office where the commander of the fort, who was also named Jones, awaited him. Their meeting began with an awkward silence. They looked at each other. Colonel Jones walked to the narrow window and stared out into the yard where some of his men were drilling. He started back toward the desk and then turned to the window again. Ensign Jones thought he detected the beginnings of a smile on the colonel's lips. Suddenly Colonel Jones wheeled about and addressed his enemy. "That was a damned splendid affair, sir!" he said. After this the two men chatted amiably for about half an hour, when they were joined by Adjutant General Hardman, his arm in a sling. He was not inclined to take the same sanguine attitude toward the night's business as Colonel Jones.

Before his departure Ensign Jones produced a letter from Cushing to General Hébert, which read:

My Dear General:
    I deeply regret that you were not at home when I called.
                                        Very respectfully,
                                            W. B. Cushing.

Hardman thought the letter "the essence of impudence," but Colonel Jones could not help grinning when he read it. He gave Ensign Jones copies of the Wilmington paper, which contained a story of the affair highly complimentary to Cushing. (There were accounts of it in many Northern newspapers, including Cushing's hometown Fredonia *Censor*.) Before taking his leave of Ensign Jones, Colonel Jones told the young officer that he would like to meet Cushing. When the gig had departed the colonel made hurried arrangements to strengthen the guard in the Cape Fear River and surrounding waters so that nothing like this might ever occur again.

Colonel Jones's meeting with Lieutenant Cushing was postponed by an event which occurred a week later. On March 6, at five in the morning, while the *Monticello* was steaming to Beaufort to replenish its supply of coal, a vessel was sighted about three quarters of a mile off the port bow, near Sheep Head Rock. Acting Ensign Joseph Hadfield, deck officer of the watch, supposed the vessel to be a blockade runner and changed his course. The ship replied correctly to his signals, thus proving itself to be part of the blockading fleet, and the *Monticello* turned to go back to its course. Hadfield seems to have thought the *Peterhoff*, a captured and converted blockade runner, was at anchor. It was not, and the two vessels met with the heavy prow of the *Monticello* striking the *Peterhoff* amidships, and the latter sank within minutes. Happily the entire crew of the *Peterhoff* was rescued.

A court of inquiry decided that Hadfield was entirely to blame. Cushing wrote later that the affair "was an unavoidable accident, arising from the strict rules of the blockade that required instantaneous signals in order to avoid being fired into or run down." But though the *Monticello* was not seriously damaged it was necessary to take her into Norfolk for repairs, and it was the beginning of April before Cushing was back with the blockading fleet.

His exploits in the Cape Fear River had not gone unnoticed by the Navy Department, and particularly by the Assistant Secretary of the Navy, Gustavus Fox. Admiral S. P. Lee, commanding the North Atlantic Blockading Squadron—its beat was from Wilmington north to Chesapeake Bay—received a cryptic letter from Fox saying that it was too bad that "Cushing's undaunted bravery and good luck cannot be put to a useful purpose in a manner to tell upon the enemy." (Writing of the expedition to Smithville, a naval historian said years later that "it was an enterprise hardly worth the risk, for the danger was great, and the capture of a dozen commanding officers at such posts as Smithville would not compensate for the loss of one Cushing.") The admiral replied asking for an explanation; he declared that he thought he had always favored Cushing's proposals as much as possible; at the very moment, he said, he was considering Cushing's plea that he be permitted to cruise outside the blockading area, on a "roving commission," in search of prizes. He was not certain, he had to admit, of Cushing's wild plan to take the fort on Bald Head by storm, although he considered it, using the official negative, "possible." Would the Assistant Secretary authorize such a project? "I have a good idea of, and good feeling for this youngster," he added. Fox replied characteristically: "What I meant about Cushing was that it was a pity that so much luck and dash had not brought fruits equal to the risk. You notice the Department never finds fault with these exploits. I believe they ought to be encouraged. To be sure, the people will say, when he is captured, 'Damn fool!' The Department will not."

As a result of the foregoing Cushing received his roving commission. He was ordered to cruise out beyond the line of blockaders with a view to catching any inbound runners who might hover until dusk around Cape Lookout Shoals before making a run for New Inlet. He was also to search for any vessels which might have slipped through the Union fleet bound from New Inlet to Bermuda. He was to calculate by dead reckoning, allowing for wind and tide, where a fast blockade runner would be in the morning if it managed to slip through during the night.

He did not have a great deal of luck in his new duty. He had never had much luck waiting for the enemy to come to him. Once he sighted a blockade runner but was unable to catch it when a main valve stem was found to be bent. Ten days later the English schooner *James Douglass* was found floating, abandoned and dismasted, six feet of water in the hold, with a cargo of rotting coconuts and bananas. Cushing had the cargo thrown overboard and towed the vessel into port, but it was hardly a great victory. A week later the ironclad *Raleigh* appeared off Wilmington, chased the blockaders away and allowed a blockade runner to steam through with impunity.

This was too much for Cushing. He at once made an agreement with a comrade-in-arms, Lieutenant Commander Daniel Braine, of the *Vicksburg:* they would proceed down the coast and if the *Raleigh* was still in evidence they would run her down in company and sink her. When they arrived off Wilmington the *Raleigh* had retired, and was nowhere to be seen.

"I feel very badly over the affair, sir," Cushing wrote to Admiral Lee about the *Raleigh*'s impudence, "and would have given my life freely to have had the power of showing my high regard for you and the honor of the service by engaging the enemy ships." If the *Raleigh* was unwilling to meet him, he went on, he would go into the harbor and seize the ram by boarding. He had been there before, he added. He enclosed complete plans, noting, however, that he still believed, despite his lack of results, the idea of having him rove outside the blockading fleet was a good one. Most of the runners were taking a more southerly route, and it was for that reason that he had overtaken none of them. The *Monticello* was a swift ship; "I trust," he ended, "that you will not cancel my permission to cruise outside after this ram business is settled."

Cushing lay off Wilmington for several days, but the *Raleigh* did not appear, whereupon he handed a letter to the senior officer present, Captain Sands, asking for permission to enter the harbor and take the ram by boarding as he had already suggested to Lee. Sands refused to give him the number of men Cushing thought necessary; Cushing begged and cajoled and promised not to come back alive if he failed. But Sands declined to take the responsibility.

Admiral Lee saved the day. His answer was tardy, though he claimed to have just received Cushing's communication, but he declared that he "heartily" approved of the plan and authorized Cushing "to apply to the senior officer" for whatever men he would need to reach his anticipated minimum of one hundred. Sands was still reluctant, even though the admiral had specified that the men should be volunteers, but in the end he concurred, though not before Cushing had taken matters into his own hands by going to Washington and sending in a letter to the Secretary of the Navy, Gideon Welles, and to Fox. He would wait, he said, until the ram came down close to the mouth of the river, when he would board and take her with a picked body of men. The low flat decks of the *Raleigh* were very suitable, he believed, for boarding; once on the deck the ship was so constructed that his men could easily capture the gundeck, which would give them the magazine hatch and the engine room. To the objection that the crew of the *Raleigh* could defy him successfully below decks, he countered that he would take with him shell and slow matches. "One shell down each hatch would be likely to bring all hands to terms," he said.

Welles and Fox were enthusiastic. The former wrote to Lee that "Lieutenant William B. Cushing has proposed a scheme with regard to . . . [the *Raleigh*] which it would be well to encourage, and you will instruct the senior officer off Wilmington to that effect. Risks to accomplish an important object ought to be taken without hesitation, and never will be disapproved by the Department if well arranged and intrusted to good officers."

Now that he had full authority Cushing decided that it would be prudent to conduct a thorough reconnaissance before embarking on the expedition. Two or three days after he got back from Washington, on June 23, he pushed off from the *Monticello* in one of the cutters with Jones and Howorth and fifteen men just after sunset. The group took two days' rations of food and an armament consisting of eleven revolvers, seven pistols, six Sharps breech-loading rifles and ammunition. Cushing himself took his pair of dueling pistols.

The moon was shining brightly though occasionally obscured by clouds; this was a disadvantage perhaps, but, as Cushing argued, it would help them to spot the *Raleigh* if she were anywhere in sight. With muffled oars the cutter rowed along the same route it had followed twice before. Past the great guns commanding the outer approaches to the Western Bar, past Fort Caswell and Fort Holmes, their cannon pointing ominously out to sea, the little craft slipped through the waves. Once inside the outer defenses the crew of the cutter anxiously scanned the water for some sign of the *Raleigh*. She was not to be seen. Stealthily the cutter started to pull past the Confederate batteries on Zeek's Island. Suddenly, looming out of the night, the outline of a rebel tug appeared against the horizon. The men pulled at their oars. The tug bore down on them, and then passed their stern, missing them by no more than twenty feet. They had not been discovered; no shots began to sting the water around them. In the distance a guard boat was seen, slowly circling, but the moon went behind clouds and again they were not discovered. They continued up the river.

For the first few miles the river, at this point more accurately an estuary, flowed slowly between low-lying banks that stretched away in a maze of swamp and marsh grass and cattails. Occasionally a fort or armed encampment was visible along the edge of the water: a signal fire burning, a few boats drawn up on shore, a stack of rifles, a heavy gun peering out at the sluggish surface of the stream gave notice that they were deep in enemy country.

About fifteen miles from their starting point the moon came out bright and strong just as they were passing the Old Brunswick batteries; a hundred yards farther upstream sentries along the bank near Fort Anderson raised the alarm. "Boat ahoy!" came the cry from first one voice, then another, until it was echoed up and down the bank. When no answer was given the muskets opened fire. The water around the cutter was lashed by bullets. Down the bank a signal fire was lit, then far in the distance another, giving the alarm to the entire area. The men in the cutter stopped rowing and looked at Cushing, their faces white in the moonlight.

"Row for that moonlit patch of water there," Cushing said, pointing a few yards away. The boatswain directed his crew, and the cutter shot across the intervening water. The fire doubled in intensity but none of the bullets hit the boat. "Now, boys," Cushing shouted, "turn on your oars, turn her downstream, we're getting out of here!" The cutter seemed to fly downstream, while around them the bullets sang, but still they were not hit. They rowed for two or three minutes and then the moon went behind a cloud again. They were now invisible from the shore, Cushing judged, and he directed the boat to turn upstream once more.

The men were startled but they soon saw the point. On the bank the soldiers were running and shouting. Far down the river the crew of the cutter could hear the rumble of the drum rolls, and could see the flames of the signal fires leaping to the sky. Soon Cushing and his men were past Fort Anderson in the darkness, and in five minutes more they were out of sight around a bend in the river. The firing continued. They could hear it behind them, fainter and fainter, as they pulled on their oars. Then all was silence again except for the swish of the water at the prow, the occasional creak of an oarlock, and the shuffle of feet as their position was changed in the bottom of the boat.

The trees grew down to the edge of the river now, and the current was narrower and deeper, and harder to row against. Still the men rowed on until just before dawn, when they selected a likely spot on the bank and hid the boat in a marsh and settled down for the day behind a camouflage of tree branches. Cushing strung the troop out along the bank, one man every ten or fifteen feet, and then lay down behind some bushes to observe the traffic on the river. The traffic was heavy

—they were only seven miles or so from the city of Wilmington.

All day the men lay in their hiding places, watching the world of the enemy pass by. Nine steamers puffed by in the first few hours, one of them, they made out with their glasses, the *Yadkin*, flagship of Flag Officer William Lynch, commanding the Confederate naval vessels in and around Wilmington. Cushing noted that the *Yadkin* mounted only two guns and seemed shorthanded as to crew. During the morning three blockade runners steamed by, one of them within two hundred yards of the band of Yankees behind the bushes, but without observing them. The rest of the steamers were small clumsy river craft, but these blockade runners were trim swift ships, and the men found it hard to let them pass without an attempt to stop them. But Cushing felt that the parade at least kept the men awake.

All day they lay hidden, from time to time chewing on the hard tack and salt horse they had brought with them. By evening they were hungry, and Cushing decided to make a foray in search of more appetizing provisions. Before they had even started two small boats rounded the point of land upstream and headed directly for them. At first it seemed that it must be an attack. The men took cover, lying behind bushes and trees with their weapons ready. The boats came closer. At any moment the party expected to be overwhelmed by a wave of gray-coated figures. Then it was clear that the boats were following the current, which swept close to the shore here, and that they were filled with unarmed fishermen and not soldiers. Cushing stood up and hailed the first of the boats. It swung out into the stream, and then came close when he repeated his call. The fishermen did not suspect for a moment that Yankee sailors could be in this part of the river, but they were soon confronted by ten men with drawn pistols. They gave no trouble. One of them said later that if they really were Yankees so far behind their own lines then they must be desperate, and it was best not to trifle with them.

The fishermen had interesting information: the *Raleigh* had run aground at high water some days before and fallen apart, when the tide fell, by the weight of its own armor. A hopeless wreck, they said. It sounded like a trick to Cushing. Besides, he was not ready to go back to the *Monticello* yet. He decided that he would keep the fishermen as guides and look for verification of the *Raleigh's* fate, as well as for any other information which might prove useful to the blockading squadron.

The fishermen seemed willing to give information about anything, but the Union sailors decided to see for themselves about the defenses of Wilmington. When it was dark they pushed out from the bank, the cutter heavily laden with its contingent of prisoners, and rowed farther upstream. They were about three miles from the city when they saw ahead of them in the water a string of obstructions lying across the channel; the only way left open, a passage about thirty yards wide, was under the guns of a battery on the left bank. Not wishing to test the alertness of the enemy at such close quarters, Cushing beached his boat and left some of his men to guard the fishermen. With Jones and Howorth and seven men he started up the bank of the river on foot. A little beyond the first obstructions was a second string, a line of half-submerged logs tied together by ropes and chains, again leaving a narrow channel which was protected by a battery of ten large naval guns. Still a third row of obstructions lay beyond this one. The city was obviously well defended. What was more, the fishermen had been correct so far. Perhaps they were telling the truth about the *Raleigh*.

Cushing returned to the cutter and the crew pulled down the river until they reached a small creek which ran through Cypress Swamp, about four miles below the city. They entered it and followed its wandering course as far as they could, though progress was slow as the craft had to be poled from time to time. They worked their way until they came to a place where a log road crossed the stream, stopping any further penetration of the swamp. The cutter was headed into the bank and Cushing took a party to investigate. The road was eerie in the thick darkness as the men walked along it. On either side the ground dropped away into the swamp, and high trees obscured their view. All around them was the constant humming of insects, the indistinct sounds of a summer night.

After about two miles they came to a main road. Drawing back into the underbrush they waited nervously, lest they had been seen when they blundered out into the open. No sight, no sound was discovered. Hurriedly they questioned the one or two fishermen they had brought with them. The road turned out to be the main turnpike between Fort Fisher and Wilmington—a good place to lie in wait for adventure. Over their heads stretched the sole telegraph line between the two ends of the Confederate defenses. Cushing ordered Jones back to the cutter and kept the others with him. Jones departed unwillingly. Howorth was happy to remain.

As dawn broke they hid in the underbrush, chewing on their unsavory rations, waiting for an unsuspecting fly to tumble into their web. One came quickly. They heard him first, whistling as he walked along the road. He carried a gun, but Howorth got behind him and disarmed him. He was a hunter named Smith, who when he was not hunting was the proprietor of a country store about a mile down the road. They were making plans to utilize this find when they heard far down the road the click of a horse's hoofs. Quickly they hid and waited; it was a mounted soldier with a mailbag. He was invited to dismount. He seemed much astonished at the request but Cushing assured him that he would be responsible for any delay in delivering the mail. The man got off his horse and turned over the mailbag; it contained hundreds of letters, some of which described in detail the number of men in the forts and the guns and provisions on hand. The soldier had heard that a boatload of Yankees had come into the harbor and up the river the night before, he said, but the alarm had been sounded and the boat had turned down river again. It was assumed by the Confederates that it had escaped to the fleet.

The rations were exhausted now and it became imperative to get food. A daring plan was hit upon to get additional provisions. Howorth volunteered to take the courier's coat, hat and horse and go to the captured hunter's store to buy food for the party. This was extremely hazardous since if he were caught in Confederate uniform he would probably be hanged as a spy, but he sallied forth to market anyway with his pockets stuffed with Confederate currency which had been found in the mailbag. He reached the store without meeting anybody but found a group of enemy soldiers in and around the building who asked him some embarrassing questions. He was able to satisfy them but his greatest difficulty came when "an inquisitive female" insisted upon entering into a lengthy discussion with him. It seems that she was attracted to him; also, early in the conversation, he had been forced to name a fictitious home town and as luck would have it the woman had a brother living there. Howorth was able to satisfy her curiosity, too. He had no trouble buying all the chickens, eggs and milk he wanted, as he mentioned the name of the proprietor, said he had met him down the road, and claimed that Smith had said to tell his wife, Lizzy, "that I tell her to sell 'em." Howorth managed to make his way back without having aroused any suspicions, and his provisions, supplemented by blackberries found nearby, "formed a meal that could not be improved in Seceshia."

While Howorth was at the store Cushing and his men at the crossroads had adventures of their own. People continued to pass along the road, and while some were permitted to go on unmolested, others were considered desirable prisoners and were detained. By the middle of the afternoon Cushing and eight men were guarding no less than twenty-six prisoners, who sat in a group some distance from the road, underneath a large oak tree, while two or three of the sailors watched over them with pistols in their laps. The conversation was general; among other things, Cushing learned that the military courier bound from Wilmington to the forts with the "evening papers and Richmond news" would pass by the spot about five o'clock. He determined to wait for this gentleman and then depart. He sent the prisoners with four men back along the log road to the place where the cutter was waiting, then mounted a horse on one side of the road, stationed Howorth on horseback on the other, with two or three men to cover them with carbines from the bushes, and waited like a highwayman of old for the courier to appear. Unfortunately the courier, in company with another man, rounded the bend just as the shift was being made. The two Confederates caught sight of Howorth's blue coat and without stopping to inquire the circumstances turned and raced back toward Wilmington. Cushing chased them for two miles but his horse was tired, as were those of the other men who had procured mounts, and the rebels escaped.

The situation was now dangerous. The couriers would certainly raise the alarm; the Yankees could expect a hot reception when they started down the river. There were forts to pass, all of which would be alerted. To keep word from being sent down river too fast Cushing ordered the telegraph wire cut. Men shinnied up two consecutive poles and took the intervening length of wire with them when the party struck off along the log road through the swamp. It was six o'clock when they left the high road. About a mile from the cutter they caught up with the prisoners and marched them quickly to the boat. It was impossible to carry them all in the cutter but the force left to guard the boat had commandeered a number of canoes and the prisoners were distributed in them. The cutter shoved off at about seven, towing the canoes behind it.

It was just at dusk that the impromptu flotilla entered the Cape Fear River. Not far away was a large island on which stood the ruins of an abandoned lighthouse. Cushing decided that since he had more prisoners than he could manage he would leave most of them in this isolated place where they would not be found until morning. When the cutter was within a few feet of the island the men saw a steamer shoot around the bend in the river above them and head directly for them. Cushing ordered the cutter pushed in among some high grass on the edge of the water and ordered the men to jump overboard and keep their heads below the water. The prisoners were told in a fierce whisper that the first one to cry out would be instantly killed. They seem to have had no doubt that the threat would be carried out, and were silent. Closer and closer the steamer came in the dusk. It appeared to be heading right for the clump of grass behind which the cutter was hidden. Whether the pilot had nodded momentarily or the channel came very close to the island Cushing never knew, but the steamer passed within ten feet of them, so close that they could easily read the name on its side—*Virginia*—and hear the sailors conversing on the deck.

Cushing now decided to turn the prisoners loose in the canoes without sails or paddles. He felt certain they would be picked up in the morning unharmed, and he did not want to spend the time unloading them onto the island. Two or three of the prisoners who were "persons of more importance," among them a pilot, he kept in the cutter. This pilot came in handy. He was forced at the point of a pistol to lead the cutter to the place where the *Raleigh* had run aground, where Cushing found that the fishermen's story had been correct, and the ironclad was a total wreck.

Cushing had not forgotten that Colonel Jones had said he would like to meet him sometime, nor that the colonel had said to Ensign Jones that his exploit in February could never be repeated. As the men rowed down the river Cushing sat in the stern writing in his log by the light of matches. When the cutter shot out into the harbor Cushing directed it toward one of the buoys that marked the channel, tore off the page he had been writing on, and attached it to the buoy. It was a note to Colonel Jones, reminding him of his words.

The greatest danger lay ahead of them now; the alarm was given once the break in the telegraph line was discovered, and the word had been passed to the sentinels all up and down the bank to "keep a close watch out on the bay." But again the Confederates supplied unwilling information. As the cutter neared the forts at New Inlet a small boat was detected making its way rapidly to shore. It was quickly overtaken, and the occupants, four sailors and two women, taken into the cutter. Cushing was annoyed at the presence of the women, but he could not turn them loose or they would give the alarm, and he could not conscientiously drown or shoot them. The twenty-six people aboard the cutter were now "more than a load," especially since only half of them were available for motive power or could be counted upon in an emergency. The new prisoners were closely interrogated and it was discovered that several guard boats were out looking for the cutter, and that one of them, containing about seventy-five armed soldiers, was posted in the narrow passage between Federal Point and Zeek's Island.

To add to their troubles the moon had now come out and was shining brilliantly; the water was illuminated almost as though it were daylight. In any case, a quick check of the time showed that it would be sunrise in less than an hour.

Since the tide was in his favor Cushing evolved a desperate plan. "I concluded to pull boldly for the bar," he reported later, "run foul of the guard-boat, use cutlasses and revolvers and drift by the batteries in that way since they would not fire on their own men." He started toward the channel, but five minutes later the plan, though desperate, had to be abandoned for one even more desperate. A boat was spotted ahead as they neared Federal Point; it was large enough so that it was probably the guard boat with the seventy-five soldiers. Although outnumbered by five to one the sailors were confidently preparing to board, certain that the soldiers would not be able to fight effectively on the water. The eight prisoners were warned and seemed willing to be passive in the coming fracas. But when the cutter was fifteen or twenty yards away and preparing to put its nose into the side of the enemy vessel, Cushing saw three more boats pull out from the bar on the left and five additional ones start from the shore to the right, thus effectively blocking all avenues of escape. He put the helm hard down, but immediately saw, to windward, a large sailboat filled with soldiers, which was keeping him right in the glimmer of the moon's rays.

None of Cushing's extraordinary little crew became panicky, and all pulled steadily so that each stroke was perfection —this after five hours of rowing and three nights without sleep.

Being veteran sailors, the men in the cutter knew where they were, which was not entirely true of their enemies. Glancing at the water and feeling the pull of the tide and the current, Cushing realized that he was at the junction of the two channels where the tide splits, the one channel leading seven miles west to Fort Caswell, where he had entered, the other leading directly in front of him past Fort Fisher, where he now determined to depart. Besides knowing where he was, Cushing had another piece of information which was not shared by his opponents—the Western Bar Channel was in fact impassable to him, since what was almost a southwest gale was blowing, and waves were probably breaking right over the bar; besides it would be daylight before he could reach the place, and the guns of Fort Caswell would have a fine fish in a barrel if he tried to leave by that exit. He decided to try to feint the enemy boats out of position so that he might run through the escape channel close to Fort Fisher. "Dashing off with the tide in the direction of Smithville," he reported, "I passed the sailboat, and by my trick of sheering the cutter so as to avoid reflecting the moon's rays, caused the main line of enemy boats to lose sight of her in the swell."

For a minute or two the cutter lay in the wash, every eye straining to see if the ruse had worked. The men were rewarded by the sight of the entire Confederate fleet rowing as fast as they could in a westerly direction; another minute and the group of boats was past, leaving its original station unguarded. Now there was nothing between the cutter and safety except the sailboat full of sailors which had come up when the cutter made its first feint toward the Eastern Bar. "That was my time," Cushing wrote, "and it was improved. Suddenly turning we approached the sailboat as if to board, when her crew lost their nerve and tried to tack. Missing stays they drifted off with the tide, while we shot around in a semicircle and cut under the stem of the line of boats in chase." The line saw its quarry escaping and turned to chase it, but the cutter was a hundred yards in advance as it headed for the channel. Keeping that distance from its befuddled and startled pursuers the cutter shot through the channel and into the breakers off Caroline Shoals. It all happened so quickly that the Confederates in the fort did not have time to train their guns while the boat was in the narrow passage. After it was through, the Confederate boats, manned by soldiers, were unwilling or unable to follow it into the breakers, nor could the land gunners see to fire upon it.

Considering that the cutter was heavily overloaded it is almost incredible that it could have ridden out that sea, yet as day was breaking Cushing and his crew hailed the steamer *Cherokee*, and were taken in tow. The *Monticello* maintained its position at the other channel, and it was half a day before the *Cherokee* could reach it. Early in the afternoon the fifteen men and three officers climbed the rope ladders and tumbled into bed. Cushing had been without sleep for sixty-eight hours, and his men had had no more than short naps in that time.

"Captain Cushing's Exploits in the Cape Fear River," as they came to be known, were widely appreciated in the North. Gideon Welles wrote Cushing a special letter of commendation. "The boldness exhibited by you in this reconnaissance," he said, "and the success attending it are most gratifying to the Department." Many Northern newspapers picked up the story, and it was known for thirty years after the war. Perhaps most important for the young man was the fact that after the event he never again had difficulty in getting official confirmation for his daring plans; the problem henceforth was not to find volunteers for them but to choose, among the many who offered their services, the few who could accompany him.

Probably the most satisfying compliment was paid by the Confederates themselves. General W. H. C. Whiting, commandant of the over-all defenses in the Wilmington area, wrote to General Hébert in dismay. "The last exploit of Cushing is pretty strong," he said, "*pas trop fort.* What do you think can be done? Can you get any help from the navy? I shall have to have a guard for my house in town." General Hébert could only plead that his force was "inadequate" to man the many strong points he was called upon to guard. He added woefully that Cushing's "two entrances into the river and safe exits, besides being a proof of my inability to guard myself, must necessarily have furnished him pretty correct information . . . as to troops and the position and quality of our works." General Whiting, in a report to the Confederate Inspector General Cooper, referred to Cushing's two exploits in the harbor as illustrating his need for more troops. He added that the young man was an "enterprising commander."

Only a few days later Cushing's impetuousness got him into trouble. On July 1, when the *Monticello* was on its station off Wilmington with Cushing himself belowdeck, a small brig, the *Hound*, was sighted and overhauled. The vessel began to drift away and several musket shots were fired across its bows. The brig stopped, but its captain appeared on deck to shout oaths at damned Yankees who would dare treat a British ship, not a blockade runner, so cavalierly. Ensign Hadfield then went aboard to check the brig's papers, and was met with more profanity, "both on deck in the presence of his men," Cushing reported, "and below in the cabin."

The papers were in order and the *Hound* was allowed to continue on its way. But when Hadfield returned to the *Monticello* and reported to Cushing, the latter felt that his subordinate had been insulted and decided to teach the Britisher a lesson. He declared later that whenever the captain of a vessel to be examined was unnecessarily insolent he always, when the fact was reported to him, had the vessel stopped again, and examined the papers thoroughly since the insolence might be only a trick to cover "informalities" in the ship's documents.

The brig was stopped again. Cushing wrote in his report of the affair—a report more revealing for what it implied than for what it said—that "the captain of the brig came aboard, and I took his papers, telling him I would look them over at my leisure, and he could remain or go aboard his ship as he pleased. He informed me he would remain, with my permission. I inquired what his conduct had been, and he answered by lame excuses and final retraction. I told him that he should see the propriety of apologizing to the boarding officer, and he expressed his willingness to do so. I then examined his papers, and finding them correct, told the captain to proceed." In defense of his action Cushing closed his official report thus: "It would have made no difference in my action had the ship been American, or other nationality, for a national ship must be treated with respect."

Cushing's highhanded treatment did not pass unchallenged. The British captain protested strongly to his government, and the British minister in Washington, on July 25, protested to the American Secretary of State. On July 28 Secretary Seward wrote Welles a letter calling his attention to the incident of the *Hound*. A letter of inquiry was sent to Cushing, but he had already been detached from the *Monticello* by Admiral Lee for other duty, and it was not until early September that the charges caught up with him and he wrote a full report. Welles read the report and replied, "The Department fails to find in your explanation any excuse for your disregard of international law and courtesy. . . ." He indicted Cushing's conduct by a bill of particulars; first, he had fired "musketry" instead of a blank cartridge to stop the *Hound;* second, he had no right to stop the ship for the second time since its papers were in order; and third, Cushing had no right to take the master off and keep him waiting some hours while he examined his papers again at his "leisure." Obviously Cushing did not really suspect the brig of being a blockade runner, Welles declared, but was merely using this as an excuse to punish the captain.

He went on to say that from time to time other instances had reached his attention of Cushing's failure to observe "the customary rules on the high seas"; therefore, he was not minded to express only mild disapproval of Cushing's conduct at this time. He did not want to place himself on record as endorsing the "offensive" conduct of the master of the *Hound*, but he wished to point out that Cushing had inflicted damage on innocent parties by detaining the ship, namely the owners of the vessel. "I must enjoin upon you to be more cautious in the future," Welles concluded. "Such proceedings repeated cannot fail to bring upon you the serious displeasure of your Government and result to your regret and injury."

What effect this letter had upon Cushing is not known, but it should have sobered him. Perhaps he learned something from it, for a similar complaint never again came to the attention of the Navy Department, as far as the records show. But the incident helped to give him a name for irresponsibility which was to dog him throughout his career. Welles, while displeased at Cushing's conduct, was still fondly disposed toward him. The affair was serious, but he could find an excuse. In his letter to Secretary Seward closing the incident Welles wrote: "Lieutenant Cushing is quite young, which fact may be pleaded in extenuation of his improper conduct. The Department regrets the occurrence and hopes it may not find cause again to censure one of its officers for failing to observe international law and courtesy." This ended the incident for Cushing also.

II

Fredonia

~~~~~~

ZATTU CUSHING, Will's grandfather, was born in Plymouth, Massachusetts, in 1770. When he was seven years old he heard that General Burgoyne had surrendered at Saratoga, and setting out from school, in Plymouth, in the middle of the night he traveled across ten miles of field and woodland, "walking, running, and leaping for joy," in order to be the first to tell his family in their upland farm about the victory. They had not heard the news, and in the joyous atmosphere he was not caned for being up so late. When he was in his middle teens he was apprenticed to a shipbuilder, but in 1791, when he was twenty, he left Plymouth for the West. Zattu's father had lost his farm owing to the inflation of currency during and after the Revolution, but in any case young people all over New England were packing their belongings and making a virtue of necessity in those years.

Probably Zattu went by water. He would have sailed from Plymouth in a coasting vessel, gone through the Narrows, and proceeded up the Hudson. We discover him north of Albany in 1795, where, in the town of Ballston Spa—it was noted as a health resort some thirty years later—he took a wife, Rachel Buckingham, of whom almost nothing is known except the remark of a contemporary that she was a "companion in every way worthy of him." In 1799 he was superintending the construction of a ship, the *Good Intent*, at the island opposite Erie, Pennsylvania, though his residence at the time was in the town of Paris, a few miles south of Troy. He returned from Erie through the wilderness with a pair of fine black horses, no doubt the fruits of his summer's work. One of the horses escaped from its fastenings in the night and caused Zattu the loss of three or four days until he found it. During the search he camped in the woods and the spot on which he built his fire was the site on which he later built the house in which he lived for many years in Fredonia, New York.

He settled there in 1805. He had collected five children in ten years, including Milton Buckingham, born in 1800, and the family accompanied Zattu on the perilous trek from Oneida County in early winter by means of ox sleighs. The trip must have taken several weeks; it was by way of Buffalo and along the frozen waters of the shore of Lake Erie. Once while they were using the ice as a highway dark night and a sudden storm came down on them. The parents were afraid to move in the darkness on account of the openings in the ice, but Zattu blew a horn he had with him at intervals. At about one o'clock in the morning two men on shore heard the sound of the horn and came to the party with a lantern and guided them to shore near Eighteen Mile Creek. By morning the quick thaw had broken up the ice so that it would have been impossible for them to reach safety. Fredonia is only three or four miles inland from the port of Dunkirk, and the family was soon lodged in a log hut there on a tract of land in what was then the backwoods of western New York.

Zattu was an ambitious man, and he probably did not remain in the log hut longer than the necessary minimum of time. In any case, his neighbors thought him reliable, and the former shipbuilder soon was given the appointment of associate justice of Niagara County Court. From shipyard to bench was not such a leap in those days as it would be now, particularly on the frontier. Cushing's New England emigrant neighbors had a solid distrust for regularly-trained members of the legal professions, since many of them were here as a result of losing lawsuits after the war. The people's confidence was not misplaced, as it happened; Zattu attended all the terms of the court in Buffalo, his ability made him the leading member of the court and he presided at the most important trials. In 1811, when Chautauqua County was set off from Niagara, he was chosen chief judge of the new county. He was emphatically a peacemaker, and it is claimed for him that he settled more cases as arbitrator in private than he did officially in his fourteen years on the bench.

In 1825 he retired in order to give his full attention to a new career. In October the Erie Canal was opened to commerce, and the frontier became an integral part of New York. Cushing was not the man to ignore such an opportunity. In 1826, together with other citizens of Fredonia, he helped build in a pasture north of his house a new ship for the canal. It was called the *Fredonia Enterprise*, and was drawn to Dunkirk Bay by a hundred yoke of oxen. The town had a gala day when the vessel hit the water. The citizens attended the ceremonies in their best clothes, and the children carried little American flags. Zattu made a speech and the ship was launched to the accompaniment of cheers and towed to Buffalo, carrying the first wheat ever sent from Chautauqua County to the New York market. A good part of the first cargo had been grown on Zattu Cushing's farm.

The remaining thirteen years of his life were spent in business and the enjoyment of material comforts. On January 13, 1839, he died peacefully in his bed. At the next term of court held after his death the bar of Chautauqua County procured his portrait to be hung in the courthouse, over the judges' bench. The picture shows a strong face with a pair of wide-spaced, straight-staring eyes, a high brow and a powerful chin. There is a calmness in the expression, as of one who found life not too difficult a proposition. A contemporary said that Zattu's most marked characteristics were "restless energy and an indomitable will."

Milton Cushing had by now grown up, taken the degree of

doctor of medicine from Hamilton Literary and Theological Institute (now Colgate University) and entered the medical profession. But the duties of a physician were too exacting for what was never a robust physique (like his sons he was a slender, nervous man), and after a few years of not too successful practice in Zanesville, Ohio, he went into business in that city and in Columbus. In Zanesville he married his first wife, Abigail Tupper, granddaughter of General Tupper of the Revolution. She died in 1833, leaving four children, all of whom died young. One was a "physician of great skill" who died in his twenty-fourth year. Two were remarkably pretty and intelligent girls who lived only long enough to marry. The oldest, Benjamin, was a law partner of Salmon Portland Chase, in Columbus; he too died in his middle twenties. Chase, who became Secretary of the Treasury and then Chief Justice of the Supreme Court, remembered him, and when he met Will Cushing after the sinking of the *Albemarle* he said to him: "You must be a connection of a very brilliant young man who was a partner of mine in Columbus." "Yes, he was a brother," Will said.

Milton grieved when his wife died but necessities are necessities, and he soon married again. She was Mary Barker Smith, of Boston, and was visiting relatives in Columbus when Milton met her. She came of exalted stock: her grandfather was a Congressman, she was a lineal descendant of John Alden, she was related to the Adams, Hancock, Madison and Phillips families. One cousin was Rear Admiral Joseph Smith, another, though a distant one, President John Adams. She had been born in 1807; Milton met her when she was twenty-nine, and married her within a matter of months.

Their union bore quick and abundant fruit. In April, 1837, Milton Buckingham, Jr., was born; Howard Buckingham followed in August, 1838; a third son, Walter, was born in 1839 but died while still a child. Alonzo Hersford was born in January, 1841; twenty-one months later, on November 4,

1842, William Barker was born. Another child whose name does not survive followed him; he was in turn followed by a daughter, Mary Isabel, who was born in Chicago. Her birth date is not known.

During this spate of new life the family by no means remained in one place. In 1837, taking Milton and his stepbrothers and sisters, Dr. Cushing moved from Ohio to the wilds of Wisconsin and settled in the small lakeside town of Milwaukee. The Potawatomi still fished and hunted in the vicinity, and the Sauk leader, Black Hawk, had only recently been driven from the country. Mrs. Cushing was fortunately blessed with "a splendid physical and mental constitution, and endowed with a passionate love for life in an open, free atmosphere, as near as practicable to nature itself." In 1838 Milwaukee contained only about eight hundred inhabitants, and these were divided by the Milwaukee River into two hostile camps, whose differences were always apparently on the point of breaking out into violence. The stream was still unbridged, and it seemed that it would form a long-lived boundary line. The problems thus ensuing, combined with the difficulties of caring for five children, became during August, 1838, too much for even Mrs. Cushing. She was pregnant, it was hot, the mosquitoes were terrible, and there was constant squabbling over the little river. Reared among the most cultivated people of the East, she was "a more than usually intelligent lady, and literary in her tastes." So she wrote a poem expressing her feeling that she would not survive the birth of her child, due in a week or so. "To Milton, with the Legacy of his Mother's Bible," she wrote on the flyleaf of the book:

> I have no gold, my darling son,
>   No wealth to leave to thee—
> Yet never light hath shone upon
> A richer, costlier, holier one
>   Than this my legacy;
> "Bought with a price," this guide of youth—
> And gemmed with wisdom, light, and truth.

Shouldst thou live on through many years
  Of pilgrimage below,
Full well I know that earthly fears
And human woe and human tears
  Attend the path thou'lt go,
And that thy soul may well endure—
Drink deeply of this fountain pure.

Farewell, my son! perchance through grace
  We'll meet again above—
Thine infant memory may not trace
Thy mother's form, thy mother's face;
  But O, that mother's love
Burns deep for thee, my first-born child!
God keep thy spirit undefiled!

In fact her splendid constitution saw her through and she
was delivered of Howard a week after writing the poem and
was up and about three days later. Her husband was a handsome man and was said to have had great charm, but he was not
strong and there was no time for Mrs. Cushing to be sick.
Besides, the family was moving again.

This time it was not far. Beyond the Menominee marshes lay
the country of the "oak openings," extending for scores of
miles westward from Milwaukee and resembling the most
carefully tended English parks. It was jeweled with lovely
lakes and ponds, from Pewaukee to beyond the "Four Lakes,"
between two of which the city of Madison was soon to rise.
The prairie grasses stood as high as the horses' knees, their
tops waving languidly in the soft wind that blew across the
sloping open land. A horseman following one of the grassy
tracks through the country would look about for the house be-
longing to these beautiful grounds, but they were without
human habitation and belonged entirely to the animals and
birds which occupied them.

The log cabin to which the family moved in 1839 was a few
miles north of the present site of Waukesha, halfway between
Lakes Nemahbin and Nagawicka, north of the Bark River. It

lay in the shadow of the Kettle Range, in the center of a charming little valley now occupied by the village of Delafield. Mrs. Cushing long afterward said that her sojourn there was the happiest period of her life. Alonzo, Walter and Will were born there, and Walter was buried there. There also her husband regained a measure of health in the clear open air.

A man with a medical degree was well educated for a frontier village, and Dr. Cushing took a prominent place in the new community. He was appointed justice of the peace, and when, by an act of the legislature, what is now the township of Delafield was set off from the town of Warren under the name of Nemahbin, he was placed at the head of the new organization as chairman of its first board of supervisors. He performed the duties, such as they were, with charm and a sort of fatigued dignity.

Neither store nor post office had been established in the town when Will Cushing was born in 1842, but the original Hawk's Tavern had been built and opened to the public in 1840, and was considered a great blessing by immigrants on their way westward along the lately-cleared Territorial Road. For table supplies it was necessary to go to Prairieville (now Waukesha), a dozen miles back toward Milwaukee. It was always a holiday for the Cushing children when the semi-monthly trips were made to the store. They traveled across the prairie by ox cart, and returned laden with sugar and flour and other necessities, carrying in their pockets what candy they had not managed to eat by the time they reached home.

In 1844 the outdoor existence, which at first had been invigorating, became too strenuous for Dr. Cushing, and the family moved to Chicago, where he resumed the practice of medicine. They lived on the water front and the doctor is said to have had a thriving practice. When Will was three he set out to see the world. Already conscious of his dignity, he left home with his father's tall black hat on his head, which was so much too big that he had to use both hands to keep it from falling down over his eyes. Some boats were leaving a dock and he ran after them, out to the end of the dock, and stepped off into the water. Despite his faith he sank. A sailor lounging on the dock was not in time to catch him before he fell, but he jumped in and rescued Will before he could drown. The sailor did not recognize Will, so he took him home, dried him off, and asked him his name. "Bill Coon," said Will, reaching for the hat, which the sailor had also rescued.

"Bill Coon?" asked the sailor. "I don't know any Coons around here. Where do you live, boy?"

Bill Coon was a nickname that Will's brother Allie had given him, and he did not see any reason why the sailor should not know it. He told the sailor again that his name was Bill Coon, and added that he was hungry.

The good sailor gave him some food and set out to discover where he lived, but Will had strayed some distance and the sailor returned at nightfall without having found the boy's parents. In the meantime, of course, the family was frantically searching for him. It was thirty-six hours before his half-sister Rowena, who was supposed to take care of him, found him at the sailor's house, safely tucked away asleep. "Name's Bill Coon," he said to the sailor before he was half carried, half dragged to his own house. He was put out that he was not allowed to wear the hat on the way home.

A year later, on New Year's Day, having exhausted the possibilities of water travel, he determined to make his way around the world by land. Unfortunately, his father had recently bought an unbroken colt which he kept stabled in the barn back of the house. Will crept silently into the building and examined the horse, and was horrified to discover that it had no shoes. He had spent the previous summer watching a blacksmith, whenever he could get away from Rowena, so he fetched a hammer and four shoes and some nails from his father's workbench and approached the horse again, opening the door of the stall and going in. The horse reared and kicked; fortunately for his victim a four-year-old body is not heavy, and the first kick sent Will flying across the floor of the barn, out of reach of the deadly hoofs.

His mother, though she was ill in bed at the time, was the only person to hear his cries. She rushed downstairs to find the nurse, whom she sent to the barn. Will was by this time unconscious. When he awoke he could not be consoled for the loss of all his front teeth. "Now, Willie can't eat tato and turkey!" he cried.

Dr. Cushing became worse in the fall of 1846, and it was decided that he should travel for his health. He set out for Mississippi in November, having remained in Chicago to celebrate Will's birthday on November 4, to visit his cousin, Judge L. S. Houghton, of Vicksburg. Again the change of climate helped at first, and in the spring he started north feeling more capable of supporting his family. He stopped off in Columbus to see what he could do about settling his two sons by his first wife, and spent a week arranging for Benjamin's short-lived partnership with Chase. The second week in April he set off again for home, but in Gallipolis, Ohio, he came down with a cold which quickly developed into pneumonia. He died in a hotel bedroom in Gallipolis on April 22. Mrs. Cushing accompanied the body to Fredonia, where it was buried.

"He was a man," a eulogist said, "of elevated character, deep piety, acute and vigorous intellect. His influence was felt wherever he was known. As a business man he was energetic, persevering and clear-sighted. As a friend, he was constant, devoted and self-sacrificing. As a man he was full of benevolence and active charity. The poor found in him a ready benefactor and the oppressed a strong and unflinching advocate. He was a conscientious and active antislavery man and gave liberally of his money, and his time and thought, to assist in bringing freedom to the colored race. He was a handsome man of fine presence and was a society favorite. His death was deeply mourned by those whose affection his kindness had won and whose regard his sterling qualities had secured." He was forty-six when he died, and had been married to his second wife for ten years.

Fredonia, New York, was a pleasant little town with tree-shaded streets, good water, substantial houses, and a relaxed air owing to the fact that the great wave of migration had passed it by and was, in the 1840's, breaking against the wilder country to the west. The population of the town was about three thousand (it is something over twice that now); the soil was sandy, the sun hot in the summer; it was a good place for grapes, and they were grown there as early as the beginning of the century. To the south and west rose the purple shadows of the Arkwright Hills, low-lying tree-covered mounds of sand and shale which once, probably, marked the limits of Lake Erie, now three miles north of town. From the tops of the closer hills the lake could be seen, especially in the morning when the sun glittered on its surface. Sometimes the lake would be shrouded in fog, and it would seem as though there were another line of hills in the distance. In the spring the fields were green and when the grass was cut in the front yards the whole town smelled sweet. In the fall dead leaves spiraled down from the elms and lay until the old men and boys raked them into piles and burned them and stood, leaning on their rakes, while the smoke spiraled up among the trees again. In October the entire town would smell of burning leaves, as would all the towns in that part of America. In winter there were great snows, and five feet of snow did not surprise anybody. There was a public high school and several grade schools, and also an Academy on Elm Street attended by the children of the wealthier families. When they had finished school, most children went to work, but an occasional boy went east to college, to Colgate or, as sometimes happened, to Harvard or Yale. The girls did not go to school for very long, learning instead to cook and sew and keep house. Once in a while a family would go to New York City, which, though it was in the same state, seemed very far away. Work was mostly farming, but the town was close to the lake and a good many men worked on the barges in the summer, leaving such odd winter jobs as they could find when the ice broke up on the lake. It was a good life, with little room for sentimentality in it.

Mary Cushing moved from Chicago to Fredonia with her family in the early summer of 1847 and took up residence on Green Street in a satisfactory house—Zattu's fine house was inhabited by one of his other children. The Cushings were sympathetic but Zattu had shared his fortune with many, and they were able to collect only a small amount of money to help the widow. This, with the small inheritance from her husband and something from her own father, allowed her a few months' leeway, but she soon realized that the total was not enough to support her large family and she determined to start a school in her home. The better class, as it used to be called, of Fredonians responded enthusiastically, and the school was a success.

She counted on her children, and her confidence was not misplaced. Her stepchildren helped out as much as they could, and Milton and Howard got jobs after school. Will and Alonzo, who were five and six, respectively, did their best. By the unspoken consent of everyone Mary Isabel, who was hardly three, was spared the details of the family's difficult existence. All the children had inherited their father's charm. They were all slender, graceful and good-looking; they were popular in the community, and jobs were always available. They were aware that they were poor relations; they knew that their mother did not buy new dresses, that they must practice economy in household matters, that the students living in the house were a necessity; but if their characters were affected it was mostly for the good, for they grew up feeling that they must make their own way.

When Milton finished school he worked on an uncle's farm for a year or so and then went to Fitchburg, Massachusetts, where he obtained a position in a relative's pharmacy. He was a sober lad, the least distinguished of the four sons, with a kind face and, in later years, a wide mustache, his hair parted in the middle. Howard was the most independent of the younger boys; he was old enough when his father died to remember him, and he appears to have taken his family's position rather more to heart than his brothers did. When he was fourteen he took the position of printer's "devil" in the office of the Fredonia *Censor*, held it for a year or two until he had obtained enough of the technique of the trade to imagine he was able to strike off for himself, and then set out for Boston, where, among its other advantages, his mother's wealthy relatives lived. They helped him to find a lodging house and a job with a printing establishment. When he was eighteen he contracted some illness that made him homesick and he returned to Fredonia to recover under his mother's care. At the end of his convalescence he left home again, to go to Chicago, where he was remembered affectionately by his family's former friends, and they managed to make it as easy for him as they could. He was lucky enough to receive the position of type-setter in the office of *The Farmer's Advocate*, and he worked in that capacity until his enlistment as a private soldier in an Illinois volunteer regiment in 1862. His only surviving photo-graph shows him in the uniform of a Union soldier, his coat thrown open carelessly at the throat, his hat tipped rakishly over one ear. He was a silent lad, much given to sitting deep in thought while the others around him talked. He had the fine clear Cushing eyes, was an excellent shot, and a brave and hardy soldier.

When the family first moved to Fredonia Will and Alonzo were not yet old enough to attend the Academy, though Milton and Howard went to it, and they were sent to Miss Julia Moore's nursery school. The difference of schools and age was naturally reflected in a pairing off among the brothers. The older boys were inseparable companions, as were the two younger, but the older brothers scorned what seemed to them Will and Allie's childish activities. Mrs. Cushing was inclined to side with her younger sons, when their plans were not too destructive. For example, there was the affair of Miss Harris, a pretty young woman who was their first teacher. It was suspected that Miss Harris was the unwilling object of the affections of a widower named Fink. Miss Harris' favorite, however, was not Mr. Fink but Will Cushing; she had discovered in him, so she later said, "a hero in embryo," and she made him her pet. He was called upon, in due course, to give his first recitation at an exhibition at school. The amorous widower would be there—indeed, the whole town would be present. Will and Allie and their mother spent a week composing verses but told no one about it. Allie sat with his mother, as he was not performing. The young orator advanced to the edge of the platform and in a high uncertain voice declaimed:

> Who with a cheerful, smiling face
> Meets her loved pupils in this place
> Each morn and never tarries,
> And though the day be wet and cold
> Hastes like a shepherd to his fold?
> Our teacher, good Miss Harris.
>
> Whose dark eye meets each little child
> Whose fun and frolic nearly wild
> Away good order carries?
> Who grieves to punish, when she must,
> And even then is kind and just?
> Our teacher, good Miss Harris.
>
> I fear we shall not keep her long
> Amid our noisy little throng,
> But blest is he who marries
> The patient, kind, devoted girl—
> A precious gem, a priceless pearl—
> Our dear beloved Miss Harris.

The piece was a resounding success and an encore was demanded. Only one among the audience was dissatisfied. Mr. Fink's retreating back was seen by Will as he stood to recite the poem again, and he announced to the crowd the departure of the harassed widower, which caused more merriment. Miss

Harris was delighted, she said, and Mr. Fink did not trouble her thereafter.

The next year Allie went to the Academy and Will continued at Miss Julia's, but the separation did not serve to part them for more than a few hours a day. Miss Julia's was finished two hours before the larger school, but Will would go to the Academy if he was not needed for some chore at home and wait for Allie to appear. Together they would walk home along Elm Street, past their grandfather's big house with the long porch on the south side, along two or three paths and then across the lot behind the Edwards place (also cousins) to their own backyard. It was clear to each of them that the other was the most important person in the world. They had never tried to frame the feeling in words, and they never would try, but they would always know it, always had known it, and nothing would ever change it. Their mother knew about it, but she did not talk about it. Their little sister knew about it too, but she did not speak of it until both were dead. "One trait, I think, was very remarkable in our family," she wrote in a letter years later; "the respect and courtesy manifested toward each other. I never received a reproof or heard an impatient word from either of my brothers [by the time she was old enough to know them Milton and Howard had left Fredonia]. They always displayed toward each other, and my mother and myself, the same courtesy they would show to a commanding officer. The petting and love I received was enough to have spoiled me for life, for contact with the world."

Will always had a belief in an overruling Providence and a firm conviction that it would carry him safely through all difficulties. By Providence he did not understand, at the age of six, what the theologian means by the word; perhaps nowadays we would say that he had complete faith in himself. It was the only subject on which he and Allie disagreed. Alonzo was never so sure about anything as Will was about everything.

Allie was a serious, practical boy, and very early in life his mother decided that he was the most reliable of her sons, picking him as the one most likely to succeed and to be a comfort to her in her old age. She loved Will with all her heart; everybody loved Will with a good part, at least, of their hearts; he was, as someone said years later, "the plague and the pride of all who knew him." Alonzo was different. He had a round, almost girlish face, with long lashes and smooth cheeks, but with a strong wide mouth that never let anyone make the mistake of supposing that his gentle disposition and unwillingness to take affront or remember an injury were masks to hide a timorous heart. But he did not have the faith that Will had. Will believed not only in himself but in the willingness of water to hold him up and of horses to be shod. Once the two boys fought about it. The actual cause of the quarrel has been lost with the years, but it involved some escapade which Allie did not want his brother to undertake, and which Will insisted was perfectly safe. The fight went on for a long time, by the standard of boys, and it was, possibly to Allie's surprise, a draw, and they never fought again. It was just as well, the neighbors said, that they had been human enough to fight once, but their mother was upset. They were contrite, and tried to please her in every way they could think of for weeks afterward, until she had to speak to them about that too. But the deep-seated disagreement about the nature of the universe remained. It is probable that Allie felt his position as the elder strongly; he was inclined to that. But Will had three older brothers to watch over him, and that tends to make a boy feel very safe.

That summer an example occurred of the way Will felt about things. His mother, wishing to get him out of the house for a spell (possibly it was cleaning time), gave him money to pay his rail fare to Silver Creek, a neighboring town, for a visit to an aunt. She kept chickens and geese which a visiting boy was always welcome to feed, and Will liked to go to see her. He liked her so much, as a matter of fact, that he spent for a present all the money his mother had provided, and boarded the train without a penny in his pocket. Entering the car, he sat down next to a benevolent-looking gentleman in a checked vest with a silver watch chain. The man was sleepy but Will soon had him interested in the duck eggs which he and Allie had found the day before. They struck up a conversation, and the man was charmed by his young traveling companion. Out of the corner of his eye Will saw the conductor enter the car, and talked even more briskly. When the conductor was three seats away he reached in his pocket as though to pay the fare, but the man insisted that he should pay it himself, since he had received more than the fare was worth in entertainment. Will said that he guessed he ought not to let the man do it, but the latter, thankfully, was adamant. It was months before Mrs. Cushing learned the story, when the aunt thanked her for the beautiful gift that Will had brought.

The next fall Will was old enough to attend the Academy, and the two brothers had even more opportunity to be together. But again there arose a difference of opinion. One of their playmates, a boy named Hartwell Dickenson, had smallpox and the house was quarantined. Their teacher warned them to stay away, describing in no uncertain terms the danger they would run if they visited the boy. For a few days Will was obedient, but he had a warm heart and imagined that Harty would be lonely. He tried to get Allie to go with him, but Allie protested at the foolhardiness of such action. Will went alone. He knew better than to go in the front door, but the Dickensons had a back porch and a maple tree, and it was easy to swing from one of the large branches onto the porch roof and into the stricken boy's window. There he would sit for hours each day, talking. Once Harty's father came into the room unexpectedly before Will had a chance to get away. "What are *you* doing here, young man?" asked the surprised parent. Will stuttered out a story, but his series of visits was soon got out of him, and General Dickenson marched the boy home. "Mrs. Cushing," he said when they reached the house on Green Street, "you must keep your boy away from our house! He has been to visit Harty every day since he has been sick, and we can't keep him out." Mrs. Cushing was horrified, as none of the family had ever been vaccinated, and smallpox was then, of course, one of the most dreaded diseases. She turned on Will and spoke to him as angrily as she ever had. He burst into tears. "It's a shame," he wailed. "Poor Harty! None of the boys will go near him, and he's so sick." His mother could not remain angry, but she waited fearfully for the day when the small red spots would appear, indicative that someone in the family had caught the disease. It was perhaps not the best thing for Will that his faith in his own star was entirely justified. No one in the family came down with smallpox.

The Cushings were Baptists, and one of Will and Allie's favorite people was the daughter of Elder Kingsbury, pastor of the First Baptist Church. Her name was Ella, and Will met her the first day the family moved to town. The Kingsburys lived in a house opposite their own on Green Street, and Will, who would have received high marks for curiosity if for nothing else, spied her through the fence and crossed the road to speak to her. At first she was shy but they soon became friends, and he brought her back and introduced her to the rest of the family. Ella spent many hours in the Cushing home from that day forth, and she recalled a characteristic of the boy. "He was very enthusiastic," she wrote in a letter, "and would talk enthusiastically about the nice things he meant to buy for his mother, who was in the habit of humoring his bright fancies and helping him along in the building of his air castles; as, for instance, he would say, 'Mother, I will buy you a satin dress, or a velvet robe, which shall it be?' She would reply: 'I think satin will be the most suitable for me.' 'Then satin it shall be,' would be his rejoinder."

When Will was ten Elder Kingsbury gave him his first regular job. For a certain weekly sum the boy was to drive the preacher's cow to pasture after the Elder had milked it in the morning. The Elder told his new hand that he should not come too early in the morning, since he liked to stay up late at night studying and reading. The first morning Will came just before school, and the Elder said that was right. But there were chickens to feed and the horse to curry, and half a dozen other chores for which Will rose before dawn, "heroically," as Ella put it, "sacrificing his morning sleep." Will seems to have felt that if he could get out of bed early then the Elder could too. Within a week he was coming every morning as soon as it was light. The Elder was usually not awake, but Will would get up on the fence, about three feet from his window, and proceed to whistle and sing and scrape the fence pickets with a stick. The Elder did not break the bargain, but after a year he hired a less enterprising cowherd.

That winter Will had his first taste of command. Between them he and Allie formed an organization which included most of the small boys in the town. The "Muss Company" was well schooled in obedience, for Allie and Will could lick any boy their size. Will, a natural leader, was chosen captain, while Allie, who was perhaps a little too old for such games, was content to be secretary-treasurer. The group wrote no letters and had no money. The public-school teacher, a harried little man with glasses perched at the end of his nose, had incurred, for some reason, the severe displeasure of the captain of the band. Therefore, Will would go during his lunch hour, mount the fence surrounding the public school, and give the special whistle which identified the members of the company. They would all rush out and form by the gate and be marched off by their young commander while the teacher waved his arms in the door of the school building. After a few minutes Will would march his men back, but though they missed little in the way of instruction, it was obviously impossible for the teacher to allow this to continue. In despair he went to Mrs. Cushing. Her son, he said, was destroying his influence. The boys were frightened of Will, he added, or of course they would not go.

"Do you know how old this 'monster' is?" Mrs. Cushing asked.

"Why, I suppose he is an older boy, ma'am," was the reply. "Else they would not obey him."

Mrs. Cushing told him that her son was not yet ten years old, and the teacher was then shown to the door after being assured that she would take care of the matter. At a word from her the Muss Company was abandoned, but its work had been done.

The fact that Will was chosen leader of the Muss Company over his older brother was not out of the ordinary. "Will was the ringleader in all the berrying, nutting and fishing frolics," his sister wrote later, "and our adventures would fill a volume. He always killed every snake, even pulling them out of their holes." He was also kindhearted, as the affair of Hartwell Dickenson had shown. "One day when he was sent by Cousin George White to take a horse, that was not very well, over to a pasture in Arkwright, he found an old wagon, and taking a lot of us children, went to Arkwright for a berrying. At every hill, great or small, we were all under orders to alight and help the horse to get the wagon up the hill." And Ella Kingsbury remembered that "as a boy he was venturesome, and even while very young, was a daring and willful leader of his young companions. He was quick-tempered and always ready to settle disputes with a fight, upon the principle that the best men won the battle."

In 1854 and 1855, when Allie was thirteen and fourteen, there was a momentary lull in the intimacy between him and his younger brother owing to the fact that Alonzo had discovered the attraction exerted by girls over maturing males and Will had not. Will was annoyed and could not understand the change that had come over his brother. Julia Greenleaf, who lived in Silver Creek and attended the Academy, was a special object of Allie's affections, and she remembered that "Will was never happier than when playing some joke upon one of his older brothers. One summer evening I accompanied his brother Alonzo to the 'mill pond,' upon his invitation to take a row in a forlorn old scow which was much patronized by the young people for what they considered delightful trips over the smooth pond. When we reached the bank we found that someone had untied the boat and set it adrift. No other boat was to be had and so we sat down on a log, wondering if someone had tricked us out of our row. Soon we heard a wild whoop in the distance and saw Master Will waving an oar and shouting to us: 'Next time you want to row, don't forget to ask your friends.' "

"Another time," she recalled, "when one of his brothers invited me to go to Methodist prayer meeting, Will offered to accompany us and we declined the pleasure of his company; he seemed to accede to our decision very meekly, but when we had been seated in the church a few minutes he came in and took a seat behind us, and when the first hymn was being sung, we were shocked to hear his fresh young voice shouting very personal remarks to us to the tune of the hymn. The sexton discovered the culprit and when the youngster was led out of church in disgrace we followed."

Unable to understand the change that had overtaken his beloved brother, Will took it out on the boys of his own age. "He had an uncle living on a farm, a short distance from Silver Creek," Julia wrote, "whom he was allowed to visit for a week during a summer vacation. After a day or two on the quiet farm, Will concluded to seek more excitement than his uncle's home afforded and so came to our house in the village and informed my mother that he thought he would visit us for a few days. Each day, while with us, he went out in quest of adventure. One day when a letter came from his mother commanding his return home, he said: 'Well, I've whipped every boy in town, so I guess I might as well go.' I am sure there was little, if any, exaggeration in this assertion."

He made his peace with Julia, however. "Shortly after this episode Will met me on my way to school one morning (we were both attending the academy in Fredonia), and with an air of great meekness presented me with a gorgeous bouquet, which, he incidentally explained, he had 'hooked' from Mrs. Gillis' garden before that worthy woman was up in the morning. The stems of the flowers were thrust through a little gold ring and among the blossoms I found a tiny three-cornered note."

It may have been that this overture of friendship was the prelude to something more serious. In any case, when Will went to Annapolis he had his picture taken in his first midshipman's suit, and sent it to Julia. However, she married a Mr. Horton from Buffalo a few years later.

One of Will's best friends in Fredonia was his cousin Mary Edwards. She was a pretty girl with brown hair and blue eyes, only a few months older than he, and they were in the same class at school. Will was always welcome at the Edwards home —Francis Smith Edwards, Mary's father, had married a sister of Mrs. Cushing—and he spent many happy days with the family. For years he wrote her letters describing his adventures, and their friendship lasted all his life.

In the fall of 1854 her father ran for the House of Representatives on the American party ticket. The party's politics were unfortunate—it is better known by its nickname of the "Know Nothing" party—but Edwards, who was a large, hearty man and a good speaker, seems to have been one of its less fanatical adherents. In any case, enough of his neighbors subscribed to its ideals to elect him to Congress from the thirty-fourth district of New York State. His term started on March 4, 1855, and before leaving Fredonia he promised Mrs. Cushing that he would do what he could to place her sons in a better position in life than they could otherwise have attained, and he was true to his word. In the summer of 1855 he called on the Cushings and after a private discussion with Will's mother the boy was called into the parlor. The occasion was obviously of some moment, and Will stood very still while his mother told him that his uncle had procured a place for him as page in the House of Representatives. Edwards also told the family that he was trying to get Alonzo appointed to be a cadet at West Point, in which he was finally successful. Will thought that he would leave immediately, but his uncle told him that he would not go until the next year, and that he should do as much school work as possible in the intervening months.

He spent the rest of the summer studying Latin, his most dreaded subject, and passed his examinations the next year well enough to graduate from the Fredonia Academy in June, 1856. Despite the fact that he had been, as he wrote years later, "a rather small and wicked student," he received a good education at the school—a better one than many of his contemporaries. His handwriting was clear, he could compose a workmanlike prose (later he would write better than average reports of his naval exploits), and though his punctuation was erratic it was better, for example, than Lord Nelson's. He knew a little Latin and more mathematics, and he was not weak in American history. And he knew many things of practical value for a boy leaving home at the age of fourteen to go to the capital of what everybody was beginning to say would be the greatest country in the world.

There was much talk of politics that summer. The main subject of conversation was the Kansas-Nebraska Bill, and occasionally someone—it was usually Cousin George White, who was a firebrand—would wonder "if it would come to a war." There were many arguments about the protective tariff, of which Edwards was a strong supporter. In this he concurred with the newly formed Republican party, although the new party was the most severe threat to his own in the coming elections. Aside from politics, iron had been discovered in northern Wisconsin and the portage of it through the lakes and down the Erie Canal was beginning to be seriously discussed; Fredonia businessmen were among the first to invest money in what became, through the impetus of the war, one of the most thriving of American industries in the years to come. The opening of St. Marys Falls ship canal had connected Lake Huron and Lake Superior, which would make the job easier.

Edwards' party, along with the Whigs, nominated Millard Fillmore for the Presidency, but he was badly defeated in November. Although Buchanan, a Democrat, was elected to the White House, the Republicans scored notable victories in the North and Northeast—Edwards lost his seat to a Republican—and the results forecast the speedy demise of the Whig and Know Nothing organizations. They also forecast something that worried people more. The election had been fought on sectional lines and decided on sectional lines, and it began to look as though it did not matter much what a man thought any more, if he lived north or south of that line which Daniel Webster had said, only six years before, that they could not draw "to satisfy any five men in the country." But now there seemed to be millions of men satisfied, or dissatisfied, if that was the way you wanted to look at it. And many did.

Congressman Edwards' defeat did not affect Will's appointment, and before he left for Washington, in the fall of 1856, he wrote a poem called "Farewell" which appeared in the January, 1857, issue of the *Academist*, the school paper. It begins thus:

> Ere I haste away to another clime,
>   A clime with promise bright,
> My heart will say in simple rhyme,
>   Dear village home, good night!

and continues for half a dozen stanzas in this vein. But in fact those he was leaving behind would miss him more than he would miss them—it was exciting to be going out into the big world at last. His mother would miss him, and so would Allie, who was left behind "bravely attending to such home duties as would be valuable in lightening his mother's work," but no one, perhaps, was sadder at his departure than his little sister Isabel, for whom he had always been a protector and a guide. Because she felt deeply about his going and wanted him, at the bottom of her heart, to stay, she wrote a poem too (she was not yet eleven, and her mother probably helped her) which, like his, was published in the *Academist*, but which unlike his has a tone of sincerity about it, and is thus, though sentimental and not very sure technically, a good poem. It was called "The Old Straw Hat."

> For a sober half an hour,
> I've been looking still at that,
> As it hangeth in the corner,
> An old forsaken hat;
> For a charm still lingers o'er it,
> Torn and shabby though it be,
> For the sake of him that wore it,
> A brother dear to me.
>
> All through the sunny summer,
> When he sought the berries red,
> That little hat hath shaded
> My merry brother's head;
> And when the thorny bushes
> Had torn a rent so wide,
> That I was called to mend it,
> How crossly I replied!
>
> I remember this with sorrow—
> For now he's far away—
> And his bright blue eyes I may not see
> For many a weary day.
> There's his likeness on the table,
> And I like to look at that,
> But there's nothing brings him back again
> Like that old forsaken hat.

"No matter what anybody says or thinks about Washington, it is us inescapably," said Joel Sayre of our national capital, and though the words were written eighty years after Will Cushing first saw the rough new city on the Potomac, they have always been true. In 1856 the American nation was raw and sprawling—Washington was raw and sprawling, too. In 1856 the nation was only half built and not too sure of itself (it made up for that by what seemed to many Europeans an ill-justified confidence)—Washington was half built too: work-men were busy putting a new dome on the Capitol, and scaffolding covered the unfinished wings which would house the Senate and House of Representatives; Pennsylvania Avenue boasted no fine buildings except the White House, and its impressive wideness, paved thirty years before by cobbles which proved too thin to withstand the increasing traffic, had long since given way to the mud and dust of the changing seasons. Mud was a problem everywhere in America —therefore it was a problem in Washington. In 1856 the nation was having trouble assimilating its new and unformed elements—Washington was having similar difficulties: it did not know where to throw its garbage, for example, and just ten blocks from the White House waste collected from the out-houses of the city was deposited on the Potomac flats. When a southeast breeze was blowing, which was practically all the time, the odor was unmistakable. Maintaining law and order in a frontier society was a notoriously hard problem—Wash-ington was notoriously negligent in its police department: it was by no means safe to be out on the streets at night, any more than it was safe to be out alone on the prairie, or along the Mississippi, or on a California mining claim. The Washing-ton fire department was as bad as the police. Quite often, contemporary reports announced with shame and sorrow, fires were left to burn without hindrance because the firemen were engaged in "stone and pistol fights" over the question of which company had jurisdiction over the fire, or just, perhaps, out of an excess of animal spirits. And in 1856 the nation was preparing for a civil war, a war of words only in that year and for five years to come, but a war that was fought more bitterly in Washington than anywhere else.

Despite its unfinished look this "sprawling and unfulfilled embodiment of national grandeur" was impressive to a four-teen-year-old boy who had never seen a city except the even more primitive Chicago of his infancy. There were statues, for example, of George Washington, Thomas Jefferson and Andrew Jackson, as well as of other heroes of the nation's youth; and though few buildings of any size were completed there was something magnificent about the unfinished structures that pointed into the sky, their exteriors covered with scaffolding, their interiors crawling with workmen. The Union Station was not yet built, but there was a station, and more trains came into and out of it in a day than Will Cushing had seen in his entire life. And there was something magnificent, too, about the way, and about the fact that, the city was planned—a grandiose plan, a giant pie with radiating avenues and circular streets with easy-to-remember names. It was probably the first planned capital to be built in a thousand years or more, since the last of the great monarchical foundations had been swallowed up by the irresistible jungles of Nepal and Mysore.

Will lived for a few weeks with his uncle and aunt in their suite of rooms near the Capitol, but the arrangement was not very satisfactory. There was a housing problem in Washington then as now, and the apartment was not big enough to accommodate an extra boy, particularly one as lively as Will. A room was found for him in Washington House, where the other pages lived, and he moved there before Christmas. He had enjoyed his stay at the Edwardses'; he had spent as much time as possible with his cousin, and after he moved he continued to see her often. His duties were not restricting. He was supposed to be on the floor of the House during debates and available for the carrying of letters and notes from one Congressman to another, but there were more than enough pages and most of his time was spent sitting as quietly as possible on the Speaker's platform, waiting to be called. This was hard for him, since he had never before been still in his life. The House was engaged in further discussions of the Kansas-Nebraska Bill that year, but Will did not listen very carefully to what was said and quickly came round to the opinion that he was not missing a great deal if he did not listen. "I heard enough nonsense in my time in the House to last for fifty years," he said in a letter some years later. It was exciting, of course, to meet, as he inevitably did, all the great men of the time; if he did not meet them, he at least saw them. Occasionally he would visit the Senate and listen to debates there, and he heard Seward, Chase and Douglas. He did his job as well as could be expected; he was cheerful and pleasing in his appearance and behavior; and everyone liked him, both the men who ran the country and the boys who served them. His natural ability to lead was in evidence among the latter; he organized excursions among the pages as he had among the boys in Fredonia, and within a few months he knew the city of Washington as well as he knew the tree-lined streets of his native town.

Among the important people whom he came to know was Commodore Joseph Smith, who had been since 1846 the chief of the Bureau of Navy Yards and Docks in Washington and in control of all naval construction. Commodore (later Rear Admiral) Smith was Mrs. Cushing's cousin, and though he was a solidly built man with iron-gray hair and "a rather frighteningly serious demeanor" the two relatives became friends. Will met him at Christmas, and it was not many months later that the boy was informed that, owing to the efforts of his Congressman uncle and Commodore cousin, he had been accepted at the Naval Academy in Annapolis, to enroll in the class of 1861.

Will did not forget his early resolutions, and his promises to his mother. The first money that he saved he sent home, directing that it be used by her for the purchase of a silk dress. She bought the material and wore the garment when he went home. He was very proud and thought the dress the prettiest his mother had ever owned, and he made her turn around so that he could examine it from every angle. "You look very well in silks, Mother," he said, so seriously that she did not know whether to laugh or cry. She managed to smile in the way a woman should who is being dressed by her fourteen-year-old son. He told her that he would get her more dresses but that she would have to wait, for his wages were not so great as yet.

He spent the summer at home, and there was hardly time to tell about all the extraordinary things that had happened. The inaugural of President Buchanan, for instance—it had occurred in March, it had been a sunny day but cold, and Will had had a seat in the grandstand. The speech was long and Congressman Edwards, who had resigned his seat on February 28 but remained at Washington until the end of the year, did not approve of much that was said. Two days later the Supreme Court handed down the Dred Scott decision and though Congress was not in session Will spent a hectic week delivering letters. He described the debates in Congress with such animation that Isabel laughed to think that her brother knew so many Congressmen and that Congressmen were such silly creatures. He described the way Washington looked, with special emphasis on the many Negroes one saw everywhere. If he said that he had seen the President riding by on his black horse a few more times than he actually had, we must not blame him. He had an instinct for drama, and drama pleases little girls. He brought messages from Commodore Smith to his mother, and she was thoughtful, remembering the days in Boston when they had been children. Isabel was interested in the clothes that the rich women wore, and Will told her as much about that as he knew, and filled out the story when it was necessary. He somehow left her with the impression that he had been a guest at a number of balls and other festivities, though he never specified which ones.

Will and Allie had long-drawn-out military and nautical conversations, speaking of General Washington and John Paul Jones as though they were friends of the family. There were veterans of the Mexican War in Fredonia, and the two boys sought them out whenever they could. They would come home late from such discussions and shake hands before they parted for sleep—they had adopted the custom of shaking hands as though they were strangers—and then salute each other "for practice." Will called Allie a "sojer" with derision and Allie called Will a "tar" with equal derision, but they gloried in the titles. Their mother insisted that they were still "boys."

It was a good lazy summer for them both, and in the backs of their minds they knew it would be the last for a long time. Commodore Smith had been quick to point out that there was no place at the Naval Academy for lazy or mischievous boys, and Allie had received the same warning from his uncle. They took advantage of their leisure while they had it, but in due course the time came to leave. They walked solemnly all around the town in their best clothes, stopping in at almost every gate to say good-by. Their mother and Isabel and Cousin George White drove them to Dunkirk, where they could catch the train to Buffalo and New York. They spent two or three days in New York as guests of a cousin and then Alonzo took the train to West Point and Will took one south to Philadelphia, Baltimore, and Annapolis, where he became an acting midshipman on September 25, 1857.

III

Annapolis

~~~~~~

THE U.S. Military Academy was founded at West Point in 1802 and received its first cadets on July Fourth of that year, but it was forty-three years later before its sister institution saw the light on the banks of the Severn River in the beautiful pre-Revolutionary town of Annapolis, Maryland. For George Bancroft, born in 1800, it had been a constant dream, and it was under his administration of the Navy Department that the Academy (called at first the "Naval School") came into existence in 1845, the year of the annexation of Texas. It was ten years more before Congress showed any enthusiasm for the project. In spite of its late beginning and its status as stepchild, and in spite of the fact that by 1861 the school had graduated hardly three hundred officers, the Naval Academy did good service for the country in the Civil War.

The school had arisen out of the disused remains of the old army post called Fort Severn, a small installation pinched between Annapolis Harbor, the Severn, and the narrow tributary of the river called at the present day College Creek. On two sides were walls intended to keep the middies in and the townspeople out. They were not very successful either way.

The inherited buildings were old and rickety. In the former quarters of the army commandant the Academy's superintendent took up residence, and though the building had "cracking walls and settling floors" from the beginning it

endured for fifty years before being declared unfit for oc-
cupancy. Adjoining it were four relatively new buildings
occupied by faculty members of professorial rank. This row
of square stone houses was known as "Buchanan Row." The
midshipmen were quartered in a miscellany of old army barracks and newer wooden dormitories distinguished for ill-
fitting doors, windows that would not open or close, and
poor construction throughout. During the superintendency of
Louis Goldsborough, in the mid-fifties, the barracks were
fitted out with steam heat (the old fireplaces had caused a
number of fires before this, though none was serious) and gas
lamps, and new buildings were built. But the construction was
usually slipshod. Once in 1858 one of the new structures lost
a wall, which collapsed at eight o'clock in the evening when
the midshipmen were hard at their studies. No one was hurt,
miraculously, but the study period came to an abrupt end.

In Cushing's time the midshipmen lived in five buildings.
Beyond them was another group of buildings, the largest of
which was the recitation hall. To the left of it was the mess
hall, in front of which were large brass cannon captured in
the Mexican War. The upper story of this building was the
library and lyceum; here the Lawrence Literary Society met
once a week. Cushing was a leading member of this debating
society, and his later fluency in addressing public gatherings
stemmed in part from his experiences here. Next to the mess
hall was the chapel, then the observatory, the store and the
gas house; beyond this was a monument erected to the memory of a group of midshipmen lost on a practice cruise. Surrounding it were British guns captured in 1812. In the belfry
of the chapel were two bells. The smaller was the fire bell, but
the larger, brought from Japan by Commodore Perry and still
in use, struck the hours.

The naval uniform of 1857 was, as the young midshipman
wrote proudly to his mother, "distinctly nautical." The jacket
was navy blue, double-breasted with a rolling collar bearing
a gold foul anchor on each side. The jacket was ordinarily

worn unbuttoned and the cap, with its silver foul anchor over the front, was worn, at least by Will, "flattened down on the top and rolled over to one side." The trousers were navy blue and cut slim. Under the jacket was a white shirt, and the necktie was a loosely flowing black handkerchief. Will was a slim five feet five inches when he matriculated at the Academy, and he must have looked well in his uniform. The record indicates that only one person ever took exception to his appearance. In his second year the young sailor visited one of his aunts, who lived in Chelsea, Massachusetts, and a neighborhood boy openly sneered at the short uniform jacket. "The battle," according to the aunt's account of it to Mrs. Cushing, "raged over the sidewalks and the dusty streets." It was a rugged and, unfortunately for the uniform, bloody fight, but Will was as usual victorious and "afterwards walked the streets of Chelsea quite free from comments on his beloved uniform."

The lack of governmental enthusiasm for the Academy had other effects besides poor living quarters. Without adequate personnel and proper teaching and training facilities it was difficult for the administration to maintain much discipline. The citizens of Annapolis more than once were shaken in their beds by the sound of the firing of the big guns which overlooked the harbor. There were not enough watchmen, and it was easy enough to inveigle the one or two charged with keeping the peace by means of decoys of plebes—there was little or no hazing until the war—while upperclassmen loaded the guns and touched the matches. In the morning the authorities would splutter, but to no avail. Occasionally, not content with noise, the midshipmen would descend on the town in person and spend half the night shouting in the streets. This was severely frowned upon, for Annapolis had a sure conviction of its dignity as capital of Maryland. The State House stood (and stands) impressively on top of a hill, and the main streets of the town radiate from State Circle, which surrounds the building. The midshipmen would attack the place as though it were a fort, and come shouting out of the radial streets to converge on the top of the hill, where they would no doubt have fired the captured cannon which still sit there if a foresighted legislature had not spiked them years before.

Such excursions into town were rare, however; the young men were more likely to express their high spirits by having all-night cigar and whiskey parties in their rooms. They would sit up and eat cheese and crackers, sing loud songs, and tell stories until dawn interrupted their gaiety. In the morning the inspecting officers would find the inevitable signs of the night's hilarity but would not, or could not, punish the offenders. By the time Will Cushing arrived at the Academy the grip had been tightened—a fact which he was to find disastrous.

Only one man in the history of West Point ever managed to survive the four rigorous years without receiving one demerit, and that man, not surprisingly, is Robert E. Lee. William B. Cushing was far from equaling that record at Annapolis. It required 200 demerits for misconduct during a year to "restore a midshipman to his friends," as the saying went. Cushing in his first year received 99. None was for a serious offense. The next year he did much better, receiving 188 demerits, again for a series of annoying little misconducts. In June of that year he almost went over the line. A midshipman spent the early hours of the evening at a girl's house in town and was incorrectly identified as Cushing when he was seen scaling the wall on his return. The boy admitted his guilt when he discovered that Will would have been dismissed, and so Will was safe for another year. The experience may have sobered him, for the next year he managed to collect only 155 demerits. It may have been that he had become cleverer.

The same instinct that made him leave the note on the buoy for Colonel Jones was at work six years before, and he rather enjoyed the knowledge that his misdeeds did not go unnoticed. For example, he was famous during his Academy years for his "tea parties." It was the practice of the cooks to prepare buckets of tea for the evening meal and set them on the kitchen window sills to cool (cool tea was a favorite beverage of a hundred years ago). Will had a room during his second and third years which was directly above the kitchen, and from his window he would lean out and drop a line with a hook on it and draw up the pails of tea. He would then invite such of his friends as, in his estimation, deserved to be invited, and when they had drunk all they wanted he would fill the pails to the top with water and lower them to the shelf again. The cooks were always baffled, and of course those midshipmen who had been treated to the beverage at full strength would be the first, and the loudest, to complain that it was too weak that night at mess. But Will was never content with this simple deception. Before returning the pails he would fill half a dozen whiskey bottles with the pale brown liquid and hide them among his belongings. In the morning the room inspectors would find the telltale bottles and haul the miscreant before the superintendent. He would act demure and innocent, which he was, since there was no rule against having bottles of tea in one's luggage.

He did not confine his activities to tea. A favorite trick and, one would think, a dangerous one, was, as he wrote to Mary Edwards, "the art of extinguishing all the gas light in the building during study hours by vigorously blowing into a burner." This was a sure creator of pandemonium, and was effective if an inspecting officer in rubber-soled shoes—they were often reduced to that—was discovered in the attempt to catch the middies in their misdeeds. Another defense against such ungentlemanly conduct on the part of their superiors was a "door salute." All the doors not in the immediate view of the poor officer were banged "in the manner of a gun salute afloat," and when the inspector turned into the next corridor all would be spick and span. Occasionally more active sports were indulged in. Every morning a gun was fired when the flag was raised, and too often for comfort the gun was found, when it was set off, to have been crammed with bricks or stones during the night. No harm could come from this since the gun was pointed away from any human habitation, but two or three times during Cushing's years at the Academy the light battery guns which faced the harbor were similarly loaded with brickbats and pebbles. These guns were fired only on special occasions, but when the salute began the boats in the harbor would flee in terror from the "shot" splashing around them in the water. The most glorious firing of the guns occurred during Will's third year, in the spring of 1860. The superstructure of the old fort was enclosed by a number of glazer sashes which had to be removed when a salute was to be fired, as in this case in honor of a frigate of the French Navy which had arrived in the harbor during the night. Whether by accident or design, the sashes were piled on the barbette of the fort and directly under the muzzles of the guns, which were lowered before the firing commenced. The sashes were not noticed, and when the salute began there was a fearful crashing and clattering of breaking glass. The salute could not, of course, be interrupted. The entire corps of midshipmen had been drawn up in parade formation in front of the fort, and they watched and listened gleefully while a hundred and thirty-six sashes were blown to bits.

"Frenching it" was a term used by the mishipmen to denote leaving the Academy grounds without permission, and a "Frenching" expedition usually went into the town of Annapolis, even when its perpetrators were bound on amusement rather than destruction. The favorite rendezvous was Rosenthal's saloon, which was "Rosey's" to the middies. At the "stuttering Dutchman's" they would drink beer and sing songs until the worthy German, who could speak his native language with no difficulty but had great trouble with English, threw them out and closed his doors. There then remained the ticklish problem of getting back into the Academy grounds and into bed without being caught. Under Captain George S. Blake's administration (he served in this capacity throughout most of Cushing's stay at the Academy, and "was a portly old gentleman, who had the habit of placing his hand upon his stomach and remarking impressively: 'I can lay my hand upon my heart, and say I have never wronged a midshipman' ") the police force was augmented by the acquisition of a huge and proportionately fierce black Newfoundland dog which roamed the lawns inside the walls all during the night, to be tied up by day behind the kitchen. Will had more than once tried to make friends with the animal, but to no avail; it did not wish to make friends with anybody and only condoned the watchman because of familiarity. If the tide was low it was possible to wade around the end of the wall, climb the east wall of the fort, and, making use of a tree limb and the roof of the unused store house, reach the first barracks, from which the others were readily accessible. This, though difficult, was usually a successful maneuver. But the tide was not always low, in which case the dog and his master had to be avoided. Many midshipmen were caught by this combination of forces and one or two were dismissed, but Cushing was fleet of foot and adept at outracing both sorts of guardians. Once he lost the seat of a pair of pants to the Newfoundland. "Fortunately," he wrote Mary, "they were by no means my best pair of trousers."

Considering the amount of thought he expended in his successful attempts to outwit the authorities, it is surprising that he had any time left over to do the work required of him, but in fact, though he was not distinguished especially as a student, he was by no means the worst in his class. He had never been studious; he was, until his third year, the youngest man at the Academy, and always the youngest in his class. The grading system in force at the time was complicated. Each boy recited every day; for recitations marks were given, from zero for a complete failure, to four for a perfect performance. Certain branches of study, such as seamanship, gunnery, navigation and other professional subjects, were given greater weight than those pertaining to general education. For example, the first year the weights were arithmetic and algebra, 20, grammar, 10, geography and history, 25, drawing, 15, conduct, 5, while the professional subjects were weighted about twice as heavily. The highest student in a class received the full weight, while the minimum received by the lowest man was usually a third of the total weight. The general merit roll was made up by adding together all the weights obtained by a student and then arranging them numerically. Since the weights for the different subjects were shifted with each year's course of study, a drastic change in a midshipman's standing could result. George Dewey, for example, who was in the class of 1858, in his first year ranked thirty-fifth in a class of thirty-eight and was, the next year, ninth in a class of twenty-nine.

Cushing's naval biographer says of him that "it is remarkable that a youngster of eighteen years should be able to stand high in his studies with so little effort." As examples of Cushing's grades, he reports that the young midshipman, in his second year while a member of a class of thirty-seven, stood "3 in gunnery, 8 in ethics, 13 in astronomy, and 9 in general order of merit, and last in conduct." The examinations in February, 1861, found Cushing "6 in ethics, 7 in gunnery, 9 in artillery, 11 in philosophy, 26 in modern languages, and 6 in general order of merit. . . ." His standing in conduct is not mentioned. It was probably not high.

His lack of studiousness was not only due to temperament. His health was not good. Will had inherited his Grandfather Zattu's indomitable will, but not his constitution. Milton Cushing passed other things along to his sons, but unfortunately for them he could not help but give them the slight figure and the physical weakness that had killed him in his forties. Will suffered, and had suffered for years, from racking colds and their complications. There were many days when he literally could not get out of bed, and sometimes he went for a week on end with a headache so bad he could hardly see. "I am not in good health now," he writes to Mary Edwards in February of 1860, "and I do not study any. I expect to go down in my studies in consequence. It does not make any difference, however; health must be attended to, and the officers and I know what I can do." In March, 1861, he writes, "Ahem! I say ahem! because I have a cold, a real consumptive cold, a cold that the most polite language (also a little of the other kind) will not persuade to abandon its position, therefore I repeat ahem! It is the first day of spring. . . ." Nothing that the doctors could prescribe was of any use, and winters were times of misery for him. When he left the Academy he was six feet tall and weighed only 150 pounds, yet he managed to lose 10 pounds every winter. No one could ever discover where his energy came from. Yet he never lost his cheerful demeanor, even in the face of the chill wet days in which Annapolis abounds from November to March. And he was amazingly strong. Once when he was visiting a cousin in Boston he caught and held a runaway horse which had escaped the clutches, his cousin wrote, "of five men who could have lifted Will over their heads with one hand." Perhaps the simplest explanation is that he was not afraid of the horse. It is not recorded that he was ever afraid of anything in his life. "All mortal greatness is but disease," said Melville of Captain Ahab. For Will Cushing, perhaps courage was as much a disease as anything else.

It would have been good for him, perhaps, if there had been any sort of organized physical exercise at the Academy while he was there. But there was none: "The rule was one endless grind of acquiring knowledge," Admiral Dewey said in later years. There was no gymnasium or other equipment to encourage athletics, a lack which has been amply compensated since. There was in fact almost no way to get rid of the steam generated by normal young men, with the uncommon exception of "stag hops" in the recitation hall basement on Saturday nights, and sailing on the bay—a sedentary occupation at best. The situation was recognized toward the end of Blake's administration, and an attempt was made to remedy it by instituting an hour's drilling each day. The new program was disastrous at first, however, and gave Cushing the opportunity to score one of his most famous victories over the authorities.

"A messmate before a shipmate, a shipmate before a stranger, a stranger before a dog, but a dog before a 'sojer,' " went the old saying, which every plebe had to recite the first day he spent on Academy soil. The midshipmen were most emphatically not "sojers"; the fact that Alonzo was at West Point was something which Will could conveniently ignore when the spirit took him. But in the fall of 1858, here they were drilling every afternoon, with rifles over their shoulders, and, worst of all, under the command of a Professor Lockwood, who had been trained at West Point itself. Ignominy of ignominies! Everything possible was done to discourage the energetic Lockwood from his task. The midshipmen slouched and sagged, and managed to keep from looking at all like soldiers. Cushing was the worst: he was able to walk more limply than anyone could have thought possible, and the good professor would throw up his hands in unbelieving despair when Cushing "marched." Even so, the drills went on. But the sailors were eager at all times to disavow any skill which Lockwood might suppose he had taught them. The strain began to tell after a few months, and the professor developed the worst of all possible defects of a drillmaster: he began to stutter. It was in February that this first became evident, and the thing grew apace. The middies, under Cushing's expert tutelage, made no sign that they noticed. "R-r-r-r-r-right face!" would come the order, and they would turn smartly when the sound finally came. "At-t-t-t-t-t-ten—shun!" and they would snap their shoulders straight. They lulled their drillmaster into a false security, but it did not cure the stutter. "Woe unto the world because of offenses! for it must needs be that offenses come; but woe to that man by whom the offense cometh!" So said Abraham Lincoln of a greater guilt, but nevertheless for Professor Lockwood the day of retribution came.

It was a fine afternoon at the beginning of March, and the drillmaster had had more than ordinary command of his words.

He was marching his charges, after an hour of close-order drill, along the steep embankment of the Severn River, in field-artillery formation. The bank turned, and the professor attempted to turn his men. "H-h-h-h-h-h-h-h-h-h-" he stuttered, but the word would not come. The men hesitated at the brink of the water, looking around uncertainly. Cushing was in the fourth rank, and a little smile began to play over his features. He quickly suppressed it, and with his head held high and his back straight he continued to march forward. It did not take a second before his comrades had the idea. Down the steep bank they marched, slipping and sliding, and entered the river, dragging the guns with them, which immediately sank in the ooze. Line after line plunged into the water, while the desperate cry sounded behind them: "H-h-h-h-h-h-h-" The midshipmen with the drag ropes started to swim across the river; the water was full of bobbing heads with uniform caps bravely on them. Finally the command came, and those midshipmen who had not entered the water stood at attention on the bank, staring disconsolately at their luckier companions. They spent the rest of the afternoon digging the guns out of the mud, but it was worth the effort.

But the next day was better still. They were practicing light-artillery formation, and the battery, dragging its "6-pounder brass Napoleon," as a schoolmate of Cushing described it, "was advancing and firing by half-batteries in the direction of the board fence in the rear of the Superintendent's house." Lockwood began to stutter a "Halt!" but the word would not come. Frantically he waved his arms, but the battery did not stop. Closer and closer they came to the fence. Each time the gun was fired a hole appeared in the fence. Before the poor man could stop them they were only three feet away from it. "Bang! went the gun, and the Superintendent's fence was reduced to kindling wood."

Lockwood became so unpopular that a group of students hanged him in effigy from the flagstaff on St. Patrick's Day. For the administration, this was the last straw. The professor was politely invited to depart, and replaced by a commissioned officer. The move worked, and, within a year or two, almost all of the faculty become regular navy officers. There was no more funny business. A West Point civilian was one thing; a gruff naval lieutenant, with his gold braid tarnished by real sea water, was quite another. But they got out of being soldiers for two or three months, which was a signal triumph. Cushing was very proud.

It would be wrong to give the impression that Cushing's years at Annapolis—important years for him in every respect —were only a series of rebellious acts. There was much gentle happiness in those years, much memorable experience, both at the Academy and at Washington, which he visited as often as possible, for Congressman Edwards had become almost a father to him. Will spent Christmas at the Edwardses' the first year. The next Christmas, in 1858, he spent the vacation at Commodore Smith's home in Arlington, and wrote to his cousin Mary (who was visiting in East Troy, Wisconsin, not far from the little town were Will had been born—mutual relatives lived there, and Mary finally married a man from East Troy): "I had a splendid time [at the holidays] this year. I went to Washington the Friday before Christmas. I was astonished when I got out of the cars at Washington by the appearance of a great darkey who came up with all the assurance in the world and called me 'Mr. C.' I had to look twice before I could believe that this lump of darkness was the 'little Andrew' that used to wait on you at Md. Beverage. I believe Andrew has been on the lookout for your father ever since he left Washington. I asked him what he was doing there and he said: 'We been watching for Mr. Edwards.' "

After going to the Washington House and seeing the people that used to be there Cushing went over to Commodore Smith's, where he remained.

"I went into the new house of Reps. and while there listened to enough nonsense to last me a year. One man spoke for three days. It was ex-Governor Smith of Virginia. He spoke with a glass of eggnog before him; and did not stop till he had tired out." A year later Cushing was in the capital again, and wrote to Mary that he would "return to the subject of Washington, as you wish particulars. I did not call upon Mrs. Roach, as I could get no clew to her present residence. Neither did I see Mrs. Wood, nor Mrs. Brigham. I had a long talk with Mrs. Beverage. At the office I saw Mr. Carnes, Mr. Leech, Dr. Hudson and our own talented Congressman R. E. Fenton, New York. I did not expect to see any of the ladies whom I knew in Washington. Our old French professor says that 'No one thing can be in two places at the same time without it is a bird.' My opinion is, however, that if it were within the range of human or I may say earthly possibilities to be in two places at one and the same time, woman alone could be at both.

"Please give my respects to Miss Carrie Stevens, also to Mr. and Mrs. Mason. I will in a moment pay my respects to your father in person. You know I have his picture and you don't know how I prize it. My best respects to your mother, and love to Nellie [Ellen Grosvenor, a friend of Mary's who married Will's oldest brother Milton], and here I will tack and stand off to bed, come to anchor in the land of dreams and then I can be at home."

It was not always necessary to go to Washington for social life. In February, 1861, Will's mother sent him a "trunkful" of Fredonia produce, and he had to go to Baltimore to receive it. "The two bushels of apples, together with the maple sugar, preserves, etc.," he wrote to Mary, "have long since disappeared. In fact, they lasted about six hours. The trunk that I had them in together with its load weighed about two hundred pounds, and many were the guesses made along the route as to what it contained. To one inquisitive 'plug-ugly' of Baltimore I affirmed that I was running off a gentleman of dark complexion; to another that it was some of A. Lincoln's private property. But I got it to Annapolis in safety, where it soon became lighter. I yesterday gave it to a classmate of mine from South Carolina. He has resigned and is now on his way with it to Charleston. So ends the history of this remarkable trunk. The fate of the apples seems to prove the reverse of the saying: 'Man wants but little here below; but wants that little long.' "

As the Academy became more and more respectable the dances, hops, and so forth became more common. During Cushing's last two years there was one nearly every Saturday night. And there were festivities in the town of Annapolis to which the midshipmen were invited. When Will was seventeen, in 1860, he was tall and not at all bad-looking, and he was a popular companion for a number of girls whom he knew in Washington and Baltimore, who came to Annapolis for weekends. Many were friends of Mary Edwards, others he met through his cousin the Commodore, still others were relatives or relatives' friends from Boston and Washington and New York. None of them seems to have made a permanent impression on him, although he tended throughout his life to be close-lipped about such things. Also, as all men know, there is safety in numbers.

On May 20, 1860, Cushing wrote to his cousin that the next Friday they would give their parting soiree, and sent invitations to her and Ellen Grosvenor, although admitting that it was only a matter of form, since they could not come on the telegraph wire. "Do you ever get the Washington papers?" he asked. "Now that you are away from home it may be that you would like to see them once in a while. If so I will send them. The Japanese ambassadors [Commodore Perry had reopened that country to the West only six years before] arrived in Washington on Monday last, and they are now the great center of attraction. They were received by the President Thursday, and we expect to see them at Annapolis before long [they came in June]. If they judge the country by what they see of this city, they will have but a poor idea of these United States. The yellow individuals attended a ball at the house of the Secretary of State night before last and flirted desperately with the young ladies of the city. Do you not wish that you and Nellie could have been there to have made some conquests?" The next day (Sunday) he continued the letter. "Yesterday I went with a party of ladies up the River Severn about two miles. We had a splendid sail. We went to a place called Round Bay and had a picnic.

"You say that you almost envy me my cruise. I think Mary, that you would make a splendid sailor, that is to say, if you were only a boy. I intend to see every nook and corner of this little world that is to be seen, if I live. I want to live on the sea and die on the sea, and when once I set foot on a good ship as her commander I never want to leave her till I leave her a corpse. A ship at sea is a complete system in itself. The captain is king, and as absolute a monarch as ever lived. The officers are his house of lords, and some five hundred men his subjects. If a seaman is ordered to do an act, it must be done. The power of life and death is in the hands of the captain and his officers. One looks with as much pride and affection upon his ship as he would upon his wife. A man cannot be happier than when he is bowling along under a good breeze at fourteen knots an hour. And, if you would see the sublime, I can imagine no place where sublimity lies more grand than in a storm at sea. I have stood on the *Preble*'s deck [the *Preble* was an old ship of the line which was used for practice cruises, and which hardly ever left Chesapeake Bay] in such a storm that our old gray-headed captain, who had been to sea since he was nine years old, said that he had never seen such a storm, and at that time I would not have exchanged my post for the most brilliant place in the land. Such is life on the ocean, for those who have the taste for it. Of course I do not speak of common seamen, for their life is at best a dog's life. But I had rather be an officer on a man-of-war than the President of the United States."

Despite the presence of more than a touch of bombast in this letter, it indicates the most important change that had undertaken the young midshipman in his three Annapolis years. He had fallen in love with the sea. His biographers have tried to find in his heredity a reason for this new love. They point out that he came from a seafaring race, though little is known of any Cushing before Zattu. They add that Zattu himself had journeyed from Plymouth by water, but he was, after all, only taking the quickest route to the West if he did so; and that for a time he built ships on Lake Erie testifies only to his skill as a carpenter. Will's father, as far as is known, never saw the ocean; he was an inland man, having been born and having died there. But somehow, sometime, the sea had reached out and grasped Will, and would never again let him go. And so the European cruise which regularly followed the midshipmen's third year, and which they looked forward to throughout their Academy careers, was for Cushing a wonderful adventure, and probably the most exciting thing that had ever happened to him.

The *Plymouth* left Annapolis early in June and sailed down the bay to Norfolk, Virginia. The journey started inauspiciously. "After heaving up anchor in Annapolis Roads," Will wrote to his cousin Mary Edwards five months later, "we stood out of the harbor under all sail; we had a very narrow channel to pass through, and as the buoys had been shifted, the first thing we knew, the ship went aground with a shock, and her keel was at once buried in the glue-like mud of the bay. Sail was at once furled and we sent out an anchor for the purpose of trying the process of 'kedging,' in order to get off. Well, we worked all day, and I was nearly tired to death when, what should come alongside but the schooner *Rainbow* with the mail bag aboard, and in that was a letter from you. You can have no idea of the pleasure with which I then read your everwelcome letter. I returned to duty much refreshed. And, I have no doubt that it was your letter which aided us in our efforts to release the ship from her uncomfortable bed. Now, just think, if one letter does so much good, why will you not write often?" The ship sailed on, a little the worse for wear, and in a few days came to anchor off Old Point Comfort, Virginia, and twenty-four hours later was moored off Norfolk. "For a few days I had abundant leisure to observe the F.F.V.'s.

I, like the renowned Yankee, failed in spite of the most persevering search to find one of the second families of that
renowned old State."

The ship underwent repairs, during which time the crew of
midshipmen "underwent the torture of an innumerable amount
of balls, excursions, etc.," including a ball given for Cushing's
first class on board the frigate *United States.* The midshipmen
whiled away the time by admiring the fleet of warships assembled at Norfolk. Among them was the *Pennsylvania,* a "line-
of-battle" ship which had been pierced for 120 guns. It was
one of the largest ships in the world, though no longer in active
service; it was used as a receiving ship where new recruits
were taught the rudiments of the nautical arts. Another giant
was building in the yard, the *New York;* it would be destroyed
the next spring in order to avoid capture by the Confederates.
The same was true of the *Merrimac,* which would be burned,
but not well enough.

While the *Plymouth* was being readied for sea the midshipmen were housed on the *Pennsylvania.* Cushing became bored
with watching the fleet, and one night after ten o'clock, when
he should have been in bed, he led a group of his comrades and
broke into the shot lockers and began to roll the cannon balls
on the decks. They made a grand noise and woke everyone on
the ship. His crime was detected, but the punishment must not
have been severe, since he was allowed ashore when the *Plymouth* reached the Azores.

Toward the latter part of June "we again hove up anchor,
and just as the sun went down, the noble old *Plymouth* was
tossed and rolled on the broad bosom of the Atlantic, and before darkness set in the last trace of America's shores had sunk
beneath the waters. Nothing could be seen on either hand
except the blue waves and perhaps a gull or petrel following in
our wake. I soon turned into my hammock and was in a
moment fast asleep. It was my watch on deck in the mid-
watch, that is from twelve to four in the night, and five minutes
before twelve I was turned out by my chum; and I hastened on

deck to muster the watch of men. I found several middies of
the other watch on deck stowed away amidship or standing in
the lee passage. They were all fellows of the lower class who
had never been to sea before. I walked up to them and said,
'Hello, youngsters, what are you doing on deck?' The invari-
able answer was, 'Oh, Cushing, I am so confounded sick!' Yes,
Old Neptune was demanding his dues, and the only comfort
that I could lend them was to tell them to 'grin and bear it.' "
The next morning they were far out of sight of land. "There
was a heavy swell from the northward and soon the lee gangway was crowded with youngsters. Youths with pale faces
and sunken eyes walked about the deck, having but one wish
in life, to find out and thrash the man who wrote, 'A Life on
the Ocean Wave.' One poor and verdant youth expressed as his
fixed determination to resign when we reached Europe, and
return to the United States by railroad."

Seasickness does not last forever, and they were soon sailing with equanimity. But it was not easy work. There was
much hardship for the young midshipmen on these cruises.
They were required to do all the work on the ship, even the
most menial. Worst of all was the food; the navy ration of the
time was "of so poor a quality that they were literally half-
starved." The diet consisted of salt horse and hardtack with
the occasional addition of "some detestable ham, salt junk,
pork and beans, weevily rice, wormy cheese, rancid butter,
and the commonest varieties of tea, coffee and sugar." And
the day's allotment of water was one gallon only from the
ship's dirty tanks for all purposes, including washing.

Each morning the watch on deck was exercised aloft at reef-
ing, furling, loosing and bending sails, and other evolutions,
and for three hours daily they worked at marlinspike seamanship. In the afternoon the watch below studied navigation,
and at 4 P.M. there was drill at quarters. The first-class men
took turns as deck officers and navigators, and, "in brief,"
Cushing wrote, "the true idea of a practice cruise was realized." The conditions on board such practice ships taught the

future officers "that sympathy with the life and endless work of the sailor which was a distinguishing feature" of the men trained at the time.

The voyage was of course not without its compensations for Cushing and his companions. There were the beauty and the endless variety of the sea. The Atlantic is lovely in June and July, and if the ship was old and the quarters crowded and one's body tired it was still a delight to hang on a yardarm when there was no work to do and search the blue horizon for birds and other ships and sway with the swaying of the masts and observe the clean white foam at the prow and the clean white line of the wake stretching far behind them, tinged pink and red in the evening by the setting sun. And there was the moon, gigantic and yellow and still, hanging in the dark sky at night. It was possible to forget the bad food and the hard work when one sat on top of the forecastle and looked at the moon rising out of the sea. And Cushing was still only seventeen.

There was excitement, too. "Things went on till the third of July. On the evening of that day as we were sailing along under a fresh breeze, and all but a quarter watch were below at mess, we were suddenly electrified by the startling cry: 'The ship is on fire.' We rushed on deck and saw the red flames leaping from the galley funnel. In one moment the sails would have been a mass of fire and the ship lost, but we manned the ropes, and in an instant the sail was beyond the reach of the fire; the pumps were quickly set in motion and the fire was soon extinguished.

"Now, Mary, I do not object to fireworks in their time and place, but it was plainly against all patriotic principles to have the fireworks on the third instead of the Fourth of July, and besides that, a thousand miles out at sea is not the place for such display. It was therefore unpleasant to have the ship burn up while I was on her." It was indeed a serious matter. Fires at sea in the era of wooden ships were no rarity; the combination of an open galley fire, a pitching ship and a strong breeze was too often fatal to whole crews and shiploads of passengers. Once a fire took hold, there was nothing to be done about it. There was plenty of water all around, and it would extinguish the fire when it reached the waterline, but that was small comfort. And in the great and pathless expanse of the oceans a burned ship, nothing but a nearly submerged piece of driftwood, would more than likely never be found. Indeed, Cushing and his companions were fortunate to extinguish their fire in only fifteen minutes.

That same night a greater danger overtook the *Plymouth.* "In the dead of night we were awakened by the hoarse cry of 'All hands shorten sail.' I literally jumped into my clothes and hurried on deck and was at once aware that we were to battle with another of the elements. A strange sight met my eyes; one that, in sublimity, cannot be equaled. One half of the heavens was bright and clear. The pale moon's rays glittered on the water, and the stars were reflected from a sea as smooth and glassy as a mermaid's mirror, and the white clouds crossed the blue and beautiful sky, but the other half of the heavens was black as the darkest night, and by the glare of the lightning I saw the great inky clouds hurled onward by the mighty arm of the storm king, while, far away on the horizon the mad waves were seen leaping forward, borne by a gale, before which prouder ships might well tremble and beneath which many a sailor has found his grave. In an instant my eye took this in, and in another I was working as for life against death. As if by magic, the white canvas was gone, and our tall spars when seen by the next lightning flash, were bare and specter-like, rising like the leafless trunks of tall, slender pines, defying the storm.

"The low moan, which was at first heard, deepened into a roar, and the storm was upon us. The ship flew before the wind like an arrow and was only outstripped by the great black waves that went by, dashing the white foam on our decks as if there to claim a victim. We were in danger. One false turn of the helm and we were lost. We clung silently but firmly to the lifeline, and waited the issue. Oh, it was a grand sight! I did not think of danger, I only thought how grand was the scene, and how tame were all the other scenes that I had ever witnessed in comparison to this. 'They that go down to the sea in ships see the wonders of the Lord.' All that night and all the ensuing day, the day of Independence, we fought the winds and waves, and our ship was tossed about like a feather in a whirlwind. Though a splendid sea vessel, her oaken timbers could not withstand such shocks, and she sprang a leak. The pumps were at once manned and every effort was made to prevent the water gaining on us, and at last with success.

"By the evening of the 5th the wind had died away and we had a dead calm. The sea was as smooth as glass, and nothing disturbed it, except the dolphin as it chased the flying-fish through the water, or the lazy movements of a school of whales in the distance. In the afternoon a breeze sprang up and we were once more on our way."

There are other reports of this storm and none of them makes it out to be as grand or as dangerous as Cushing's does. He was writing the letter four months after the event, and he had a vivid imagination; besides the imagination, he had a sure ear for every cliché of his century, particularly for the idea of the "sublime." There is something awe inspiring about any storm at sea: there seems so little defense against it, one feels totally at the mercy of wind and water, and yet it is doubtful the *Plymouth* was in such dire straits as indicated—she had had a leak before, for one thing, and the new one was not terribly serious. But there is no doubting Cushing's emotional reaction to the event. It was his first large storm and he was determined to enjoy it.

He was determined, too, not to fear it, and it is perhaps the most significant thing in the letter that he was successful in this. He had heard about storms for years, he had read about them and no doubt imagined their terrors before he ever saw them; but when it came the storm had no terrors for him, only grandeur.

At 8:10 on July 17 land was reported three points off the *Plymouth*'s starboard bow. It was a beautiful morning, clear and bright, with a pleasant wind from the eastward. A strange-looking white cloud, far ahead, broke away and the top of an immense mountain appeared in view. It was then about forty miles distant. It was the island, or rather mountain, of Pico, one of the Azores. The mountain is about eight thousand feet high, an extinct volcano; as the ship neared land the crew could see that the entire side of it was covered with vineyards. By five o'clock in the afternoon the vessel had come to anchor off the town of Horta, on the Island of Fayal. The sails were furled, hammocks piped down, and all made snug for the night. The American counsul came aboard, and with him the health officer; upon examination the latter told the men they might land as soon as they pleased, as their "health bills" were all right, but as they could not take advantage of the opportunity so late in the evening they quietly turned into their hammocks. They had been out of sight of land for twenty-two days.

"Early the next morning a crowd of blue-jacketed middies might have been seen besieging the gangway to get at the boatloads of fruit, fresh milk, and goat butter that had come off from land and now lay alongside. These are termed 'bum boats,' and are to be found in every port. The Portuguese proprietors of these boats were loudly proclaiming to the great world and middies in particular that all their wants might be satisfied there so far as fruit, goat's milk and jackass cheese were concerned.

"At about eight o'clock in the morning the boats were piped away, and we set out for the town of Horta. I noticed as we neared the shore that the town was protected by two covered batteries on the beach, the appearance of which, though formidable at a distance, loses caste as you approach. In fact, a boatload of Uncle Sam's tars might take and hold them against the town. The landing was massive, and was crowded with a noisy set of Portuguese who proved to be beggars. 'Oh, Mr. Shentlemens! give me one dump!' 'Mr. Yankees take a jackass!' 'Only one pistareen!' These and other similar cries rang in my head until I was almost crazy. One old woman about eighty years of age, begged me in the most abject maner 'to have pity on a poor orphan.' Seeing that it would be almost impossible to escape from the crowd unless I complied with some of their demands, I made the best of a bad bargain, and mounting a jackass I incontinently fled. Two of my shipmates were in company with me, and we determined to cruise around the island for the day, so going to the hotel we ordered dinner for six to be ready at three o'clock and then set out. We were all mounted on small mules, and seated in saddles, without stirrups, and which had projections both forward and astern not unlike the back of a chair. While speaking of our equipments, I must not forget the very important item of three guides, one for each mule. The guides or dagos were each armed with a long pole, in the end of which was a spike. This is used as a gentle reminder to their muleships that their pace does not accord with the state of the age. Away we went down the paved streets at a rate that bid fair to leave our guides to shift for themselves, when all at once, our diminutive animals came to a halt, as if by common consent, and with a suddenness that caused my chum to take up a horizontal position some ten feet in advance of the rest of the party. As this had immediately succeeded to a loud hiss, which I heard in our wake, I concluded that the mules had been told in the lingo of the country to stop and that the animals knew more Portuguese than I did. However, I immediately exhausted my vocabulary of horse words to induce them to go on, but not a foot would they budge until they were reminded by the spike and the cries of 'Lakayeux! Carramba!' and others, when we again got under way. All this not only reminded me that these were not Yankee mules, but that I was not in Yankee land, and as I remembered the maxim 'When you are in Rome, do as the Romans do,' I concluded that instead of taking the guides with me I would go with them for the remainder of the day. At last we were fairly on the road to Mount Chalders, a volcano which still smokes. . . .

"We now proceeded to the hotel, and if the three of us did not do justice to that 'dinner for six' such a thing was never put on record by the landlady. Indeed, I had it from her own lips that she never took six dollars with a greater consciousness of having earned them than on the afternoon of the 18th of July, 1860. I then took a last look at the narrow streets, the houses with their red-tiled roofs, and the churches, and then went down to the boat. In going to the ship I ordered the coxswain to lay me aboard a whaling ship that lay in the harbor. I then procured a whale's tooth and a cane made of beautiful white whalebone sawed by hand, and with great care, by one of the crew. This cane, I designed to present to your father, but I lost it overboard one day in the old Atlantic, and the Gulf Stream now carries it to some distant part of the world. Thus terminated my first visit to the Island of Fayal. The others are so nearly the same, that I will now drop Fayal, heave up anchor, make sail, and be off for Cadiz."

It had been planned to continue the cruise eastward but it had to be curtailed owing to the difficulty of getting clearances from local health officers. As a result the *Plymouth* returned early to American waters. But the diet did not improve when the ship cruised in Chesapeake Bay to give the midshipmen additional instruction in seamanship. "Even after reaching Chesapeake Bay," one of them wistfully remembered, "our breakfast consisted of one spoonful of potato soup, one piece of potato, and one cup of coffee, with all the wormy hard tack we cared to eat—and this while in full view of the beautiful summer restorts and the many market gardens at and near Hampton Roads!"

When the ship arrived back at Annapolis Will sent Mary Edwards a small piece of dried seaweed as a souvenir of the trip. He was almost eighteen now and had reached his full height of something over six feet. His face and body were even thinner than when he first entered the Academy, and he wore his hair to his shoulders; all in all he was a handsome young man, with his most striking feature his deep bright eyes.

"I can assure you that political affairs look decidedly squally at present," William Cushing wrote to Mary Edwards from Annapolis on December 12, 1860; "even here, in Maryland, there is tremendous excitement. Men are arming in every portion of the State; all the banks have suspended; and the blue cockade may be seen in every nook and corner. Within the Academy, where there are representatives from every State in our Union, the huge weight of the crisis has penetrated. Midshipmen are every day resigning. Each Southerner has orders to resign as soon as his State secedes. Secession speeches are made by the South Carolinians and Georgians, and there is not a Southern man but hopes and believes that the world now views for the last time this great Republic.

"There is no money in the treasury; the United States officers cannot be paid and even if Congress does issue treasury notes no one will take them. Here a government check is not worth five cents to the dollar. I have seen them repeatedly refused. Matters cannot be improved except by a miracle, and unless that miracle happens, the 'Ship of State' which has been so long on a lee shore, must go down, carrying with it the naval academy which is but a speck on its deck.

"But if it comes to blows between the North and the South, I will shed the last drop of my blood for the State of New York. If this place does break up, I will get my graduating papers. If it does not, I will get them all the same, but in one case it will be in June, and in the other it will be—well, may be, in less than a month."

Five days later he was writing again. "To-day South Carolina goes out of the Union, and this will be the new Fourth of July for a Southern Confederacy. Taking this into consideration, and having nothing to do, I am going to write you a note.

"I am in another man's room, and writing on another man's paper. I have just come back from Spanish recitation, and it is very near dinner-time. Christmas is coming, but we cannot get leave. June is only six months off, and I am going to graduate. The military are out in the city to-night, and making a great noise. That is all that is going on. . . ."

But there was a great deal more going on. Marylanders favorable to the new Southern Confederacy were quick to show their sympathies. One of the strong pro-Northern men at the Academy was William S. Sampson, honor man of Cushing's class. One day he walked by a group of Southern midshipmen who were discussing the situation. "You say," he slowly and deliberately repeated the words of the last speaker, "if the capital of the nation is attacked, Northern troops will not be permitted to march through Baltimore to protect it? Well, then," his voice, usually so quiet, rang out, "the North will march *over* Baltimore—or the place where it stood!"

Companies of volunteers who were ready to aid the South strolled and marched within sight of the Academy grounds. "I can see from my window," Cushing ended his letter, "passing along, a barbarian from the 'Eastern Shore,' calling himself, I believe, a Zouave. He is clad just at present in smiles and red flannel. The latter intended to represent by its color, I suppose, the blood of thousands of Northerners to be slain in time to come. I tremble as I write!"

In the Academy as a whole there was maintained a surprising tone of moderation on the subject of secession and the coming dissolution of the Union. Midshipmen with Northern sympathies did their best to convince the others to remain loyal; the "secession speeches" by Southerners were measured and rational; they were attempts to settle the problem without hard feelings. Neither side had much success in its efforts. However, the Southern midshipmen usually did stay at school until their States actually seceded, although with increasing feelings of divided loyalty. Some took to wearing secession badges, but were soon relieved of them by the authorities. Indeed, many of Northern persuasion felt the South had a case. "I believe that the South has been deeply wronged," Will

William Barker Cushing, when he was about twenty-one years old

Admiral David G. Farragut

Gideon Welles,
Secretary of the Navy

The *Albemarle* going down the Roanoke

A contemporary photograph of the *Albemarle*

The *Sassacus* ramming the *Albemarle*

The *Sassacus* disabled after the ramming

The sinking of the *Southfield*

Inside the *Albemarle* casemate

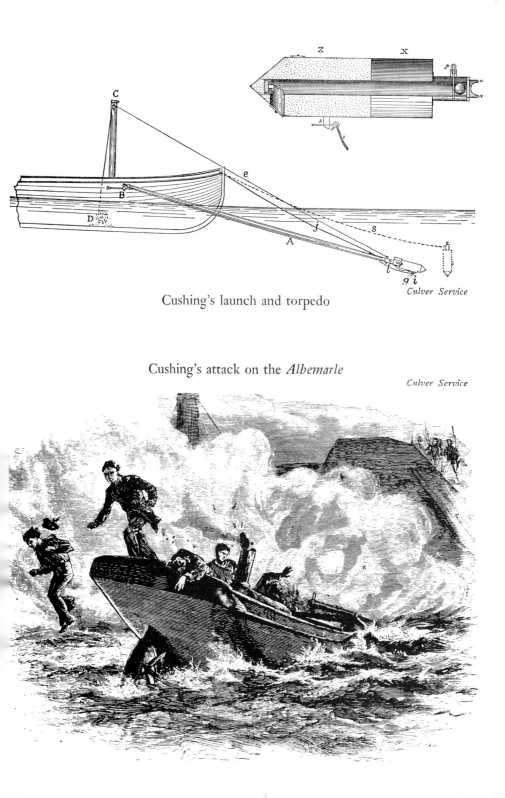

Cushing's launch and torpedo

Culver Service

Cushing's attack on the *Albemarle*

Culver Service

The blowing-up of the *Albemarle*

wrote: "and that unless it can procure security for the safety of its slave property: That it would be cowardly for it to stay in the Union." And aside from any question of principle, the departures of Southern comrades were often a source of much emotion. On the 11th of January Alabama left the Union, and the next evening Cushing's class, the first, assembled in the dusk and marched solemnly with honor man Sampson at its head to bid good-by to a departing Alabaman. The Southerner was himself an honor man and popular with his classmates. Arm in arm the young men marched together, in full uniform, singing a slow and quiet song of farewell. As they walked past the commandant's house, Lieutenant Rodgers, the adjutant, emerged and sharply asked:

"What is the meaning of this rioting on Sunday night?"

"No riot, sir," replied Sampson; "we are only bidding our classmate good-by."

The lieutenant stood for a moment, and then sighed. "Go on, gentlemen," he said gently, and the troop marched on to the railroad station. The barracks were quiet that night, and the inspecting officer reported that he could find nothing out of order.

A few days later the irrepressible spirit of Will Cushing erupted once more, and this time with serious results. For more than a year there had been an undeclared war between the young man and his Spanish professor, Edward A. Roget; a war in which the student, it would seem, had won more than his share of the engagements. Cushing had often mimicked his professor, a dapper little man whom the midshipman considered an effeminate dandy. Once Roget had dressed in his best clothes to meet a young lady and Cushing had prepared a bucket of water at the top of the doorway through which the swain had to pass on the way to the party; he was deluged and angry. Cushing was not punished, perhaps for want of certain proof. In any case, the midshipmen occasionally got away with murder. Not long before they had imprisoned a professor of botany in one of his glass cases and escaped without even a reprimand. Of course, the bucket of water over the door was a time-honored Academy custom.

But this time Professor Roget took it upon himself to be seriously angry. One cannot blame him. The facts of the matter are that on the 14th of January he was severely bitten on the left shoulder by a horse. The next day he came into class, his shoulder swathed in bandages, to find his students laughing at a well-executed sketch on the flyleaf of Cushing's textbook. The haughty little professor, his Latin blood boiling, demanded the book and found that the drawing depicted him in the act of biting the horse's neck, with the inscription, in clear, bold capitals, "The poor old Don, he bit the hoss!" He began to wave his untethered arm in the air. "I did not bite the hoss!" he shouted angrily. "The hoss bit me!" The class was of course convulsed with merriment, and remained so throughout the hour; the teacher could find no way of quieting them. When he did get a measure of silence at one time he ended it himself by muttering that it was absurd that anyone should make the stupid mistake of assuming that he would have any interest whatever in biting the neck of a horse. The class was again convulsed. Whether or not Roget ever got the joke, Cushing was found to be deficient in Spanish in the February examinations. Superintendent Blake forwarded the following report to the Navy Department: "Deficient at February semi-annual examination, 1861. Midshipman William B. Cushing. Deficient in Spanish. Aptitude for study: good. Habits of study: irregular. General conduct: bad. Aptitude for Naval Service: not good. Not recommended for continuance at the Academy." He was ordered to leave the Academy, and his enforced resignation was signed on March 23.

The reason for his dismissal is somewhat mysterious. "It certainly was an unusual proceeding," Stewart, his official biographer, states, "to dismiss a first classman, standing high in his class, for being unsatisfactory in Spanish, and one is forced to conclude that some personal resentment entered largely into the motives for prompting summary action in his case." It is possible that a recent run-in with the commandant may have had something to do with it. Cushing had obtained a week's leave early in January to stay with one of his aunts, who was alone in Washington and confined to bed with an illness; at the end of the week he asked for and obtained an extension. During this time Captain Blake, the superintendent of the Academy, met Commodore Smith, Will's cousin, and, supposing that the aunt in question was Mrs. Smith, asked after her and discovered that she was in perfect health. When Cushing returned to school Blake charged him with lying. This infuriated the hot-blooded midshipman and he countered with a like charge. The incident was smoothed over when the facts were discovered but it may have left a scar. The official report on the dismissal, on the other hand, stated that Cushing had been ill "for a considerable time." It is true that he had one of his racking colds during January and February (he cannot have been a very cheerful companion for his aunt), but he had had colds before. The report goes on to say that the illness "affords no palliation for neglect of study . . . nor for continued delinquencies in conduct throughout the term." Cushing had built up the respectable score of 147 demerits by the first of February. A few more failures to get out of bed on Sunday and he would have been automatically dismissed in any case.

Perhaps the most likely cause of the action is that the tension in the country was beginning to tell on authorities and midshipmen alike. The Academy was almost an armed camp. No one was entirely sure on which side Maryland would jump; if it did choose the Confederate cause, the Naval Academy, with its big guns and large store of ammunition, would be a rich prize. Academy personnel went into Annapolis armed; at night the gates were guarded by details of armed men, soldiers as well as future sailors. But whatever may have been the true cause, Gideon Welles, writing in 1876, when the war was long over, could say that Cushing had been dismissed for reasons "insufficient to justify such severe treatment."

On April 12 Beauregard fired on Fort Sumter, and the

Academy became, *de facto,* a Union stronghold. All classes were suspended, and the grounds were made ready to withstand siege either by land or water. The remaining midshipmen were kept under arms in order to guard their ammunition and guns and also to defend the famous "Old Ironsides," the *Constitution,* then aground just beyond the Academy's shore. Within a week or so help came in the person of Benjamin Butler and his Massachusetts volunteer regiments. The Academy and its remaining students, after the last of the Southerners had left, were removed to quarters in a Newport, Rhode Island, hotel, from which the first, second and third classes were graduated in early May and sent into active duty.

IV

Master's Mate Cushing

WILL CUSHING was stunned by his enforced resignation from the Naval Academy in March, 1861. It was impossible for him to believe that his dream of becoming a naval officer had ended, and yet there was the fact of his dismissal and the hard looks of Captain Blake to remind him; that he had been allowed to resign at all, he was told, was merciful. It seemed silly to Will. He had nothing against Professor Roget—he would have been glad to say so, if they had asked him. He had in fact been sorry about the horse. But when he thought of his cartoon he could never keep from laughing. When he bit the hoss, or the hoss bit him—what was the difference? As to Spanish, the war was going to be fought between men who knew the same language. He could learn Spanish later, if need be. The authorities were obdurate. Will's record was not a good one, they said. He evidently did not have respect for the service, he did not take it seriously. They would not listen to his appeals.

He went to Washington and stayed with Commodore Smith, who was very busy and was seldom at home. This was a relief to Will, who felt guilty whenever he met his relative. He stayed away from the house as much as he could himself, wandering along the streets and visiting the places he had known when he was a page, seeing old friends. He met several of his fellow midshipmen en route for their Southern homes, and was invited, sometimes playfully, once seriously, to enlist in the Confederate Navy—he would be given an ensign's commission, they told him, and would command a gunboat after a few months. For a moment he considered the offer. It would be poetic justice, he thought; the Academy would know then what it had done. But the idea was fundamentally repugnant to him, and he turned it down.

A few days after he had arrived he met, at the Naval Department, about which he lingered disconsolately, Lieutenant Charles W. Flusser, an old teacher at Annapolis whom Cushing considered a close friend. Flusser had heard of his dismissal, of course, and was more sympathetic than Will could rightfully have expected. Flusser was a native of Maryland and a citizen of Kentucky, and was having some difficulty in determining his own allegiance; they spent several days together, during which time the lieutenant decided for the Union. Later he said that Will had helped him to make the difficult decision. And he helped the young man also, reviving his enthusiasm for the navy and starting him on the course which led eventually to his reinstatement. Flusser was stationed at Annapolis, but he came to Washington several times in the next few weeks. Once he presented Will with a little book, entitled *Naval Enterprise, Illustrative of Heroism, Courage and Duty,* containing stories of brilliant naval deeds and heroic cutting-out expeditions. The young would-be sailor read it avidly— some of its phrases appear in his reports of his exploits—and the desire to be a naval officer was again fanned to a bright flame.

He was not without friends in the navy. Commodore Smith, despite his disapproval of Will's character, had consistently maintained that his failure was "scholastic rather than naval— not essential to his profession. . . ." Gideon Wells himself, the Secretary of the Navy, who had informed the young man of the final decision as to his dismissal, later remembered how "saddened disappointment and grief . . . shadowed his face" when he was told the news.

After the firing on Fort Sumter Cushing presented himself to the Navy Department and asked to be given a place in the

naval service—where, he said, he did not care. Welles was a
Yankee and by no means a fool, and considered himself,
accurately, a good judge of men. He was mild and even benign
in appearance, with his white wig and whiskers, but he was by
no means softhearted. Lincoln called him "Father Welles," and
the navy always referred to him as the "Old Man of the Sea."
The only thing that displeased him about the young midshipman was the fact that pressure was being exerted on his behalf;
Welles was able and willing to stand up to legislators, and did
so many times during the war. But despite the fact that Blake
and the chief of the ordnance bureau, Captain Magruder, were
of the opinion that Cushing was not officer material, Welles
was impressed by the sincerity with which the young man approached him. He agreed that an appointment was not out of
the question, but said that it would be difficult to arrange.
Cushing left him with the beginnings of hope, but it was some
days—they seemed an eternity—before he was recalled to
Welles's office. The old man was stern. The young man was
very contrite, and promised that the department would never
be sorry if it reinstated him. "Sympathy for the youth,"
Welles wrote years later, "whose perseverance, enthusiasm
and zeal impressed me, had probably as much influence as the
recommendations of his friends. . . ." Cushing drew himself up
to his full height. "The navy, sir," he said, "is my life—and
I was, and am, determined to serve in it."

In an appointment back-dated to April 1, Cushing was
made an acting master's mate in the United States Volunteer
Navy, and assigned to the U.S.S. *Minnesota.* Master's mate
was a rank which had not been in use for many years, but
owing to the peculiar circumstances of the emergency it was
revived. Before 1845, in the "Old Navy," the midshipmen
were taught the rudiments of seamanship while on actual sea
duty with the fleet. With the founding of the Academy most
midshipmen were sent there for instruction and the number on
active duty declined almost to the vanishing point. The older
officers never felt that this situation was desirable; it left a gap,

among other things, in the ranks of the junior officers. With the coming of the Civil War many of the new volunteer officers were given the rank of master's mate along with Cushing. It was not exalted; it paid only forty dollars a month.

The frigate *Minnesota* was one of the largest ships in the navy. She carried forty-seven guns and a crew of 540; she was powered by both steam and sail, and could manage twelve knots. Though built only in 1858, she had been sent to the East Indies and on her return was found to be "rotten as a pear," and in need of extensive repairs. When the situation in the country grew menacing, she was ordered to be made ready for sea. The work was costly, and a new steam sloop could have been built with the money; it went slowly, as the Charleston Navy Yard, at Boston, was, according to an official report, not equipped with water closets, and the workmen were forced to take many times out. When Cushing arrived in Boston to join his ship, toward the end of April, he found nearly a thousand men at work on her, her decks covered with gear, her rigging dismantled, and he did not think it possible that she could be ready in six months, much less the two weeks that the work actually required.

He spent the time marveling at the patriotic fervor that had overtaken the city. Recruiting for the navy was proceeding apace, and police details were necessary to control the crowds which stormed the recruiting station in Hanover Street. Many former seamen, merchant sailors and boys who had never been to sea at all vied with each other for places in the service. Those who were fortunate enough to be chosen (many were turned down because of the high standards then in application) were assigned to the old receiving ship *Ohio*, from which, after a few weeks or days, depending on previous service and the exigencies of the moment, they were sent to sea. Many such men were among the crew of the *Minnesota*; Cushing was stationed on the *Ohio* himself, and helped to train the new sailors.

The navy yard looked only half finished itself. It was a

beehive of activity, though not as well organized. One of the principal egresses was blocked by a nearby private wharf; a suit was in progress to remove this obstruction, but it was months before the navy could get some of its ships out into the bay. Although much of the ground around the dry dock was paved with round cobblestones, the underfooting in places was damp, oozy mud from the April rains. More than one pompous Boston merchant, come to comment on the progress of the work of the government, found himself sitting on the ground, much to the enjoyment of the young sailors on the decks of the *Ohio.*

But the *Minnesota* was finally ready for sea, and on the morning of May 8, long before the hour of her departure, the wharves and vessels in the vicinity of the yard were thronged with spectators. At half past nine, everything being in readiness, the order was given for slipping the cables, and the head of the vessel slowly swung from the dock. As she gathered headway and cast off her lines, she was cheered by the densely packed onlookers, many of them the relatives and friends of crewmen. The boatswain's whistle tweeted out over the water, and in a moment her rigging was covered with hundreds of her crew, who returned the cheering at the top of their voices. The shrouds of the *Ohio* were manned, and the *Minnesota* was cheered from that quarter also. As the frigate passed, the wharves of all Boston, crowded with people, greeted her with enthusiasm and good wishes. As she moved slowly past Fort Independence, the great guns fired a salute, which the *Minnesota* answered, the smoke from her cannon drifting slowly across the bay. In an hour she was in the open sea.

Cushing was placed in charge of the berth deck—"the lowest of all positions," he said later, "in a man o' war." The senior officers of the *Minnesota* were all from the old navy; the weather-beaten old captain, Gersham Van Brunt, had begun his career in the navy as a midshipman shortly after the war of 1812. His six lieutenants all had had many years of service; most of them had started in the navy before Cushing was born. The chaplain had been in the navy for nearly thirty years. The other three master's mates, however, were not much older than Cushing, and had come into the ranks of officers very recently, like himself.

"I am an officer aboard the splendid steam frigate *Minnesota*," Cushing wrote to his cousin. "We have just left our moorings, and as I write we are moving under steam and sail out of Boston harbor. I am going to fight under the old banner of freedom. I may never return, but if I die, it shall be under the folds of the flag that sheltered my infancy and while striking a blow for its honor and my own.

"I cannot tell you exactly where to write to me. This is the flagship of the 'Home and Blockading Squadron.' Wherever there is fighting, there we will be, and where there is danger in the battle, *there will I be*, for I will gain a name in this war. I must now say good-by. God bless you, Mary." It is the letter of an eighteen-year-old boy, no doubt; but it is boys who fight in wars; long before they can write with any knowledge of death they are involved in it.

The *Minnesota* arrived off Fortress Monroe, Virginia, six days later, having enjoyed an easy trip. The vessel entered Chesapeake Bay in the morning with guns loaded and run out, and all the men at their quarters. They expected that Confederate batteries had been constructed on Cape Charles, but if such was the case "they were afraid to use them." The ship entered the bay without opposition of any kind and came gallantly up to the fort. The guns of Monroe thundered forth their welcome, and the great guns of the ship replied with a shotless broadside. Another steamer was landing a regiment of Vermont volunteers at the fort, and cheer upon cheer pealed over the quiet waters of the bay. In a letter to his mother describing the scene, Will wrote: "We will remain here several days, and it is now considered as certain that we will have some hard fighting in a day or two. *This is no idle rumor.* We have quite a fleet of U.S. Men of War here, and a strict blockade of the harbor is observed. My motto is: 'Death to the traitor!" It is the first in a long series of bloodthirsty letters from son to mother. One can imagine that she would have been willing to forgo the gory details, but Will never forbore to tell her of the dangers he had passed and of the ones to which he eagerly looked forward.

The other vessels in the blockading squadron were the sloop of war *Cumberland*, 1,700 tons, with a crew of 228 and 24 guns (she would be sunk by the *Merrimac* in not too many months in the same channel which she was now defending); the screw steamer *Monticello*, 655 tons, with a crew of 96 and 3 guns (Will Cushing should have looked carefully at her, for she would be his own ship in a year or two); and the *Quaker City*, a side-wheel steamer of 1,600 tons, a crew of 129, and a battery of 4 guns.

It was not long before the blockading squadron captured its first prizes, three schooners laden with tobacco and bound from Richmond to Baltimore; the three were caught within a period of twenty-four hours, on the 14th of May. Flag Officer Stringham was short of junior officers, and Cushing was assigned to take one of the prizes, the *Delaware Farmer*, under the overall command of Lieutenant N. C. Bryant, to Philadelphia.

The trip was not uneventful. A storm came up during the second night out from Hampton Roads; the crew "were a lubberly set, and did not know how to work in so much confusion." The battering of the wind and waves caused the vessel to spring several leaks. The men were about to give themselves up for lost, for the pumps did not work properly, when in the midst of all the trouble a flash of lightning revealed a large vessel bearing down on the *Delaware Farmer* in the darkness. A "despairing cry went up from the men" in the schooner and they stood frozen with fear. Cushing sprang to the wheel and put the ship hard over to port, but he could not avoid a collision. But his quick action had managed to keep the oncoming ship from striking the schooner bows on, and instead of cutting her in two the other ship tore off her starboard bulwarks, and after thumping her heavily, dropped astern, taking with her the spanker boom and three or four backstays.

Their reception in Philadelphia made up for the distress they had suffered. The ship was the first captured Southern vessel to be brought to the port, and crowds lined the wharves to get a look at the contraband. Cushing was feted as a hero and assured that the prize was worth at least $75,000. In the end he received nothing from it; the owner argued successfully that the ship had been seized illegally, and the *Delaware Farmer* was returned to him.

Cushing was rewarded when he returned to the fleet by being given another prize, the bark *Pioneer*, which had been seized by the blockaders because both ship and cargo were Southern-owned; he was to take the vessel to New York. The assignment was hazardous, since Flag Officer Stringham could not spare a crew, and it would be necessary to sail the *Pioneer* all the way to New York—a journey of from three to four days—with Cushing and one other officer, Master's Mate Harrington of the *Cumberland*, alone against the sixteen members of the ship's original company. The two took turns standing over the men with loaded revolvers. Not wishing to deprive his mother of any thrills, Will described the scene in a letter to her: "As I write, I feel the weight of a brace of revolvers in my belt, and I know not at what moment the crew may try to retake her; but your boy is ready, and I trust no son of yours is a coward." Poor Mrs. Cushing! "Now I must go," the letter continues mercilessly, "and have the pumps sounded . . . to see that none of the crew have scuttled her."

The *Pioneer* arrived off the Narrows without trouble. Flag Officer Stringham was aware of the danger his two young officers had undergone, and he personally commended them on their return to the fleet. The ship was worth twice as much as the *Delaware Farmer*, and Cushing felt justly proud of having brought it into port successfully, and began to dream of a promotion.

His return was delayed. In order to rejoin the *Minnesota*

he found that he would have to go to Boston by train and take passage on the steam frigate *Colorado*. When he arrived he found that the *Colorado* was not yet ready for sea, and he took advantage of the time to visit his mother's Boston relatives, of whom there were many. Several of his uncles were bankers, but more important to Will was the discovery of some "handsome young lady cousins." The cousins were hospitable, and when the *Colorado* was ready for sea, they combined to give a party for him. There was much hilarity and, once, an embarrassed silence when someone at the party stated that "we will whip the rebels in three months," and Will replied, "I have spent four years with Southern officers and midshipmen at Annapolis, and I know something of their character and ability. They are a brave and valiant people, and not only shall we not whip them in three months, but it is probable that it may be three years before they are finally conquered." It seemed, he remembered, that they thought it shocking that an officer of the United States Navy should say such a thing.

The *Colorado* sailed on the early tide, and they were out of the harbor before the sun was fully up. Cushing was glad to find Harry Blake, a schoolmate for three years at Annapolis, aboard. They spent what time they could spare from their duties remembering the days at the Academy. At seven o'clock in the evening of June 25, Will was writing a letter to his cousin. He was called to go on watch, and he laid down his pen and put on his hat to go to the forecastle. There he met Blake, and stopped for a moment to talk to him. The man on the foretopsailyard sang out: "Sail ho!" "As we are off the Southern coast," Cushing's letter went, "every sail is an object of curiosity. Young Blake ran to get his sea-glasses. One of the ladders was unshipped as he went below, and he was precipitated a distance of forty feet, head first into the hold. Down, down, he went until his head struck with a dull crash on the edge of a cask. He was picked up senseless with the whole top of his head split open, and his spine injured. He is now dying. I have been for two hours standing over him, fanning him and trying to ease his pain. Poor Harry! It will kill his father and mother. He was a tall, noble, dark-eyed boy, and he has been a schoolmate and shipmate of mine for three years. It has left an impression on me that can never be erased. It brings forcibly to my mind the thought that I may never see home again. I have faced death, but I never felt as near it as I do now.

"Oh! how sad it seems to me to see one of my messmates cut off in such a manner. You must excuse me for talking so much on this subject, but it is on my mind, and I cannot shake it off."

Despite Cushing's vivid description, Harry Blake did not die. He appeared to be much more badly hurt than he actually was, and he had the benefit of two skillful surgeons who were being transported to the fleet by the *Colorado*. In fact he was back on active duty two months later, and led a small-boat expedition off Fort Pickens.

When the *Colorado* arrived at Charleston it was discovered that the *Minnesota* had returned to her station at Hampton Roads, and Cushing was sent aboard the steam frigate *Wabash*. The ship remained off Charleston for several weeks, while Cushing chafed at the inactivity. He suffered both from boredom and hunger, for there was no friendly land base nearby and the Union ships were on short rations. Will wrote his cousin describing the hardship and adding that the Confederates were suffering in the same way, but this was largely wishful thinking, since the blockade was not yet so effective off Charleston. The captain of the *Wabash* reported to Stringham that he had Cushing aboard, but there was no room for him on northward-bound vessels, he said.

By the end of July Will had returned to his own ship, and in time for adventure. The Back River, General Benjamin Butler had told Stringham, was the site of an enemy buildup, and the general requested five boatloads of men to raid the concentration of troops. Cushing volunteered as soon as he heard about the expedition. Stringham sent five launches, three manned by men from the *Minnesota* and two by the *Roanoke*'s sailors, under the command of Lieutenant Pierce Crosby. Cushing rode, characteristically, in the first launch. Together with four boatloads of soldiers from Fortress Monroe the force went up the river at noon on July 25. Confederate scouts checked their progress from time to time, but no serious effort was made to oppose them. They burned ten small vessels, and captured a schooner "heavily loaded with corn, provisions, and other articles." This they brought back with them to the squadron in the morning. Cushing described his part in a letter to his cousin, but he could not help exaggerating the importance of the expedition. "In this action I had the supreme pleasure of burning one of the vessels with my own hands," he said, "and capturing gun, plume and powder of a red-shirted individual who was persuaded without much trouble to beat one of those masterly retreats which should be handed down to posterity a theme for every poet, painter, and historian. The musket is a curiosity in itself being over seven feet in length." He told her that twelve ships had been burned, which was stretching the truth a bit; he also described the capture of a rebel battery on the river, whereas in fact no resistance had been offered except by snipers.

The letter is more significant for the other things it said than for its exaggerations, which can be put down to over-enthusiasm. "I don't know but I may resign before long and go into the land service," he writes. "I have no doubt but that I can procure a captain's berth in the volunteers. I so long to be near Allie." But he adds, "I will see the war out." In fact he was beginning to discover that war is mostly waiting, that action is rare and when it comes disappointing and chaotic. The Battle of Bull Run had only recently taken place; from this distance it seemed that service on the land would be much more exciting. And, too, he was in a depression, had been in it since he had left Boston. He had frequent headaches and his temper was short and he got into arguments with his fellow officers. He felt that his friends had deserted him, for he had received no letters for over a month (in fact it was hard to deliver letters to the ships of the blockading squadron). In this bitter mood he struck out at everyone within reach. "Why does not Fredonia give at least one company to the war?" he asked his cousin. "Are the people cowards, or are there no officers to lead them. Why! I would come home and raise a company myself if I thought it could be done." Such statements were eminently unfair. In the early months of the war several companies were raised from the town, but the state authorities felt they did not need them. Many men from Fredonia served in the Union forces, although there was never a Fredonia company.

One reason for Cushing's dissatisfaction was that conditions on board the *Minnesota* were not to his liking. It was the commanding officer's ship, for one thing, and every sailor knows how much extra "spit and polish" that entails. But Cushing had a lieutenant stationed over him who was, he felt, particularly offensive. He was obnoxious to all the young officers on the vessel. One night this officer fell asleep on watch. Cushing hastily summoned witnesses, and to prove beyond a reasonable doubt that the man was really asleep, swung a lighted lantern in front of his eyes. Cushing decided not to bring this evidence to the attention of his superiors, however. But the lieutenant learned what the young man had done, and before long the situation had become unbearable. Cushing decided that his only recourse was to challenge the lieutenant to a duel. Dueling was still sometimes practiced in the navy, though it was against the law. But the code under which naval officers operated provided that if a junior officer challenged his senior the latter could honorably decline; in order to force the lieutenant to fight Cushing determined to resign. "As long as I live," he wrote to his cousin, "*no man of any rank* shall insult me with impunity." If he resigned, he decided, he would join the army. He hoped for a commission, but failing that he was willing, he said, to go to West Point. "It seems foolish," he told her, "but I have got to like the army better

than the navy, because . . . Lon is in the land service." "I don't
care how the whole thing turns out," he added. "I am going to
make as broad a path as I can through the world for myself.
And if I come to the conclusion that I prefer to be a lieutenant
in the army, at twenty-two, to be a Lieut. in the navy at thirty
—I shall act on that conclusion."

Whether or not he actually tried to resign from the service
in order to go through with his fantastic plan, the navy could
not spare him at the moment: a major combined sea and land
operation was in the offing. Two forts, Clark and Hatteras,
guarded the Hatteras Inlet, off the coast of North Carolina.
The inlet was strategically of the first importance: it furnished
a haven for Confederate blockade runners, and was also the
entrance to the extensive inland waterways of the North
Carolina sounds. On August 28, 1861, Flag Officer Stringham
led against the two forts "the largest fleet that had at that
time ever sailed in company under the American flag." General
Butler was in command of the accompanying troops.

At seven minutes of seven in the morning the fleet got
under way and moved slowly in toward the forts. As the haze
of morning gave place to the full light of day, long rows of
tents could be seen lining the shore, while over all floated the
Confederate flag. The Union ships gradually neared the inlet,
with the *Wabash* first in line; at 10:15 the first shot was fired
from that vessel. The first shot was followed immediately by
a broadside; it was possible to see the balls making a graceful
curve in the air and dropping directly into the rebel camp.
Then, as though one of the shots had been "a perfectly elastic
body, and had rebounded," a shot came skimming over the
water toward the fleet. For ten minutes the *Cumberland* and
the *Wabash* seemed to be one mass of fire and smoke, and
then the *Minnesota* stood in between them and the forts, and
opened a heavy and well-directed fire. The action now became
general. Most of the Union shells struck in the forts or tore
through whole rows of tents and wooden buildings. Three
times the secession flag was shot down, and three times it rose

again on improvised poles. Toward three o'clock in the afternoon it fell again on both forts, and at the same time the garrison of the smaller fort, Clark, deserted their posts and rushed
along the beach. Shell after shell exploded in their midst,
throwing them dead and wounded into the air, and at every
explosion their terror seemed to increase tenfold. Finally, seeing
that no flag waved from either fort, Commodore Stringham
signaled the fleet to cease firing, and once more all was still,
while the thick clouds of smoke rolled off inland, clearing the
air.

In the meantime troops were attempting to land about two
miles from the fortifications, but with little success. As fast
as a company of soldiers reached the beach the boats were
stove in or beached by the breakers. By three o'clock only
318 men had been landed, and it became clear that no more
could be put ashore. An advance guard was sent out from
the beach head, and the small fort taken possession of. The
men raised the Union flag to the top of the pole. It was the
first time the United States flag had floated over North
Carolina territory for nearly six months.

The men of the fleet looked anxiously to see their flag
appear over the larger of the forts, Fort Hatteras, but they
were disappointed. The gunboat *Monticello* was ordered into
the sound in the rear of the fort; to do this it was necessary
to go through the channel, which ran under the fort's guns.
No sooner had the vessel started to obey, and reached the
nearest point to shore, than the guns opened fire. The observers
on the fleet were thunderstruck. The secession flag was down
and the ships had ceased to fire, and had given the land a wide
berth. It was impossible to stand in and give aid to the
Monticello, and it seemed that she must be sunk where she
lay. But the gunboat gallantly returned the fire until, at
length, having received several shot in her hull, several of
them below the waterline, one in her mainsail yard which
tore the topsail to shreds, and with one boat shot away, she
stood once more out to sea.

It was now nearly dark, and impossible to continue the action until morning. The prospects were far from encouraging. Steamers behind the forts were rapidly bringing reinforcements from New Bern; the three hundred Union soldiers could not be taken off again or protected, and were surrounded by more than two thousand enemies.

At four o'clock the next morning the *Minnesota* hove up anchor, fired a signal gun, and stood in toward land followed by the rest of the fleet. The troops, to the glad surprise of the Union forces, had not been attacked during the night; in fact only a small proportion of the reinforcements had been landed. The fleet sailed in and engaged the shore batteries, opening a terrific fire which soon drove the defenders from their guns to seek shelter in the "bomb proof" tent erected in the center of the fort. Only two or three guns returned the Union fire after the first few minutes. At half past eleven the white flag was hoisted over the fort.

In a letter to his mother, Cushing supplied some "incidents of the battle." "In the hottest part of the engagement one of our men who was sponging out his gun lost the sponger overboard. His position was over twenty feet above the water, and we were steaming ahead at the time, but the brave fellow, preferring to lose his life rather than see his gun cease to work, sprang overboard, recovered his sponge and by a miracle as yet unexplained, again got on board. For this he was advanced.

"I have been informed by the rebel officers, that no less than *twenty-eight* bomb shells exploded in their fort in one *minute*, such was the intensity of our fire. They say that we made the place a 'Hell upon Earth.'

"One of our bombs blew the secession flag to atoms—a piece was preserved by one of their officers, and presented to me. I enclose a portion of it.

"One of the rebel officers presented me with his sword belt for my kindness to him. While another, the Captain of the 'Morris Guards,' gave me his bowie knife with these words: 'Sir, accept this in remembrance of the Morris Guards.' Such things are worth more to me than gold, for they show that though I fight to the death my country's enemies, yet I also soothe the sufferings of a wounded foe."

The entire operation could not have been more successful, or more admirably carried out by Stringham and his men. Cushing himself witnessed, on August 29, the surrender of the three ranking Confederate officers, who came aboard the *Minnesota* to sign the articles of capitulation and to surrender their swords. Nearly seven hundred prisoners were carried by the *Minnesota* to New York for incarceration in Northern prisons, and a large number of heavy guns were captured along with a vast store of ammunition. Many defenders were killed and wounded. The Union forces suffered only one casualty. A fragment of a shell struck Private Lembrecht, of Company G, 9th New York, making a painful wound in the hand.

Cushing's part in the engagement was to act as commanding officer of a quarter-deck division of eight eight-inch guns on the *Minnesota*. "This was a great moment for me," he wrote some years later, "a youngster who had never been fairly under fire—and I shall never forget or again experience the wild pleasure and excitement that I felt, as the stern challenge and response passed over the blue water on that sunny August day." He was amazed at his own coolness. In fact he was never in great danger. The Confederate commander of the two forts, in his report, said that the ships' guns were so much more powerful than his own that after the ships had got the exact range with their eight-, nine-, ten-, and eleven-inch guns, they did not find it necessary to alter their positions; "not a shot from our battery reached them with the greatest elevation we could get."

This engagement had been, as Cushing said, wildly exciting to him; but the excitement did not last, nor did its effect of diverting his thoughts. The *Minnesota* carried the Southern prisoners to New York and then returned to its post off Hampton Roads, and the boredom and monotony again became unbearable for the ship's youngest master's mate. He whiled away the time in making up names for the senior officers, and among his inventions was a nickname for the commander of the fleet. One wonders why the name had not been applied before, but it seems that Cushing was the first to refer to Stringham as "Old Sting 'em," and the haughty old sailor, who had come to the fore through years of service in the old navy, heard about it and could see nothing funny about this action on the part of a junior officer whom he had treated courteously. Cushing had decided to go through with his plan of resigning his commission, though he had given up the idea of the duel—he expected to be reinstated as a midshipman in his class instead—and he resigned on September 13. But Stringham was not to be appeased, and he forwarded the resignation with "a cruel endorsement," as Cushing saw it.

It was accepted, and Cushing anxiously went to Washington to see if his services had won him reconsideration as a midshipman. His brother was stationed in the city at the time, and the two young men spent as much time as possible together. They had seen each other little since they had left Fredonia, four years before, and their reunion was a happy one.

Alonzo had graduated from West Point in June, 1861. His career was in marked contrast to that of his brother at Annapolis. Allie did not escape demerits altogether, but he never collected many of them, and he graduated twelfth in his class and was a captain of cadets during his last months at West Point. He was "approved by his superiors and beloved by his fellows," says a West Point historian. "Modest in demeanor," says another, "he was always efficient in his work, and kindly towards under-classmen." No doubt these estimates are just. The qualities which his mother had seen ten years before, and on which she counted as a bulwark against her old age, had become more and more evident as he grew older. He was then in his twenty-first year but looked considerably younger (whereas Will looked older than he was); he stood five feet ten or eleven inches high in his stocking feet, and was well but slimly built. He had very long legs, a contemporary stated, so that he appeared, when on horseback, to be below medium height. He had a smooth face with dark skin and black hair and blue eyes which were usually laughing; in fact his good nature "was so unusual on the part of young regular officers that it captivated every volunteer with whom he came in contact," including the volunteer who met him outside of Washington and wrote that sentence more than forty years later. Although he worked his men hard they all loved him for his smiles and frequent infectious laughter, "which were potent factors in smoothing the grim front of grizzled war."

On June 24 Alonzo was commissioned a second lieutenant in the 4th United States Artillery, and was promoted to first lieutenant before leaving the hall in which the graduation ceremony took place. The first of his class to receive orders, he proceeded directly to Washington, where he was assigned the task of drilling the green volunteer troops who would man McDowell's guns a month later at Bull Run. He worked hard, taking almost no rest from his labors; if the artillery did not behave itself in the battle it was none of his fault, but rather because he had only three weeks in which to train them. In any case, his own battery, the 4th United States, could have done no more than it did. On July 18 he was at the front in the reconnaissance at Blackburn's Ford, near the Stone Bridge over Bull Run, and there fired the first Union gun. Three days later he was in the thick of the disastrous fight on the other side of the stream. His conduct on that occasion was said to have been admirable, but his position was not yet sufficiently advanced to secure him mention in the reports of general officers, such as became a matter of course as soon as he fought on his own responsibility, whether in command of his battery or detached for important staff duty at corps and grand division headquarters. Immediately after the battle, in the early hours of July 22, and despite the fact that neither he nor his men had slept for more than twenty-four hours, his battery joined two infantry regiments in a reconnaissance near Fairfax Court House which established that the Confederate Army had abandoned its pursuit of the routed Union forces. Having reported this, Cushing and his battery set out for Washington. "In company with some thousands of other infantry soldiers," the above-quoted volunteer recounts, "I was floundering along the vile wagon road from the Long Bridge to Bailey's Cross Roads, where our regiment was to make its headquarters for several weeks afterwards, sending out scouting parties from time to time, and establishing picket posts in what appeared to our uneducated eyes to be appropriate points of vantage. On the Monday just mentioned, a copious rain set in at a very early hour, and the roadsides were strewn with knapsacks, blankets, and other impedimenta of the returning soldiers who plodded along towards Washington from the battle of the day before. Many of them had marched all night, and very few of them had taken more than short intervals of rest during their night exit from the vicinity of Bull Run. One battery was distinguished for its fine appearance, however; and that was Battery A of the Fourth regular artillery. Cushing was in command of it when it met and passed us, and even the events of the preceding twenty-four hours had not been sufficient to take away his smile— although it might have shown a sarcastic side to a closer observer than I then was."

The remainder of the summer was spent by Allie, in company with 70,000 others under the skillful hand of General George McClellan, in making secure the defenses of Washington. New regiments poured in from Ohio and Indiana and New York and Rhode Island and Pennsylvania and Massachusetts; from all over the North they came, until at the end of October there were more than 100,000 men in Washington, the mightiest army the world had ever seen, under the command of "the young Napoleon," who still felt, with his passion for defense, that the capital was not yet safe.

> Marching along, we are marching along;
> For God and our country we are marching along;
> McClellan's our leader, he's gallant and strong,

they sang as they marched, drilled, dug earthworks and constructed trenches. Alonzo pitched in, though he would rather have been fighting. His Fourth United States achieved perfection and then went beyond it; after that it went even farther. The men could load their guns in the dark, with their eyes shut, almost with their hands tied behind their backs. It was boring, but it paid off in the end. McClellan seems to have been fascinated with the problem of perfection; he has often been criticized for it, and was so at the time. But he created the first modern army. If he could not fight it effectively, there would be others who could.

In September, when Will came to Washington, Allie had just been promoted to the temporary rank of captain on the staff of General E. V. Sumner. Will was a little envious. He spent his days at the Navy Department, anxiously hovering around offices, while Allie went through his duties, but in the evenings they met and talked. If the navy should turn him down, they decided that Will should join the army. They might be able to serve together, since Allie was high in Sumner's favor and imagined that he could take care of any necessary arrangements.

But this was not to be. Will's friends in the department were working hard to obtain his reinstatement. Stringham was later compelled to admit, though a trifle grudgingly, that Cushing's work as a master's mate had been "in some respects meritorious." Even Cushing's old commandant at Annapolis had relented and now stated his belief that the boy could become a good naval officer and recommended that he be restored as a midshipman. Secretary Wells was favorably disposed, though he was not inclined to take lightly the pranks that seemed inevitably to accompany the praiseworthy conduct of his young protégé. In the end Cushing was warranted a midshipman on October 19, 1861, the warrant to be dated from

June 1, and ordered to the *Cambridge*. He thus received the same rank as if he had stayed on and been graduated with his class, for at that time students at the Academy were only acting midshipmen, assuming the higher grade upon graduation. Later the rules were changed so that graduating midshipmen were given the rank of ensign. Despite his resignation, Cushing is listed as having stood twenty-first among the twenty-six members of the class of '61. He did not miss any appreciable amount of schooling, since his class was sent into active duty early because of the emergency. By the middle of October, he had seen at least as much action as any of his classmates.

Shortly after he arrived in Washington he received a letter from Mary Edwards, inviting him to her wedding and asking him to be best man. He discussed the request with Allie at length, and finally wrote that he could not come. "It is needless to say that in seeing your happiness complete," he told her, "one of the dearest wishes of my heart is gratified." The letter does not mention his resignation, or the anxiety with which he was awaiting reinstatement. No doubt he was embarrassed at going home as a civilian, and he may have thought his presence in Washington would be advantageous to his hopes. He decided with Allie that under these circumstances it was best not to go.

Alonzo went in his place. He had done his work well, and had earned a leave. Will accompanied him to the railroad station, and when the train pulled out he felt very sad that he had not gone after all. But a proud man of eighteen cannot change his mind.

In the spring of 1861, only two or three weeks after the beginning of hostilities, Milton, the oldest of the Cushing brothers, enlisted in the navy. He had not been happy as a drug clerk, and he was glad to get away. He had administrative abilities and he was used to handling money, so he was immediately assigned to the paymaster corps, and served with distinction through the war in that branch of the naval service. When the war broke out his brother Howard organized a company of his fellow newspapermen in Chicago, of which he was elected captain. But there was a mixup, for some reason the company was not needed at the time, and Howard was turned down. He went back to work, but without his heart being in it. Finally, in March, 1862, he could stand it no longer and enlisted as a private in Battery B of the 1st Illinois Artillery. Living in Chicago through the summer and fall of 1861, he was often able to get home to see his mother and she came to depend on him during this time. He was also able to attend the wedding of Mary Edwards at Fredonia, and was there reunited with Alonzo, whom he had not seen for several years. When the two brothers parted, Allie returning to the war, Howard to his job in Chicago, they were seeing each other for the last time.

V

The *Ellis* and the *Barney*

~~~~~~

THE *Cambridge* was a screw steamer of about 850 tons which had been purchased from a civilian owner and commissioned in August. "It is a fine, large gun boat," Cushing wrote, somewhat exaggerating its merits, "mounting four sixty-four pounder guns on the main deck, and two large rifled guns on the spar deck." He reported on board toward the end of October, and the ship left Hampton Roads the day after and steamed to the mouth of Rappahannock River, where it relieved the vessel which had been on blockading duty.

The first few days were uneventful; the men spent most of the time shooting ducks and going after oysters. Occasionally a boatload of escaped Negro slaves appeared in the river, and the *Cambridge* would pick them up. "In the short time we have been here, we have received on board over one hundred contrabands, all stout and healthy, and valued in good times at over one hundred thousand dollars. I have got one of them for my servant. They are as happy as flies in a sugar bowl. They dance and sing every night, till my sides ache with laughter." One of the boatloads of fleeing slaves reported that "there was a vessel loaded with wheat and wood . . . anchored some six miles from the mouth of the Curatoma branch of the river, or about twenty-six miles from the mouth of the Rappahannock." Captain William A. Parker of the *Cambridge* judged rightly that this was a blockade runner preparing to escape, and he determined to cut it out before it would have the chance.

"The 1st lieutenant came up to me and asked me if I wanted to go on an expedition," Cushing wrote. "Of course I said yes. When he told me that he and myself were to take thirty men in the small steam tug, and cut out the schooner, I at once made preparations for the work—put on my sword, loaded my revolver, took a Sharps rifle and off we went." Cushing neglects to mention that two masters, who outranked him, also accompanied the expedition. The tug, the U.S.S. *Rescue*, encountered no opposition on the way up the river. The Union force reached the *Ada*, a schooner of about 120 tons, only to find that a recent gale had driven it firmly aground. Cushing was the second man aboard, and expected to be fired on, but the guard had "considered discretion the better part of valor, and retreated." After breaking two hawsers trying to get the vessel off the mud bank where she lay, she was set on fire, along with some huge piles of wood on shore, "all the property of Captain Pritchard, a notorious rebel." The marauders remained with the schooner for an hour, to be sure that every part of her was in flames, and then set off down the river.

The Confederates had rallied and were determined not to let the *Rescue* escape unscathed. When the Union vessel was opposite Mary's Point she was fired upon by a rifled cannon and by a number of riflemen concealed along the bank. The first shot from the shore carried away the guy for the boat davits on the *Rescue*'s port beam. "Struck once!" said Cushing, who was in charge of the little vessel's thirty-two pounder smooth bore cannon. "Now, my lads, aim just where the smoke came from and let fly." The thirty sailors commenced firing, and canister from the gun drove the Southerners from their artillery piece, but they kept up a hot fire from a large house located on the shore nearby. The *Rescue*'s gun threw a well-placed shell directly into the house, killing about twenty-five of the defenders and effectively putting an end to the opposition. The tug continued back to the *Cambridge* without further resistance. Union losses were two wounded. As the tug neared the larger ship the crew, who had listened to the heavy firing with much anxiety, knowing that there would be odds to contend with, sent up a cheer. "We were heartily congratulated upon our safe return by the officers who had remained on board. I returned safely, although my coat did not, for a splinter torn off by a round shot struck that useful garment, and knowing that it was impossible to wound a midshipman, much less to kill one, it only tore the coat and lodged in the vest, where I found it when the action was over. It was not a large one, not larger than my fist, and I have kept it." This in a letter to his mother—if the fragment had been as large as his fist it would certainly have killed him. He starts the letter thus: "I think that it is about time that I should write to you. I do not know when the letter will go off, but if I do not write now, I may never have a chance, for we are fighting quite often now, and I will get my letter ahead of any stray ball."

That winter the *Cambridge* did blockading duty off the Virginia capes. Cushing, as a midshipman, was boarding officer and he found the duty "very severe." He was required to board stopped vessels in order to check their papers. "I was frequently out in open boats," he wrote, "for five and six hours at a time with the icy seas and sleet dashing over me continually. Several times I was too stiff upon return to step over the ship's side and had to be hoisted on deck." He also had little faith in the seaworthiness of his ship. In fact the *Cambridge* had had a serious mishap toward the end of November which, coupled with the ordinary wear and tear of continuous blockade duty, had considerably lessened the vessel's efficiency. "We ran into a schooner which we sunk, not without losing our bowsprit, and in a gale, out at sea; the vessel was strained and now leaks. I only hope we will go to Boston, for I long to see my friends there. If the vessel should, however, go down the Southern coast in the condition she is in now, I might as well bid all my friends good-by at once, and begin to describe the oyster, not coral beds, that are to be my future residence." The ship was less seriously damaged than Cushing hoped, and it continued through the winter in active service. The coastline was long and Union vessels few that winter, and the Navy Department felt constrained to keep the *Cambridge* at her station.

All of Cushing's letters to his mother were not bloodthirsty, and some, like one he wrote from the *Cambridge* on February 24, 1862, might have been soothing. "My Dear Mother," it began. "It is blowing as if all the Nor' westers in the world had been tied up for the last twenty years, and had just broken loose. The waves have been rolling twenty feet high all the afternoon, dashing against us, and making the old ship shiver like a freezing giant.

"Yet, how calm I feel, just the same as in the most beautiful calm that ever fell upon the bosom of old ocean.

"A huge, roaring foam-crested mass of water comes dashing over the bows and sweeps the deck, fore and aft. Yet here I am with only six inches of plank between myself and the wild, deadly, sublime wrath of Nature's moving throne.

"If there is one time more than another when one realizes God's greatness and His mercy, it is at such a moment as this. A man who has a heart must think of the time when Christ said to such a sea, 'Peace! Be still.'

"Often, I feel as in the hand of God.

" 'They that go down to the sea in ships, that do business in great waters; these see the works of the Lord and his wonders in the deep.'

"As usual it is very late. Give love to all dear ones. Your affectionate son."

On March 8, 1862, the lookout on the *Cambridge* spotted the *Merrimac* (the Confederates called her the *Virginia*), iron-coated and with a vicious ram beak, coming around Sewell's Point, escorted by two or three smaller vessels, to challenge the entire Union fleet in the Roads. The *Cambridge*, with a crew of ninety-six and only five guns, was hardly a fitting adversary. She was ordered alongside the *St. Lawrence*,

an outmoded sailing frigate of fifty-two guns from the old
navy; the idea was that the *Cambridge* would tow the larger
ship into position for a broadside. It was late afternoon of that
fateful day before the *Cambridge* could get the *St. Lawrence*
into position. By that time the *Merrimac* had done most of the
damage it was to do: the *Camberland* had been rammed and
sunk, the *Congress* badly mauled and captured after its commander, the son of Commodore Smith, had been killed, and the
Minnesota, Cushing's old ship, which had run aground, was
in imminent danger of being destroyed. To compound the
Union difficulties the *St. Lawrence* also ran aground. The
Cambridge took it in tow again, but soon found that it was
under the fire, along with the larger ship, of the Confederate
ironclad and the attending steamers. Fortunately for Cushing
and the U.S. Navy, the sun was setting, and the rebel ships
withdrew, confident of a victory the next day.

The *St. Lawrence* was again afloat, but the *Minnesota* was
helplessly aground and listing at a severe angle so that its guns
could not be fired effectively—an easy prey for the ironclad
when she should choose to come and take it. Union hopes were
not high that night; the gloom that hung over the fleet
pervaded the land troops at Fortress Monroe as well, and
reached even to Washington. The *Monitor*, however, had
arrived in the afternoon and, not being able to get into action
before nightfall, was ready to fight the next day. The battle
lasted most of the 9th and ended in a stalemate that saved the
Union fleet. The *Merrimac* retired without destroying the
Minnesota, which was refloated and escaped to safety. The
age of wooden ships was ended.

"We have just come out of action with the rebel fleet,"
Cushing wrote his mother. "Two of our frigates are destroyed,
and the *Minnesota* is terribly cut up. We did some good
fighting—were struck a number of times. I am the only man
on this vessel that was wounded. A hundred pound Armstrong
shell from the *Merrimac* burst over my head, and a splinter
has taken out an inch of flesh; it is slight, but bled considerably.

I am all right for tomorrow's fight. I was highly complimented by the Captain and Commodore. The Captain said, 'You are highly honored in being the only officer wounded.' I *do* feel so. My hand is very stiff and I can't write more. The rebels took us by surprise and we were much cut up. Some of the frigates must have lost a great deal of life. Two were destroyed. You can imagine how hot the fire was. *I shot the rebel flag staff away*, on the Sewall's Point battery with my rifle gun, and I will try to do as well tomorrow."

He missed the great battle the next day, however, as the *Cambridge* was ordered to drop down the bay and start for duty off Beaufort, North Carolina. The *Nashville*, a swift Confederate blockade runner, was bottled up in the straits. Captain Parker proposed to prevent her escape by blocking the channels; Cushing thought the plan absurd, since there were several channels to cover, and the *Cambridge* was slow and had for support only a small sailing vessel, the *Gemsbok*. The young midshipman proposed, though his hand had become infected and was very painful, to lead a cutting-out party into the harbor to capture or destroy the rebel steamer. Parker would not hear of it. On the night of March 17, a dark and cloudy one, the *Nashville* made a dash for the open sea and easily eluded the *Cambridge*—the lookout did not even see the escaping ship. The *Gemsbok*'s lookouts sighted her, but the night was calm and the combined efforts of the two Union ships were to no avail, and the *Nashville* vanished into the darkness.

The Navy Department was angry and frustrated at this incident. "This is not blockade," wrote Assistant Secretary Fox to Commodore Goldsborough. "It is a Bull Run to the Navy." Commander Parker was ordered to Hampton Roads to make a full report to his superiors. For the first time in his life Midshipman Cushing did not have to say anything. All that he might have said was painfully clear. In any case, he could hardly speak, for he was a very sick man. His hand was badly infected, and he had a deep, racking cold and cough and could not sleep. He was therefore extremely pleased when Captain Parker told him that he was being sent home on sick leave. The two men did not part friends. Cushing's low opinion of the *Cambridge* had been transferred to her skipper, and he was glad indeed to leave him.

He arrived in Fredonia at the end of March and was immediately put to bed by his mother. It had been a long time since he had been in a comfortable bed which did not sway with the motion of a ship, and he was not unhappy to have a nurse to take care of him. For the first two weeks he was glad enough to remain in the house. His cold would not leave him, and his hand ached and throbbed despite all that his mother could do for it. Toward the end of April the weather turned warm and sultry, and then clear and springlike, and he could not endure the confinement that his mother insisted upon. One evening he climbed out of his window, as he had used to do, and, shinnying down the porch column, spent two or three hours at a gathering in the Baptist church. When he returned his mother smiled at his escapade—if he could climb down that column, she said, he must be well. He agreed. But the town was very quiet. His cousin was in East Troy with her husband and there were hardly any young men about. He was not unhappy when his orders came, at the beginning of May, to return to duty. Before leaving he visited the offices of the Fredonia *Censor*. He described the actions in which he had been engaged, with a few embellishments, and the story was printed on the first page. He was surprised that his mother was not impressed. He was able, however, to get her to agree to give his letters to the editor after she had read them, and they were printed regularly thereafter; the fact may account for the bloodthirsty tone of some of them. It was late in May when he left Fredonia to report aboard the *Minnesota*, then in Hampton Roads. He swung up the ladder like a veteran, and indeed he felt like one. He had burned powder more than once, and had been wounded in the most famous naval action of the war.

The Peninsular Campaign had started, and the *Minnesota* was soon involved in stirring events. This ill-fated attempt to take Richmond from the south, by way of the James River, had begun in March, but after the capture by siege of the great roadblock of Yorktown, the campaign had turned into a series of terrible frustrations. McClellan was held at Williamsburg by Longstreet, giving General Johnson time to concentrate his forces. McDowell's force at Washington was not able to join McClellan by water, as the latter had hoped; instead McDowell was ordered to march overland through the rough Virginia terrain. The terrain was rough, but Stonewall Jackson was rougher; he attacked the Union troops covering Washington, McDowell was detained to defend the national capital, and the meeting was never effected. Starting on the last day of May there was a series of bloody battles in which the Union forces, though outnumbering their foe at least two to one, were hard put to it to hold their own. Jackson had caused particular trouble by his sneak up the Shenandoah Valley, the move which detained McDowell. To frightened Washington politicians he seemed at one point within an ace of taking the city. Then he dropped back into Virginia to reinforce Lee, who had taken command of the Army of Northern Virginia before Richmond. The last week of June, the Seven Days, was terrible. On July 1 they fought at Malvern Hill. The rebels, believing that the Union troops were demoralized by six days of retreat and near-disaster, made the mistake of attacking the Federal artillery face on. They lost about seven thousand men, and got nowhere. McClellan saved his army in the end, but in doing it he merely showed his talent for defense and retreat. In any case, he had been sent to take Richmond, not to save an army. The South was discouraged too. "The campaign was nothing but a series of blunders," papers on both sides said. Altogether nearly thirty thousand men were lost.

Alonzo Cushing missed none of it. He had been promoted to chief of ordnance of General Sumner's staff, with the

temporary rank of captain. "He is in perfect health," Will
wrote his cousin, "weighing now one hundred and seventy
pounds. I don't know where he is going to stop in promotion.
He ranks far above every man in his class. I am proud of his
success, for I think such rapid promotion for a boy of twenty
is entirely without precedent in the regular army." At the
battle around Williamsburg Alonzo displayed great bravery;
he was constantly up front under fire. Once a horse was shot
from under him, but despite a heavy fall he remounted and
went back into action. As the Army of the Potomac inched
its way up the peninsula he was constantly in the thick of
the fighting. At Fair Oaks, on May 31, he was hit by a Minié
ball while standing only a few feet from General Sumner.
The ball struck him in the breast but was turned aside by a
bulging dispatch book and a pistol, chipping a piece off the
butt of the weapon. Despite his dislike of war he was excited
by the battle. It "was the grandest sight I ever witnessed," he
wrote his mother. "Just as it was getting dark, the muskets
were much heated, there were two long parallel sheets of
flame from the opposing lines, and I can conceive of nothing
more grand than the spectacle presented—nothing so exhilarat-
ing as that splendid bayonet charge. I never expect to witness
another so beautiful a fight, if I live to be as old as Methuselah."
As the action warmed, he continued to range the front with
dispatches, paying no attention whatever to the enemy fire.
On June 30 at Glendale he had another horse shot from under
him; another was killed under him the next day, at Malvern
Hill. For his extraordinary heroism his name was sent in to the
President for two brevets: one for gallant conduct at Williamsburg and Fair Oaks, the other for Malvern Hill. The recommendations do not seem to have been acted upon, however.
The practice of giving brevets for bravery or meritorious
service entitled the recipient to a nominal rank higher than
the one that he held but without any additional compensation,
and was an honorary recognition. A presidential brevet also
entitled the recipient, at least during the first years of the war,

to wear the uniform of his brevet rank, to be addressed by his brevet title, and to serve as of his brevet rank when specially detailed. Under later laws the officer could not wear the uniform of rank above that which belonged to him by regular commission. In Alonzo's case, if the two brevets had been acted on, he would in effect have had the temporary rank of major, although receiving only a first lieutenant's pay.

In the early part of July Flag Officer Louis M. Goldsborough went up the James River to meet with General McClellan, taking with him as a member of his staff Will Cushing. The President himself came down to confer with his general, arriving at Harrison's Landing on the 8th. McClellan took the opportunity to give Lincoln some unsolicited political advice, but Lincoln did not have to be told anything about politics, and listened in silence. He asked, instead, if it were possible to disengage the army and do something with it. McClellan said no, and his generals agreed. To make up for the lack of action a review was ordered, and Cushing rode on the President's staff. He sat very straight on his horse, very proud and young, as he trotted along behind Lincoln and his generals. The President was immensely tall, he said, and wore a high black hat that made him look even taller. The young officer was moved by the way the men stared at their commander in chief, as though he were made of something different from the stuff they were made of. And when Lincoln rode away they cheered him until the valley rang with the sound.

Will stole away without permission soon after arriving with his commanding officer at Harrison's Landing, to visit Alonzo. He hoped to be able to fight at the side of his brother in any future action; he could handle an artillery piece as well as any landsman, he said, and could do more good for the Federal cause behind a howitzer than he could on the *Minnesota*. But his warlike anticipations were disappointed. Lincoln, having lost confidence in McClellan, decided to withdraw the Army of the Potomac and entrust further operations to other generals. During this time, and at the review, Will had the chance to see "every regiment in the army," and was introduced by General Sumner, Alonzo's patron, to Generals Sedgwick, Hooker, Couch and Peck, and to Colonel Hunt, later the great Union artillery commander, as well as to a number of other officers. When Will had ascertained that there was nothing he could do he returned to Norfolk. Goldsborough was not overjoyed to see him, and he was placed under suspension. But the commodore "was a typical seaman of the old school, imposing in person, loud in voice, genial in temperament, and very much inclined to let the youngsters have their own way up to a certain limit." He had been commandant of the Academy during the period when discipline was at its lowest ebb, and had consequently a poor opinion of midshipmen; he was thus willing to grant Cushing his liberty after a nominal punishment. "As a midshipman is hardly considered a responsible being," Will wrote, "I was soon released."

The summer heat off Norfolk was intense and unremitting; typhoid fever was the scourge of the fleet that summer, and Cushing fought a bout with it. "I suceeded in losing eight pounds of flesh in one week, and then concluded to get well." When he was on his feet again he varied the dull existence by riding back and forth in the pilothouse of the mail steamer, which recreation came near, on a hot evening in the middle of July, to costing him his life. The steamer, while chugging up one of the little rivers that line Chesapeake Bay, came too close to the shore. Confederate sharpshooters had crept down to the edge of the water; they opened fire and sent five bullets through the pilothouse. One of them came within inches of Cushing's head, while another took off three of the pilot's fingers.

The increase in naval personnel under the act of July 16, 1862, created opportunities for promotion, and Cushing, along with many others, waited hopefully. Despite his pranks and his seeming disrespect for naval discipline the young officer believed himself to be worthy of promotion, and hoped for the rank of master, or if not that, at least ensign. The navy was not unaware of his potentialities. Gustavus Fox and Gideon Welles were both of the opinion that he could be a valuable naval officer. As a result Cushing was elevated to the rank of lieutenant in August, thus skipping the two ranks for which he had hoped. He was overjoyed, and extremely proud; such a rank was exceedingly rare for a young man of nineteen, if not unheard of. "Perhaps it will interest you, Mother," he wrote, "to know that I am the only man who has ever reached this rank at anywhere near my age. I am not yet twenty," he added, as if she could not count.

Along with his promotion Cushing was given the right to choose what officer he would serve under. It was not a difficult decision, for he considered his old friend and benefactor, Lieutenant Commander Flusser, to be the ablest of the younger commanders. "He is the fighting man of the North Carolina Sounds," Will wrote; "he is daring to the death and chuck full of fight." His request was granted subject to the recommendation of Flusser and the commander of the blockading force in the Sounds, H. K. Davenport, and Cushing set off for New Bern, North Carolina, to secure their permission. Davenport was absent when he arrived, but Flusser was glad to see him again, and when Davenport arrived back on the scene the transfer was affirmed. Cushing was named executive officer of Flusser's ship, the *Commodore Perry*. She was not a large vessel, being a fourth rated sidewheel steamer with a crew of only twenty-nine and but four guns; with Flusser and Cushing in command of her, however, she was ready to give the Confederates much trouble.

Conditions of service in the sounds were not exactly what Cushing had hoped for. They were "vastly different from the ideal naval life of the period," a naval expert of the nineteenth century wrote; "the lofty frigate shortening sail and clearing for action under the blue sky far out in the open sea was then the symbol of naval glory, but no such spectacle cheered the

eyes and exalted the patriotism of the seamen. . . . The vessels
were small and smoky, redolent of engine oil and innocent
of snowy canvas and glistening spars; instead of the bright
blue sea of nautical romance, one saw the muddy, shallow
flood of the far-reaching inland waters, stained and poisoned
by the ooze and vegetable decay swept down by numberless
rivers and creeks from the surrounding swamps." Indeed,
the sounds and the country around them are uninviting.
Separated from the sea by a narrow strip of sand, pierced here
and there by inlets most of which are so shallow as to allow
only boats of the lightest draft to pass through them, the sounds
are of vast extent but never more than a few feet in depth.
Though the terrible storms that turn the Atlantic into a
very hell in winter from Norfolk to Cape Hatteras to Cape
Fear do not greatly disturb the inland waters, still the choppy
waves are hard to manage in the small ships which are all that
can maneuver in the shallow water. Swamps line the western
side of the sounds, and are pierced by slow, meandering rivers,
over which the thick, almost jungle trees nearly close in summer, to drop their leaves into the muddy, dark currents. Sailing
is out of the question up these creeks and rivers; sometimes
the only means of water transportation is by poling. And to
make the terrain even more uninviting, ten thousand Confederate infantrymen were stationed here and there in the
swamps, and were likely to begin firing at any moment when
one's ship rounded a bend. The only consolation was that the
enemy was equally uncomfortable—and that the blockade,
despite its difficulties, was beginning to work.

It was even hotter than at Norfolk, and typhoid attacked
this part of the fleet also; it was regarded as a vicious killer.
One of the *Perry's* sailors contracted the disease after seeing
several of his shipmates die of it; as a consequence, he had come
to think of it as inevitably fatal. Cushing visited the man in the
sick bay to which he had been removed on one of the larger
ships outside the sounds. "You are a good deal better today,"
the young lieutenant said cheerily. "Oh no, I am not," the man

replied. "I will bet twenty dollars I will die before tomorrow morning." "Done!" cried Cushing. He took twenty dollars out of his pocket. "Well, where's your money, man?" he asked. The sailor pointed to his knapsack, and the officer left the sum with the doctor. "I thought of course that it was a jest," Will wrote. "But I went back the next day to collect my money and found to my dismay that he had won his bet."

Whether through this contact or another, Cushing again came down with the disease within a week or so, and spent ten days flat on his back. Flusser came to visit him toward the end of this time, and said that he had better get well because there was fighting in the offing. Will smiled weakly. "Aye aye, sir!" he whispered. The news was better than medicine. Within forty-eight hours he was up, and back on the *Perry* after two more days.

Major General John A. Dix, commanding the Seventh Corps with headquarters at Fortress Monroe, had requested the navy to supply two or three gunboats, Flusser explained, for a joint military-naval operation against the town of Franklin, Virginia, on the Blackwater River (the Blackwater flows into the Chowan River, which empties into Albemarle sound, the large northern section of the sounds). According to inaccurate Union intelligence this town was being used as a concentration point for ten thousand rebel troops which would be used to attack the Union base of Suffolk, Virginia, twenty miles east. The gunboats, the army believed, could ascend the Chowan and Blackwater rivers as far as Franklin, where the railroad to Suffolk crossed the river, and there co-operate with an army force to destroy the enemy concentration. Flusser telegraphed to General Dix that he would be at Franklin by six in the morning of October 3, agreeing with the army officer who had brought the dispatches that this would leave sufficient time for the necessary preparations.

General Dix, however, did not agree. He sent a special messenger asking Flusser to wait a few days, but the messenger was delayed and did not arrive at Plymouth until five hours after the *Perry* had started up the river. The messenger hastened back to Dix with this information; Dix then reported to Admiral S. P. Lee, over-all commander of the North Atlantic Blockading Squadron, that all was not lost, for he had two thousand men under Colonel Samuel Spear who could make a reconnaissance in force toward Franklin. Spear, unfortunately, was able to bring only about thirteen hundred men into action. Happily for the Union troops the reports of the Confederate force had been much exaggerated.

Spear's men did not arrive on the scene until the afternoon, and then fought so halfheartedly that the bulk of the rebel defenders were able to give their full attention to the gunboats, which were having a merry time of it. The *Perry*, with the *Hunchback* and the *Whitehead* following behind her, had reached a point three miles below Franklin the night of the 2nd, and after a hasty breakfast were on their way again at 5:45 A.M. Confederate riflemen lined the banks and poured a hot fire into the three ships. Their task was made the easier by the fact that the river was narrow and flowed between high banks so that the decks of the ships were often on a level, or even below, the enemy rifles. The crews of the three gunboats aggregated barely two hundred men, some of them soldiers who had replaced sailors sick with the fever, and their fourteen guns had to contend against numerically superior fieldpieces. Nevertheless they made their way up the river without suffering too many casualties until they reached a sharp bend in the stream. This had occurred before: the standard procedure was to heave lines ashore, make them fast to trees, and thus swing the bows of the vessels around the bend. This was extremely difficult in the circumstances, however, with a withering fire pouring down on anything that moved on the deck, and Flusser ordered his men to cover and attempted to steam around the bend. The river was very narrow, and the *Perry* drifted into the left bank of the stream.

The situation seemed desperate. Cushing looked over the side of his ship in time to see a mass of infantry preparing to board. He called for volunteers and dashed out into the open and cut loose the howitzer, which rested on a field carriage on the after deck. Assisted by six men and the master's mate, Mr. Lynch, he wheeled the howitzer into position. By that time the young lieutenant was alone, for the seven men had all been hit by the fire from the bank, and were lying dead or wounded at his feet. The piece was loaded with canister, and without waiting an instant Cushing sighted the weapon and sent the full charge crashing into the mass of attackers, who were by this time only about thirty yards away.

The effect was terrible. The troops, who had been cheering as they ran with their rifles held high over their heads, suddenly stopped and milled about in confusion, with surprised looks on their faces, stumbling over the bodies of their fallen comrades. Their leader, however, "a splendid looking fellow with long curly hair," came on, waving his sword, seemingly unconscious that he was not being followed by any of his men. Cushing reached for his pistol, but found that he had dropped it in the effort of pulling the howitzer into place. For a long moment the two men seemed to hang in space without moving, staring into each other's eyes, and then there was the crack of a musket from the rail near where the lieutenant stood, and the Confederate officer fell, his face buried in the mud only ten feet from the side of the grounded vessel. Cushing looked down, astonished, to see that one of the wounded sailors had risen to his knees and was leaning on the rail, his smoking weapon in his hands. He looked up. "Close one, sir," he said, and winked. Cushing winked back, and then ran to the pilot-house, where Flusser was swearing at the man who had run the ship into the bank.

The entire action had taken no more than a minute or so, and it was hardly five minutes more before the *Commodore Perry* was freed and able to steam around the bend until she could bring her guns to bear on the point. She struck back fiercely at her attackers, and it was soon their turn to take cover. Under the shelter of her fire the *Hunchback* succeeded, though not without difficulty, in rounding the bend; it covered the banks with its heavier guns while the *Whitehead* navigated the turn also.

The Union flotilla was not yet out of trouble. A quarter mile up the river and still about half a mile from the town, it discovered an obstruction thrown across the stream. Such obstructions—usually, as was this one, two or three large trees cut down across the river—could have been moved under normal circumstances, but with Confederates everywhere in the woods and raking the decks of the ships with their rifle fire, it was out of the question. The gunboats sat stationary for some time, hoping to hear the welcome sound of the Union guns from the east, which would signal that the army had arrived at the town. The position was safe enough, since impenetrable marshes lined the banks on both sides of the river at this point. At 10:15, more than four hours after the agreed time, Flusser reluctantly concluded that the land attack must have misfired, and decided that his only course was to retreat. The Confederates had spent the time in felling trees at various points down the river, but with the current helping them the three gunboats were able to steam through all the obstructions (the *Whitehead* was now leading, and had a heavy prow; the *Perry* brought up the rear). A harassing fire was continued from the banks until 2:30 in the afternoon, but with remarkably little effect.

The expedition was a fiasco when viewed by Admiral Lee and General Dix, but it had an important effect for Lieutenant Cushing. Flusser, in his report, described his executive officer's bravery in glowing terms, and for his part in the enterprise Cushing was offered his own command. He accepted it eagerly. The ship was the U.S.S. *Ellis.* "She was of iron," Cushing lovingly described her, "three-eighths of an inch in thickness, measured about one hundred tons, and mounted an eighty-pounder rifle forward, and a twelve-pounder rifle howitzer aft." She drew about six feet of water, which made her extremely handy for duty in the sounds.

   Cushing was the first Union commander of the *Ellis;* she had been captured earlier in the year from the Confederate fleet in the sounds. She was at New Bern when he received his orders, and Flusser sent him in to the docks at that city in the *Perry*'s launch. It was with a feeling of great pride that the young lieutenant was piped over the side of his first command. Her crew of twenty-eight men was lined up on the foredeck when he came aboard, and though they seemed surprised to have a boy—so one, at least, later called him—for a captain, they snapped smartly to attention while he read them his orders and then walked in front of them, shaking hands with the officers and nodding gravely to the men. In fact all but six of the crewmen were older than he was, and a master's mate named Edward K. Valentine was more than twice as old. They all came in time, however, to respect him for his seamanship and his bravery. His rashness was personal. Though he was never one to take his own safety into account, he was extremely solicitous of his ships and his crews, and though he was a severe disciplinarian he never drilled his men beyond a point which seemed, in the sequel, to have been good for their own safety. In the end no commander in the navy had more loyal crews than Will Cushing. The same was true of his brother's artillery batteries, although the two officers went about achieving what is after all the end of all military commanders in different ways: Allie got results by kindness, Will by daring (though it would be wrong to imply that Allie was not daring or Will not kind).

   On October 18 Cushing wrote his cousin a letter which points out the two significant facts of his character at this time: on the one hand, that he was an extremely mature person, quite capable of commanding a ship of war in enemy territory and causing that enemy a great deal more discomfort than they could cause him in return; on the other, that he still lacked nearly a month of being twenty years old. "It [the attack on Franklin] was a very fortunate action for me," he wrote. "I am the only officer mentioned in Captain Flusser's official report for special gallantry in action. The official report will probably be published, in which case you will see it. I could tell you what it says, but will not do so, for fear you might think me too 'set up.' I will only say that I have since been given command of this gunboat for my services. I can justly be proud of having command of a steamer at the age of nineteen. It is a thing before unheard of in the service. Three days ago, I left New Berne, steamed down the Neuse River, across the sound, and out to sea. I anchored at the city of Beaufort for one night, put to sea again and ran down here [Bogue Inlet]. I am alone, inside the outer bar. The nearest friendly vessel or citizen is forty miles away. Three miles off, up the inlet, is the rebel town of Swansborough.

"I am going to run up and take possession in a few days, when I have burned up enough coal to lighten my vessel so I can cross to the other bar. Yesterday I fired a shot to the right of the town from my eighty-five-pound rifle gun, and they ran up a white flag on one of the public buildings. There is an eighteen-gun fort a mile and a half off, but they have no guns in it at present. My main object is to stop the trade the admiral thinks is carried on through the inlet. I think I shall have a fight before I leave. I find it somewhat lonesome here and would like sometimes to be with my friends in the North. The truth is, I find myself a boy yet, and it is hard to be contented away from society.

"In the few weeks that I remain here I expect to write so many letters as to astonish all of my correspondents.

"This is a fine country for forage. I send ashore every day and kill a cow, a horse or a sheep. I understand that schooners run into New Topsail Inlet, thirty miles farther down the coast, and that they are protected by a battery. I shall run down there in a day or two and try to cut out a schooner or two. You see that I have a sort of roving commission, and can run around to suit myself. For the present I am my own master. If under these circumstances I cannot stir the rebels up in more places than one it will be strange indeed."

Bogue Inlet was a bore; nothing, despite Admiral Lee's belief, was going in or out of it. In any case, Will Cushing had never had a great respect for admirals. Thus it is not surprising that the day after he had written to his cousin his intention of "stirring up rebels," he steamed down the coast to New Topsail Inlet, one of the more important of the inlets along the coast, it being deep enough to allow rather large ships to cross over into the sounds, and being also only twelve miles north of the busy port of Wilmington. He ran close in to the inlet, and seeing nothing moving on the far side of it, called for full speed ahead and slid over into the shallow waters beyond. His intrepid action was rewarded: a mile away a Confederate schooner lay at anchor, with no protecting vessels in sight. Although the *Ellis* had no pilot aboard who knew the channels (the Union ships were constantly at a disadvantage in these shallow waters because of their lack of pilots), Cushing set his helm directly for the schooner and succeeded in drawing within a hundred yards of her before running aground. The captain and crew of the schooner had no mind to deal with an obvious madman and, having clumsily attempted to set their ship afire, escaped in two or three small boats, at which the *Ellis* fired, but with no effect. A boarding party led by Valentine soon extinguished the blaze aboard the prize, which was discovered to be the *Adelaide*, lately out of Halifax, and carrying a cargo of about six hundred barrels of spirits of turpentine in the hold, with thirty-six bales of cotton and some tobacco on the deck.

The sun was setting as the last of the flames was extinguished and even Lieutenant Cushing did not feel equal to the task of taking the schooner out of the harbor in the dark. There was nothing to do, therefore, but to remain by her through the night. At dawn no resistance had been encountered and the *Ellis* began to tow the captured vessel out of the bay. Since it drew three feet more than the gunboat it constantly ran aground. After having spent the best part of the day in this fruitless activity, and finding that the tide was low, making it quite impossible to get the *Adelaide* to sea, Cushing fired the turpentine and destroyed the schooner, which was worth, it was later estimated, upward of $100,000. Realizing that he had somewhat exceeded his authority in leaving Bogue Inlet, he reported to his superior that he felt himself justified under the circumstances. Commander Davenport approved of his action and told him "to continue to act in accordance with the dictates of your best judgment. . . ."

This, of course, was like waving a red flag in front of a bull, and a week later Cushing was back at New Topsail, having established, by a visit to Swansboro, that there was little or no trade in Bogue Inlet. He steamed through the passage once more and made for the shore where, about three-quarters of a mile from the inlet, his lookout reported a large building with smoke and signs of activity. It was a salt work, capable, Cushing reported gleefully, of supplying the whole city of Wilmington. With an armed party, he went ashore in small boats. The Confederate workers made their escape. "We tore down the brickwork," Cushing wrote, "destroyed their large copper and iron kettles and pans, cut holes in their flatboats and lighters, cut through the cisterns and waterworks, and burned the buildings; 10 or 15 bushels of salt that had been made that morning I turned into the ditch." Such is the illogicality of war that even salt becomes a weapon.

The destruction had taken too much time, and the escaped Southerners returned before it was finished with a force of Confederate troops, with two artillery pieces. The landing party was into its boat in a flash and pulling for the *Ellis* before the rebels could get the range; when they did, they succeeded only in splashing water on the oarsmen. Cushing turned his gun on them as soon as he reached his ship, and after a few moments exploded a shell in the midst of them. They at once limbered up, he said, and took the road for Wilmington.

Back he went to Bogue Inlet, but there was still nothing doing. He remained a dutiful three weeks and then, toward the end of November, he was taking the *Ellis* into New River Inlet, and beyond it, up the New River, having successfully negotiated a narrow and shallow place called "The Rocks" (he had found a pair of pilots for this much more hazardous endeavor). He was going "to sweep the river, capture any vessels there, capture the town of Jacksonville, or Onslow Court-House, take the Wilmington mail, and destroy any salt works" he might find on the bank. In other words, he was bored, and hoped for some action, the more varied the better. He found it.

He had steamed up the river about five miles when his lookout reported a vessel outward bound. Before the *Ellis* could reach her she was in flames; it was cotton and turpentine again, a highly inflammable mixture, and in the confusion her crew escaped in small boats to the bank. This vessel was worth $30,000. Leave him alone, and Cushing would take care of all the turpentine south of Richmond. After making sure that the vessel was well fired, he continued up the river until he reached Jacksonville, the county seat of Onslow County. He arrived in this sleepy little town at about one in the afternoon. His sudden appearance in the river was, to say the least, a surprise to the inhabitants. A landing party was sent ashore under the leadership of the redoubtable Valentine, which took possession of the public buildings and raised the American flag over the courthouse. It flew gaily in the wind, and the men remaining on the *Ellis* cheered. The townspeople were silent. Twenty-five stand of "public arms" were discovered in a storeroom in the courthouse, and seized, along with all the mail in the post office, and two small schooners tied up at the one dock. The Negro slaves of the Confederate postmaster were "confiscated" and taken to be freed later.

After about an hour and a half Cushing decided that he had occupied Jacksonville as long as it was safe to do so, especially since several Confederate officers had escaped down the road to Wilmington before the landing party could reach them, and would undoubtedly return shortly with reinforcements. Up went the anchor, and off the *Ellis* steamed, with her two prizes sliding along behind her.

About two and a half hours downstream a Confederate camp was discovered on one of the banks. The *Ellis* turned her big gun on it and shelled it vigorously for several minutes, and then continued on her way. When she reached the spot where the blockade runner was still burning and filling the air with a pall of black smoke, Confederate rifles opened fire on the gunboat from the banks. Again the big gun was swiveled about, and again it silenced the rebel opposition.

But the sun was setting, and Cushing's pilots declared that it would be impossible to take the *Ellis* over the bar in the darkness; Cushing would have to wait for light and high water. No one slept that night; all along the shore the Confederate watch fires were burning, and ominous sounds carried across the water, seeming to indicate that an attack was to be expected at any moment. But morning came without a shot having been fired, and the *Ellis* started off down river once more. She had almost reached "The Rocks" when two artillery pieces opened from the right bank. In the course of an hour's sharp cannonading the *Ellis'* large accurate gun was able to drive the rebels from their position, and the ship passed within a hundred yards of the abandoned strong point. Her captain drew a deep breath. His luck was still with him, then. And the tide was high; the two schooners were still being towed bravely behind; this would be indeed a feather in his cap.

But his pilots were not made of the same stuff as their commander. Within two or three miles of the inlet they mistook the channel, and ran the ship aground at the top of the tide. Cushing swore angrily and sent his men scurrying to try to lighten the vessel. Anchors were cast into the mud and the engines strained against the lines, but without success. Valentine reported that the water was going down, and that there seemed no hope of freeing the ship until the next tide.

It was the middle of the afternoon—it would be dark in less than three hours. "Mr. Valentine, I want you to go and secure those guns," Lieutenant Cushing ordered. "What guns, sir?" "The guns they were shooting us with, man!" Valentine set out in the launch with ten men, but returned in an hour to report that the guns the Southerners had abandoned the night before were gone; they must have come back in the darkness for them. "We didn't waste our time, though, Captain," said Valentine grimly. "We found another of them salt works, and burned it." "I saw the smoke. I wondered what you were up to." "We found ten or eleven boats, too, sir, and stove 'em in. They won't use 'em to board in the night."

"Good man," Cushing said quickly. The situation was desperate. He ordered one of his prizes alongside, and everything that was movable was transferred from the *Ellis* except "the pivot gun, some ammunition, two tons of coal, and a few small arms." Still the ship would not budge. Her headway had forced her over a shoal and into a position where, in the middle of a little pond of deeper water, there was a circumference of shoal all around.

When Cushing had done everything that could be done he called the men onto the deck and spoke to them. "Officers and men!" he said. "I see no chance of getting this vessel off." The men nodded, and looked at one another. "We will probably be attacked in the morning, and that, too, by an overwhelming force." The men nodded again. "I will try to get her off at the next high tide if I am not attacked in the interim. In the meantime it becomes my duty to provide for the safety of you all." The men stood silent. "If we are attacked by the enemy in the morning and he overpowers us, either by boarding or otherwise, the only alternative left is to go up with the vessel or submit to an unconditional surrender." He smiled grimly. "To do the latter is neither my desire or intention. I will not do the former except as an absolute resort." It was the men's turn to smile. "I wish all the men, except five or six—and these must be volunteers—to go on board the schooner. I wish the schooner to be dropped down the river to a point without the range of the enemy's fire from the bluff. It is my intention, with the five or six men who may volunteer to remain with me, in the event of an attack, to work the pivot gun in the morning, and fight her to the last. I will not surrender [to] the enemy, while a magazine or a match remains on board."

He paused, and turned away to allow the men to choose. It had been an overdramatic speech, he knew; he was not unaware that to a cetain extent he was playing a part out of Flusser's *Naval Enterprise, Illustrative of Heroism, Courage and Duty*. But the facts as stated were true enough, and he was not going to leave his first command to be towed ungraciously away by a Confederate barge. He turned back toward the men, who had remained silent. At first he was astounded to see that the ranks were unbroken; had no one volunteered, then, would he have to fight that pivot gun alone? He opened his mouth to speak. He suddenly realized that the line of men was two or three paces closer to him than it had been. His face broke into a wide grin. "By God!" he said. "I won't forget that, men. I won't forget it, as long as I live!"

Valentine smiled back, showing the gaps in his front teeth. "Guess you'll have to choose, sir," he said. "Don't seem to be nobody that trusts that schooner to get us out of this bay." Cushing stepped forward and chose Valentine and five of the older sailors. They clustered around him and waited as the rest of the crew climbed into the schooner. "Save yourselves, boys," Cushing called across the widening stretch of water, "if they get us. But don't leave unless you're sure!" A cheer answered his words. The schooner dropped down the river and came to anchor about half a mile away. Cushing turned as Valentine plucked at his sleeve. The old man was grinning wryly. "Only one thing bothers me, Captain, and that's the magazine. If we had a cover for that I'd feel a little easier about them shells flying onto the deck." Cushing nodded. "Well, we'll just have to trust to luck. There's nothing to do about it now." The magazine was completely exposed; it would not have to be a very lucky rebel shell which would explode it, and blow the *Ellis* and her defenders into the sky.

The first ball struck the *Ellis'* iron sides before it was properly light. "I don't see how they can see us before we see them," Cushing muttered, but it was some time before another shot hit the ship. When it was bright enough to make out the situation it became evident that the Confederates had four heavy artillery pieces which could, and did, pour in a cross fire that was very destructive. The pivot gun did the best it could, but its range permitted it to reach only two of the enemy positions, both of which were well protected behind earthworks. Holes were knocked in the *Ellis'* hull and her engine was disabled by a shot that pierced her boiler and sent steam boiling out into the foggy air. The only alternatives, since, even if the engine had been in working order, the tide was still not high enough to float the vessel, were to surrender or to try to escape in the ship's boat. The schooner had dropped another mile downstream, but was still waiting. It was a long pull, half of it within range of the Confederate guns, but it was worth it. The halyard to the flag was cut, insuring that the rebels would have to shoot the standard down if they wanted it down, and the ship was fired in five places. Before leaving the pivot gun, the piece was loaded and trained on the enemy with a slow match "so that the vessel might fight herself after we left her." Cushing and his men shoved off and started down the river, the six men pulling for all they were worth.

The Confederates had had no trouble in hitting the *Ellis*—indeed, their fire had been more than ordinarily accurate—but a moving target seemed to be beyond them, and though they kicked up a good deal of spray and once sent a wave into the boat which set the oarsmen to bailing furiously, they did not do any damage. Within ten minutes, as they rowed with the current, the boat was out of danger. When it was clear that the enemy shells were falling farther and farther behind, Cushing took off his cap and held it high over his head. "I'll say one thing for the navy," he said through his teeth. "They teach men how to row a boat." Valentine grinned as he pulled on his oar.

The captain of the *Ellis* fell silent then, and the men rowed on in silence too, not wishing to obtrude upon his grief. Within an hour they were aboard the schooner. Her sails were set and she was straining at her anchorage, and by noon they were out to sea.

It was hardly necessary, Flusser told him, but Cushing ended his report on the loss of the *Ellis* with a request that a court of inquiry look into his conduct "to see if the honor of the flag has suffered at my hands." Commander Davenport and Admiral Lee refused, saying there was no need. The Navy Department approved their decision, saying: "We don't care for the loss of a vessel when fought as gallantly as that." Nor were the Union officers the only ones impressed by Cushing's conduct. Captain William Harwar Parker, once of the U.S. Navy and now of the C.S. Navy, wrote that "Young Cushing had been a pupil of mine at the Naval Academy in 1861. He was first brought to my notice during the war by my happening to get hold of his report of the loss of the U.S. Steamer Ellis, under his command at New Inlet, Nov. 24, 1862. I was impressed with this part of his official report (the italics are mine): "and the only alternatives left were surrender or a pull of one and a half miles under their fire in my small boat. The first of these was not, *of course*, to be thought of.' Knowing him to be at that time but 19 years old, I comprehended his heroic qualities and was not at all surprised to hear more of him."

The affair had an unpleasant aftermath, though not a permanent one. The Confederate general in charge of the area reported immediately after the vessel's destruction that its "armament, ammunition, small-arms, and many articles of value will be saved." This could be done, he said, because although the crew had "attempted to fire her, being of iron . . . little damage was done." This report conflicted with Cushing's

statement that as a result of the fires he had set the *Ellis* had
exploded, making it a total wreck, and the young lieutenant
was unhappy about the seeming contradiction, and wondered
if the ship had been salvaged after all. Later the facts of the
incident were discovered. In April, 1863, the schooner *Odd
Fellow* was captured running the blockade off Wilmington.
One of her crew was James T. Sayle, who had been in charge
of salvage operations on the *Ellis* the previous January. Papers
found on his person established that the Confederates had
arrived at the wreck expecting to raise the vessel, only to find
that there were too many cannon holes in it. Moreover, as
Cushing had reported, the starboard side of the ship had been
blown out when the magazine exploded. All that could be
done was to salvage some few items of equipment; the gun and
carriage, a few pieces of hawser and cable and some odds and
ends of pipe, and a small amount of ammunition were all that
could be saved.

One of the most flattering results of the action was the offer
by Major General John G. Foster, commanding the department of North Carolina, to Cushing to command a squadron
of five army steam gunboats. Cushing refused, though he was
extremely pleased by the confidence it indicated in one just
twenty years old. "I did not wish to relinquish actual naval
service," he said, "and desired one vessel of the navy more than
a fleet of army boats." General Foster said that he understood.

When he returned to the fleet Cushing found that an attack
on Wilmington was being contemplated. The most important
obstacle was the lack of pilots who knew the complicated
channels, which had been made even more complicated by the
Confederates' sunken ships and other obstructions. Cushing
had not been in New Bern three days before he had a plan. He
reported to Commander H. K. Davenport. "I have a schooner,
sir," he began. Davenport squinted at him. "The *Home*, the
one you captured at Jacksonville?" "That's it, sir. Well, sir, I'll
capture you some pilots with it."

"And how is that, Mr. Cushing?"

"Disguise her to look as much like an English blockade runner as possible, sir. That's what she is, so it wouldn't be too difficult. Then we'll play a game: I'll run and you chase me right into New Inlet, they'll think I've slipped through the blockade, a boat will be sent out to pilot me to Wilmington, and there are our pilots." "And how will you get out again?" "We'll see, sir, when the time comes. I'm sure I can make it." It would be difficult; the Confederates had batteries on both sides of New Inlet.

Commander Davenport took the plan under advisement, and in two or three days informed Cushing that he must present it to Admiral Lee; he himself, he felt, did not have the proper authority. Off went Cushing in his *Home* to tell his story to the admiral; he spent an hour with the old man, and told him about the *Ellis* and his other adventures. The admiral wrote to Gustavus Fox: "Cushing's account of his past action impresses me very favorably. [The plan for capturing the Wilmington pilots] may succeed if the idea has not leaked out. . . ." The reply came, asking for more information, and Lee ordered Cushing to Washington to present his plan to the Navy Department in person. In any case, the young lieutenant had lost all his clothes in the *Ellis* except the uniform he was wearing. It would be a chance to visit a tailor.

Fox liked the idea for getting pilots. "I told him he might go at any scheme you consented to," he wrote Admiral Lee. "Rashness in a young officer is rather commendable." Incidentally, he added, "Young Cushing went off to New York not to get clothes, but to see his sweetheart." The day Fox wrote his letter Cushing was in Fredonia having an argument with Charles Smith, Cousin Mary's new husband. Alonzo, Sister Isabel said, had written that the army was marching south, and that there would be a big battle soon. Charles Smith said it might be the end of the war; at least that was what they were saying in Chicago. Will did not agree. He also discovered the whereabouts of Howard, who was in Grant's army in the West, near the Mississippi town of Vicksburg. Will remembered it as the city where his father had gone the winter before he died.

Will remained only two days in Fredonia, not wishing to try Gideon Welles's patience. The night before he left for Washington there was a party for him, and Mary played the piano while they all sang the war songs, old and new. The best of them, as he remembered it, was a song they had seen in the *Atlantic* magazine; he had heard men singing it, but as yet had not learned the words.

Mine eyes have seen the glory of the coming of the Lord;
He is trampling out the vintage where the grapes of wrath are
  stored;
He hath loosed the fateful lightning of his terrible swift sword:
His truth is marching on.

On November 5 Ambrose Burnside replaced McClellan and shortly thereafter reorganized the Army of the Potomac into three "grand divisions" under the commands, from left to right, of Generals Franklin, Hooker and Sumner. The right grand division was to take the initiative in future movements, and Sumner wanted Alonzo Cushing for topographical work at his headquarters. The young officer had commanded a battery of artillery at Antietam, and had McClellan's and Sumner's high praise. The Topographical Engineers was considered the most scientific and technical organization in the army, and Alonzo was willing to serve in it as long as nothing else was happening. His first official duty was to prepare a map of the field of Antietam. Late in November the army started south, with Alonzo Cushing on General Sumner's staff. On the eve of the battle of Fredericksburg, which took place on December 13, he was transferred to the staff of General Darius N. Couch, as an aide at the time of the actual fighting. During the battle Alonzo performed his duties as courier and dispatch bearer so gallantly and with such disregard of his own safety that Couch praised him above all others in his official report. "Lieutenant Cushing," he wrote, "was with me throughout the battle, and acted with his well-known gallantry." Again a recommendation was sent to the President, and this time it was acted upon. Lincoln brevetted Alonzo captain, to date from the 13th of December, "for gallant and meritorious services at the battle of Fredericksburg."

Admiral Lee was willing to let Will Cushing angle for pilots if his superiors would take the responsibility. "Young Cushing's scheme ventures more than it promises," he wrote to Fox, "but liking the morale of the thing I would not stop the project." He sent the young man down to Davenport with orders to carry out the plan, and when the *Home* was suitably disguised Cushing was ready to make the effort. But his luck was poor. He took the schooner out to sea and then sailed it as fast as it would travel toward the inlet, with two or three puffing blockaders in pursuit, but the wind died suddenly, and three times the vessel was becalmed within sight of the watchers on shore. It was obvious that he was part of the squadron. Having failed three times at both the eastern and western bars of Wilmington harbor anyone else would have given up, but Cushing had another idea. He had heard that there was a pilot station at Little River, some thirty miles below Fort Caswell, close to the boundary between North and South Carolina. With his schooner still disguised he set sail down the coast, reaching his destination early in the morning of January 5, 1863.

He waited until dark and then shoved off from the *Home* with twenty-five men in three cutters. The Little River was narrow and the banks were thickly wooded. When the party had gone about a mile up the river a burst of fire surprised them from a bluff on the left. Cushing stood up in the stern of his boat. "Follow me in!" he cried, and swung his bow in toward the bank, the others following. He leaped out and gathered his men in formation about two hundred yards from the concealed enemy position. "Forward; double quick;

charge!" he shouted, and ran forward toward the fortification, without firing a shot.

"At the enemy we went," he wrote several years afterward, "yelling like demons, and coming out into the open space saw, by the light of a camp fire, an earthwork looming up in front. It was no time to turn back, another yell and we were through the ditch and over the parapet, sole possessors of a fort and blockhouse, from which the frightened garrison five times our numbers, had run away deceived by our boldness into the belief that *they* not *we* were the surprised party." He and his men were doubly pleased to discover that not only had the retreating Southerners, who went up one side of the fort while the attackers scrambled over the other, abandoned a stack of small arms and piles of clothing, but had also left a supper of pork and greens upon the table in the middle of the blockhouse. While they ate the hungry sailors examined their prize, and realized quickly how foolhardy they had been, for in fact the captured fort was "an earthwork surrounded by a ditch about ten feet broad by five deep," the blockhouse had been pierced so that the defenders might fire without exposing themselves, and it was a strong position in every way except that no artillery had been mounted in it, and it might have successfully withstood an attacking force ten times the size of Cushing's.

But they had come for pilots. Mr. Valentine went a short way farther up the river but found no sign of anyone. When he returned all the captured property that could not be carried was destroyed. A shot whistled through the air as they were about to leave, and they knew that the defenders had returned. The sailors manned the ports of the blockhouse and traded shots until the Confederates' ammunition ran out (they had left most of it behind them when they ran). The sailors were out of ammunition too, so they ran along the beach and got into their boats and successfully returned to the schooner, their sole casualty being one of the seamen, who had a slight flesh wound in his right leg.

They met a greater foe this trip than Southern riflemen. Once aboard the schooner Cushing decided to remain anchored at the mouth of the river until daylight. By midnight a heavy swell was rolling in from the south and west. A storm in those waters in the winter was never to be taken lightly, particularly in a small vessel of only four tons, carryonly fifteen fathoms of chain and a single anchor. By two in the morning it had started to rain, the drops driven fiercely into the faces of the worried sailors by a wind of nearly gale force. The vessel was straining at her anchor chain, and seemed in danger of being blown against one bank of the river, where in the darkness they could see ominous rocks rising out of the water. There seemed two alternatives: to go ashore under the guns of Fort Caswell and surrender vessel and crew as prisoners of war, or to put boldly out across the thirty miles of stormy space between the shore and the shoals, and, allowing for all the leeway made, endeavor to strike the mere vein of a channel that was the only way through them to the sea. Lieutenant Cushing chose the latter course, although, in such a gale, he was aware that the breakers must be very high even in that narrow channel. It was an extremely dangerous chance to take, for should the schooner veer to the left or right and miss the passage by as little as ten or twelve yards, it would certainly be pounded to pieces in the surf, and the crew tumbled and drowned in the great waves roaring in from the Atlantic.

Cushing called Valentine to his side. "We are going to go out," he said quietly. "It is our only chance, other than surrendering the ship, which I will not do." Valentine nodded. "Tell no one else of the danger," the skipper went on, "but take the helm yourself. If anyone can handle the vessel you can." Valentine turned to the wheel without a word. The anchor came up and the schooner started on its desperate journey.

There was no trouble for several hours, and though the gale seemed to increase in intensity it was some help that day broke, although not much was to be seen but clouds and spray. "All at once," Cushing said, in relating the affair, "I saw the old quartermaster at the lead turn deathly pale as he sang out, 'Breakers ahead! For God's sake, sir, go about!' In an instant the cry was. 'Breakers on the lee bow!' then 'Breakers on the weather bow!' and we were into them. All seemed over now; but we stood at the helm, determined to control our boat to the last. A shock—she had struck. But it was only for a second, and she fairly flew through the great white breakers. Again and again she struck, but never hard. She had found the channel, and in twenty minutes we were safe, and scudding for Beaufort."

The trip to the Union outpost was uneventful, but Cushing did not look forward to having to report another failure. He need not have worried. Any young man who was sufficiently crazy might have performed the exploits in the Blackwater River or in Wilmington Harbor, but only an exceptionally able sailor could have brought the *Home* back to Beaufort in such circumstances, and instead of berating him, Admiral Lee highly complimented his young lieutenant. As the best earnest of his praise, Cushing was promptly given a new command.

Before taking over his new ship Will was given a twelve-day leave which he spent in Washington. The city was full of activity—he wrote to his cousin that "mud and contractors were thick in the streets"—which appealed to him after the lonely days on blockade duty, and when he arrived at the Navy Department he discovered that his brother Milton, whom he had not seen for several years, had been there recently. He had "been foolish enough to go to Boston to see a cousin married," but would return in two days. Milton was now stationed in Washington, and had a room in a boarding house near the Capitol. Will was able to convince the landlady that he was related and she let him stay in Milton's lodgings until their rightful tenant came back.

"In two days Milton returned and we at once commenced

to be as jolly as circumstances would permit. There are three regular theatres in the city now, and the star actors don't shirk it as they used to, so I patronized them extensively, laughing at the farces and comedies, and looking grave, sometimes, at the tragedies. Sometimes, I say, for that brother of mine was almost sure to set me off into convulsing laughter by some absurd remark just in the thrilling part, much to the amazement, and sometimes indignation, of the surrounding multitude. And then my cousin and her spouse [the Boston newlyweds] came to Washington and I called upon them at Brown's hotel (they call it Metropolitan now), and of course I had a splendid time—but if I keep on in this way you will think I had a splendid time all around and will be but illy prepared to hear the story of my woes. I had woes—Ay! tribulations and trouble followed me on this pleasure trip, and proclaimed there was no rest for the wicked. The thing that I had most set my heart on was a trip to Falmouth to see Alonzo. One night I got a pass and early the next morning started off for the foot of Sixth Street, to take the boat for Acquia Creek, and to go by railroad from that point to the Army of the Potomac. The hackmen were disposed to cheat me, so I got on my feet and dignity, and determined to walk. The farther I went, the deeper became the mud, but I swam along without much trouble until I reached the wharf. I struck bottom four times on the way, or rather I ran into that number of sunken hacks, and I no longer wondered at the extravagant charges of the jehus in front of Kirkwood's. The provost marshal had told me the name of the boat that was to run that morning, and so I went on board and made it my first business to get rested, but I had not been seated long, when I was informed that if I proposed to go to the tents of the wicked at Falmouth, I would have to make tracks for the next wharf, as I was on the wrong boat, and the right one was there. Off I started in a great hurry, and off started the object of my search in a greater hurry.

"I can remember that when I was a small but rather wicked

youth, I used a reader in school in which was a picture of a fleshy gentleman standing at a depot, the picture of despair, and gazing after a train of cars that seemed just to have left. Under the picture were the words, 'Just one minute too late.'

"Picture to yourself a tall, slim young man, to whom these words will apply, and knowing him to be your cousin and a fellow with a temper, just imagine the young man on the rampage. I forgot to mention that there was a carpet-bag connected with the story—a carpet-bag that was filled with sherry, cigars, and other promoters of happiness, that were to have been consumed in the tent of Alonzo, 'The Indian,' who dwells in the camp at Falmouth. On my way to the wharf, the load, though heavy, was lightened by the thought that a jolly good time was ahead, but think what must have been its weight in the three miles back. When I got back to my quarters my hands were covered with blisters, and my clothes soaked with mud."

It is often the smallest things that break hearts. The argument with a cab driver, the mud in the streets, the wrong boat chosen, the sherry and cigars—all of the slightest consequence ordinarily, yet it was the last chance he would have to see his brother alive.

Within a few days Will Cushing was called into Gideon Welles's office and offered his choice of two ships. One was the *Violet*, a small, fast steamer intended to be used to harry the blockade runners off Wilmington. The other was the *Commodore Barney*, larger and with a heavier battery, but much slower. Cushing asked where the *Barney* would be serving, and was told that the department wished to keep her near enough to Hampton Roads so that her superior fire power could be effectively used. She was too slow for the blockade, and her guns would be wasted. Cushing asked Welles if it was true that General Longstreet had been given command in eastern Virginia, and if it would not be reasonable to suppose that there would be fighting south of Nor-

folk before very long. Welles said that he was not sure that
Cushing was supposed to know that, but he admitted that the
War Department thought it was true. Cushing then said that
he would choose the *Commodore Barney*. He had found
blockading duty a trifle dull, and he was glad at the opportunity of action. He asked Welles if he might have Valentine
in his crew, and this was arranged. The *Barney* was waiting
for him in Norfolk, Welles said.

   Cushing set out for Baltimore to get a ship for Norfolk.
"When within five miles of Baltimore, the train broke down,
and I at once dismounted from the iron horse, and turning
into an infantry force marched on Baltimore. If I shall ever be
called upon as a defender of General McClellan for his not
pressing the enemy after Antietam, I shall impress the mind of
the court that Maryland soil is not favorable for the marching
of troops. At last I reached the 'Monumental City,' but found
that the 'Old Point' boat was crowded and that I could not
get a stateroom. Armchairs were at a premium too, and I
only succeeded in securing one by resorting to a little piece
of military strategy; I see a seedy individual in a comfortable
armchair near the fire. A friend of mine asks seedy individual
to 'smile.' The wearer of the threadbare apparel falls into
the trap. I fall in the chair—he goes to the bar—I go to sleep.
When I wake up in an hour or so, I see the lover of strong
drink on the deck in the arms of sweet Morpheus. Moral—
never travel without a flask of whiskey in your pocket. If
this rule is observed, you can bid defiance to any bit of
military strategy like the one here recorded."

   The *Commodore Barney* was a powerful steamer of 512
tons with a very heavy battery consisting of five one-hundred-
pounder smoothbore guns, a one-hundred-pounder Parrott
rifle and a twelve-pound howitzer, and carried a crew of
thirteen officers and about a hundred and twenty-five men.
"The command of her belongs to some officer of higher grade
than myself," Cushing wrote his cousin, "but they (the
powers that be) are pleased to think that I have earned the

distinction—of course I am proud as a peacock at being the only Lieut. in the regular Navy who has a [separate] command."

The first two months were dull; the Barney patrolled the Roads for enemy shipping, and found none; in any case there were larger ships which would have taken care of it if there had been any. But spring was early that year, and things began to pick up in April. Longstreet was interested in moving into Southeastern Virginia and the coastal regions of North Carolina in the expectation that supplies could be gathered easily by foraging on the country. He also had it in mind that the Union posts of Norfolk and, particularly, Suffolk were possible bases for the attack that was shaping up, no one knew from what quarter, up the James River to Richmond. While moving into southeast Virginia, then, he reasoned, why not capture Suffolk on the way? His force numbered perhaps thirty thousand men; Union Major General John J. Peck had roughly half that number in and around Suffolk, though his troops were later reinforced.

On April 11 Longstreet appeared outside the line of Peck's fortifications. His position was strong except for his left flank, which faced on the James River; the Union fleet held the river. He asked for Confederate naval units to come down from Richmond, but they had so obstructed the stream that it was impossible, they said to get there in weeks. He therefore pulled back his left flank to the spot where the Western Branch joins the Nansemond River, and fortified his position along these banks. His center was led by General John B. Hood; it faced both south and east, in conformity with the twisting contours of the Nansemond. The right flank was held by General George Pickett, whose division rested on the north edge of Dismal Swamp.

Peck telegraphed to Admiral Lee that he desperately needed naval support, and Lee replied that he would send what he could. "Who do you suppose was selected," Cushing wrote his mother, "to perform the dangerous task of guarding the

rear and preventing the crossing of ten thousand of the
flower of the Southern army? Who but your son! That ex-
midshipman, ex-master's mate, hair-brained, scapegrace, Will
Cushing! Yes, it is even so."

Lee ordered Cushing to take the *Barney* to the Suffolk area
to assist the land forces, and sent with him four other vessels:
hardly a formidable force, since the *Mount Washington* was
a river steamer, the *Stepping Stones* a converted ferry, and
the *Cohasset* and *Alert* were tugs. Commanding the *Mount
Washington* was another lieutenant, R. H. Lamson, junior to
Cushing in service but several years older, a tall handsome man
with a neat black beard and serious eyes. The two lieutenants
soon became fast friends, and co-operated in every stage of
the actions that ensued with the greatest affability and efficiency. Cushing was nominally in command of the flotilla
("Who do you think is the naval commander in the Nansemond?" wrote Captain Chaddock, a Fredonian penned with
his Union troops inside Suffolk, to his wife. "None other
than the little boy who lived down on Green Street—you
remember him—Willie Cushing!") but Lamson knew the
territory well and was at first given responsibility for the ships
that could cross the bar and ascend the upper reaches of the
Nansemond.

The *Barney* was stationed in the lower part of the river,
outside the bar. Cushing's first dispatch to Admiral Lee after
arriving at his position was characteristically impatient: could
he lighten his vessel and cross at high water if fighting broke
out above the bar? He added that "If it comes to a fight, it
will be a hard task to remain at anchor within sound of rebel
cannon." Lee sternly forbade any such thing. "You are to hold
the lower bar," he ordered. He sent the *Cohasset* to assist
the *Barney* in this task.

As soon as the gunboats arrived, General Peck pulled his
artillery from the Union bank of the river, depending, he
said, on the navy to defend that quarter. Admiral Lee objected
strenuously. It would be impossible for the lightly armed

craft to hold the line if the Confederates attacked in sufficient force and were willing to pay the price entailed. The argument had no effect on Peck; he was trembling inside Suffolk, and wanted all the fire power he had within his sight.

There was desultory firing throughout April 12 and 13, but on the night of the 13th the action picked up, and rifle fire from Confederate sharpshooters caused several casualties on the *Mount Washington*. This was merely a taste of what was to come. The next day Lamson's vessel, leading the *West End*, an armed army steamer, and the *Stepping Stones*, was attacked at Norfleet's Point by seven concealed artillery pieces from four hundred yards range—artillery which could not have been there had Peck maintained his position where Admiral Lee had said he should. The fire was accurate, and a shot hit the *Washington's* boilers, sending boiling water splashing over the deck and endangering the lives of half the crew. After a few moments of confusion they pulled themselves together and stood to their guns. The vessel lost headway, however, and grounded against the bank. To complicate matters the *West End* also ran aground. Lamson signaled the *Stepping Stones* to tow his ship out of range of enemy fire, and amid great difficulty and with heavy casualties this was done.

The *West End* was also freed, and the three vessels started down the river, Lamson's vessel still in tow. Confederate sharpshooters kept up a heavy fire from the bank, but with little effect. When the flotilla reached the bar they attempted to cross it into the lower Nansemond, where the river was much wider and the ships could maneuver to protect themselves. Unfortunately in crossing the *Mount Washington* again ran aground, and the Confederates opened a terrible cross fire with at least seven pieces of artillery. Lamson ordered all the men who were not needed to man the *Washington's* guns into the *Stepping Stones*, since his ship was hopelessly aground until high water. The converted ferry dropped down the river with the *West End*, which was perilously short of coal, behind it.

Cushing could observe all that was happening from the other side of the bar, and he brought his ship as close as her heavy draft would allow and began to fire at the attacking artillery. The two gunboats fired as quickly as possible. In a letter to his mother written the next day Cushing described the action graphically: "I had but two vessels afloat, but I silenced their fire in an hour. In a short time they again went into action; this time unmasking a regularly constructed battery not five hundred yards from us, and so situated as to rake the narrow channel completely. It was impossible to get our disabled steamer off from the bar until high water, five hours ahead, and I determined to fight on the spot as long as the *Barney* was above water. I sent the light steamer down to guard another coveted point, and was soon exchanging death calls with the enemy.

"Well, it was a hard fight, and at close quarters most of the time; so close that their infantry riddled the two vessels with bullets. *Crash!* go the bulkheads—a rifle shell was exploded on our deck, tearing flesh and woodwork. A crash like thunder is our reply—and our heavy shell makes music in the air, and explodes among our traitor neighbors with a dull sullen roar of defiance. Up goes the battle flag, and at once the air is filled with the smoke of furious battle, and the ear thrills with the unceasing shriek and whistle of all the shell and rifled bolts that sinful man has devised to murder his fellow-creatures. *Crash! Crash!* Splinters are flying in the air; great pools of blood are on the deck, and the first sharp cry of wounded men in agony rises upon the soft spring air. The *dead* cannot speak—but there they lie motionless, lifeless, and mangled, who a moment ago smiled on the old flag that floated over them, and fought for its glory and honor. Sprinkle ashes over the slippery deck—the work must still go on. The rifled gun—my best, is disabled, for three shots have struck it—the muzzle is gone, the elevator is carried away, and the carriage is broken. Steady men, steady! Fill up the places of the killed and wounded—don't throw a shot away. The wheel of the howitzer is torn off by the shell, and the gun rendered useless—never mind! Work the remaining guns *with a will*—for we can and *must* be victorious. And so the time wore away, until the rising river promised to release the imprisoned steamer, when I signaled to the *Stepping Stones* to move up and take her in tow. This duty was gallantly performed, and the old *Barney* remained alone under the rebel cannon.

"And here let me pause to give credit to one who will never earn more glory than he grasped in our desperate combat then. Lieutenant Lamson is one of the class next below me, and commanded the disabled steamer. . . . I fought within a hundred yards of him and we are sworn friends for life. Well, I silenced the battery, and anchored at night where I had fought all day.

"My vessel is riddled with cannon balls and bullets, and I have lost three killed and nine wounded—four of them mortally—men who lost arms and legs. The loss on the other vessels is proportionately severe. I am no braggart, but I challenge the world to furnish a more determined fight, or a victory more richly earned. The enemy *shall* not *cross* here. I will not give way one inch. Even now the thickets on the banks are alive with their sharpshooters; and as I write the quick whirr of the rifle bullet is often heard, sent from the bank five hundred yards ahead, in the vain hope of injuring the hated Yankee. A good providence seems to watch over my fortunes, though I do not deserve its protection. I may go into action again at any moment, probably tomorrow. I have every confidence in my gallant crew and officers, and do not doubt the result if my life is spared. Love to all. In haste, Your affectionate son."

Perhaps a note on this letter is desirable. It is difficult to believe that his mother could have read it without fainting, but in fact it was intended more for the editor of the Fredonia *Censor* than for Mrs. Cushing, and it was reprinted in a number of Northern newspapers. It was written the day after the battle, when the writer was still under the influence of the tremendous excitement of the fighting, and contains some exaggerations. The loss on the three ships was one-tenth of the men engaged—five killed, fourteen wounded, and one missing and presumed dead. The damage to the *Mount Washington* was considerable, that to the *Barney*, despite Cushing's remarks, only superficial, although her battery suffered: she lost the services of the Parrott rifle but a spare wheel was found for the howitzer and it was used in the next day's fighting. Finally there is considerable doubt whether the Confederates were, in fact, attempting to cross the river; probably they were trying only to destroy the two Union gunboats, although of course if they had been successful in that they could have crossed at a later date with little or no hindrance. However, the action was an extremely gallant one. The gunboats had won it, against greatly superior odds, and had inflicted serious damage on a force of veteran troops and two artillery batteries. And the close co-operation between Lamson and Cushing, with no rivalry over the command and no desire to gain prestige at the other's expense, was unfortunately rarer than one could wish in such circumstances. Cushing had nothing but the highest praise in his report for the way in which Lamson had handled his ship, and the latter said of his friend that "it was owing in a great measure to his well-directed fire, causing the enemy to shift his position, that the *Mount Washington* was not entirely destroyed. His vessel was fought in the most effective manner, and he sent his gig to me to ask if he could do anything more."

On the 15th the fighting flared up again. Late in the afternoon Lamson, who had transfered his command to the *Stepping Stones*, tried to get over the bar but failed, and then joined Cushing in shelling Halliday's Point. The *Barney* got too close to the shore and ran aground. Lamson's vessel got the *Barney* off but came under very heavy fire, and suffered three more casualties.

The next day Lamson succeeded in crossing the bar and

under the cover of the *Barney's* guns went up the river with
the *Cohasset* and the *West End.* The resistance was beginning
to weaken, and the Confederates had not re-erected batteries
in the lower river. Cushing was sure that the main enemy
effort was elsewhere. He wrote to Admiral Lee to this effect,
but asked for assistance in any case. Lee sent four vessels.
Two, the *Yankee* and the *Primrose,* drew so much water that
Cushing felt they could not go over the bar; he kept them
with the *Barney* to protect the lower river. He sent the *Coeur
de Lion* and the *Teaser,* along with the *Alert,* one of the
original flotilla, to join Lamson. The next day Cushing and
Lamson attempted to land troops on the north side of the
river to capture the enemy batteries, the *Barney* aiding the
attack with long-range artillery fire since she could not
cross the bar. The army troops withdrew, and the expedition
was a failure. Cushing then telegraphed Lee that if the Admiral
would give him two launches and fifty men, he could capture
the rebel batteries near his part of the river, but Lee refused
to take the chance.

The *Teaser* now disabled its engine, and Cushing decided
to lighten the *Yankee* so that it could be sent to Lamson as a
replacement. He was confident that the *Barney* could hold
the lower river with the help of the *Primrose;* he eventually
decided, however, that the *Yankee* was too unmanageable and
would ground in the narrow upper river. The situation was
extremely frustrating: he was evolving a plan every ten
minutes, but all of them were either turned down by his
superiors or were found to be impractical because of the
physical conditions of the river. To insure his own safety
he sent out pickets every day along the Confederate side of
the stream in order to avoid being taken by surprise by a
sudden attack. Once these pickets captured a Confederate
lieutenant who had come within three hundred yards of the
gunboats in order to make a reconnaissance; he was found
to have on his person a map showing in detail the strength and
disposition of all Union troops in the area. Cushing wrote to

Lee that he felt that this meant the Confederates, since they knew the army strength in Suffolk, would not attempt a direct assault, but would surely try to take the town through his own position if they tried at all.

Lamson, on the other hand, was still preoccupied with his project to have the army land from the gunboats and by a surprise attack take the Confederate batteries in the upper river. He worked out a set of signals with Cushing so that the latter, who could not cross the bar, might aid the expedition with long-range artillery fire. Again and again the infantry were not ready, and over and over the plan had to be delayed. Cushing and Lamson were furious at the army. They strode their decks angrily, waiting for someone to tell them to do something. Meanwhile the admiral was beginning to fear that the situation was exposing his gunboats to too much danger, and he sent Captain Pierce Crosby to determine if they should be withdrawn. The army was horrified at this proposition, calling the gunboats indispensable. Indispensable for what? Lee asked. Are you going to do something with them or are you not? Yes, answered the army, noncommittally. The gunboats remained.

Meanwhile Lamson and the army were finally getting their expedition against the Confederate batteries under way. The rebel defenders had neglected to take proper precautions against a surprise attack, and as a consequence Lamson was able to land troops under General George W. Getty, which captured 5 guns, 7 officers and 130 men at Hill's Point. During the attack Cushing engaged a heavy Confederate battery on his side of the bar. The enemy's shooting was accurate, he reported—they put a hole in his hull with one shell, and fatally wounded one of his men—but with the aid of the Union batteries across the river he was able to report on the next day that the battery had been abandoned. That threat to the gunboats being removed, it was now possible, he believed, to hold the position Getty and Lamson had gained on the enemy bank almost indefinitely.

"Well done, good, faithful officers!" came the reply from Admiral Lee, but the army decided that it could not hold the hard-won position, and evacuated it the next day over Cushing's and Lamson's strong protest. The army had strongly strengthened the fortifications during their short tenancy and the Confederates had only to post a strong battery, Cushing complained, and the Union gunboats would be driven out of the river. He did not believe that it mattered greatly, however, as he continued to feel that a withdrawal was taking place. The army stated that it had to abandon the position because of Lee's order to withdraw the gunboats from the upper river, but the admiral replied that in fact the gunboats were withdrawn only after the army left.

The frustrating situation was momentarily relieved by an incident which spurred Cushing to one of his most extraordinary exploits. While patrolling the river on April 21 the *Stepping Stones* was signaled from the enemy bank by a man who seemed to the crew to be waving a white flag. Five sailors in a small boat were sent out to see what was wanted. A heavy rifle fire opened on the boat when it arrived near the shore, and one of its occupants was killed and the others captured.

The Confederates later explained that they felt this action to be justified. They maintained that some free Negroes had been tricked into telling how they signaled whenever they had information for the gunboats, that they had sent one of their number to signal the *Stepping Stones* with a handkerchief, and that when the small boat came near shore the Northern soldiers became suspicious and two of them raised their rifles. Thereupon the Confederates fired. This explanation did not come to Cushing's attention until a month later; at the time he was furiously indignant at what he construed to be a misuse of the flag of truce. He roared all night in his cabin; he could not sleep, and he did not let anyone else sleep. In the morning he took his ship, along with the *Yankee*, to the point in the river where the *Stepping Stones* was moored.

From the various vessels he chose an expedition of ninety men, including fifteen soldiers from the *West End* who brought with them a twelve-pound howitzer, and shoved off for the shore in the early afternoon. Under cover of the gunboats the seven small boats pulled as rapidly as possible for the hostile bank. Quickly it was gained and a skirmish party sent forward. The boat from which the four men had been captured was found abandoned in the rushes, along with the sailors' rifles and the body of their slain comrade. Leaving a handful of men as a guard Cushing and the main portion of the party pushed rapidly ahead. Three buildings owned by men who had helped the Confederate troops in the area were burned, and the troops continued toward the village of Chuckatuck, some three miles inland. A mile and a half from the village they encountered pickets and drove them off after capturing one; four hundred cavalry were stationed in the town, he said, and the other pickets would alert them. Leaving the man tied to a tree they hastened on. A farmer came along the road driving a pair of mules hitched to a cart. Cushing confiscated the cart and the mules and hitched them to the howitzer, thus becoming a mobile unit in a matter of seconds, going forward at double-quick time. He left half the men at a crossroads outside of town for an ambush and a support, and pressed on with the remainder. Coming up the street ahead was a troop of about forty Confederate cavalry, swords drawn, giving vent to the rebel yell. Cushing loaded the howitzer with shrapnel, aimed, fired—but he had missed them, shot behind them, they were coming too fast. The noise of the howitzer frightened the mules, and they ran off with the cart toward the charging horsemen. This was serious—all the extra ammunition for the gun was in the cart. Cushing started off after the mules with two or three men, but soon saw that he could not catch them. He turned and shouted to his men. "If the mules can charge cavalry, sailors are braver than mules!" They got the idea and started after him at a run. "Charge!" he shouted, and his men yelled behind him. The cavalry halted, stood in confusion—who ever heard of a band of forty sailors charging a cavalry troop? They must be madmen. Even the cavalry does not fight madmen—they turned, called for the retreat, did not stop for the dead, and galloped out of town. They left two dead men on the field of battle, which was the main square of the town, along with three horses fully equipped and six cavalry pistols fully loaded. Chuckatuck was in the Union hands. One "landsman" was killed in the charge.

They were a little out of breath, though, and they sat down to laugh (they did not know until later that one of their number had been killed). "I guess the army should have had some sailors at Fredericksburg," Cushing said to Valentine, who laughed and then became serious. "But they'll be back in force, sir," he said. "We ought to get back to the boats." Cushing nodded. "Just let me breathe a minute," he said. "Those horses ran very fast!"

It was too bad they had not come two or three hours later. It was four in the afternoon when they left, and early in the evening General Pickett, of the perfumed ringlets, came posting into town. Lasalle Corbell was the object of his courting— as often as he could wheedle permission from Longstreet, and sometimes when he could not, he took the long nocturnal ride from division headquarters to see his "charming Sally." The sailors were gone when he arrived, alone. If they had still been there, the charge on the last day of Gettysburg would have had another name.

On the way back from the town Cushing had more horses than officers. "Who'll ride this extra horse?" he asked the men, and a weather-beaten old tar stepped forward. "I haven't been on a horse in ten years," he said. "I'd like to try him." He mounted the animal, who seemed skittish. They started down the road. On the way through a wood they were attacked by a small band of the enemy. The attack was beaten off, but the sound of the firing frightened the old sailor's beast and it turned and started to gallop toward Chuckatuck.

"Whoa!" he cried, and pulled on the bridle. "Where do you think you're going? Whoa!" He was furious. But the horse, perhaps unaccustomed to nautical oaths, would not stop. The rest of the men were sitting in the middle of the road, unable to move for laughter. The sailor was almost out of sight when he reached one of the pistols in the saddle holsters and shot the animal dead. The falling horse threw him headlong, but he scrambled to his feet, stripped the saddle and other equipment from his mount, and plodded toward his companions. "We thought you was goin' to enlist," one of them called. "How do you like the cavalry?" "Want to join Jeb Stuart?" "We guessed you forgot somethin' in town," were other comments which assailed his ears when he caught up with the little troop. He mumbled something about liking to get that horse on shipboard, where he could show it a thing or two, but it was not sufficient. His adventure was the subject of humor for weeks.

The return to the boats was affected without further incident, and Cushing immediately sent to Admiral Lee to tell him that Longstreet's left flank was weak, and that this meant a frontal attack on Peck's army if an attack at all. He also rode nine miles across country "in a dark night and drenching rain" and reported to General Peck. Longstreet must be retreating, he said; only a shell of skirmishers had been left behind to give the appearance of a siege. Peck was a cautious man and would do nothing in the way of a reconnaissance in force.

In any case it is certain that during this time Longstreet gave up any idea he might have had of taking Suffolk by storm. Less than a week later he was reporting to the commandant of the North Carolina department that he felt he could *hold* his "position against any attack from the front." That very day, however, April 27, General Hooker crossed the Rappahannock with 130,000 men, and General Lee telegraphed to Longstreet to come as fast as he could. Leaving sufficient men to keep Peck occupied for the better part of a week, Longstreet disengaged his main force and hastened to join Lee. Before he could get to the meeting place the battle of Chancellorsville had been fought. Peck still remained cautious, but finally raised the siege. Cushing and his ship gave all the aid they could. The navy had received a request from Lincoln to help the army; Cushing, who adored the President only this side idolatry, fought all the harder.

He uncovered a new enemy battery that challenged Union control of the river and shelled it for a day and a night, although two of his ships were ordered to another station just when he could have used them most. Nevertheless he continued to harass the battery, which had been erected as a screen for the departing Southern army, even stationing a "range light ashore" so that he might shell them by night as well as by day. The second morning a white flag went up on the position and a man came to the top of the earthwork and waved. "What does he want?" Cushing asked Valentine, who reached for his glasses, and then handed them to his commander. "Why, it's Otey Bradford!" the captain of the *Barney* said. He waved his hand high in the air, and called for a megaphone. "We'll get you out of there!" he called, but the man cupped his hand to his ear. A boat was sent out to bring Bradford to the ship under a white flag. The two officers had been classmates at Annapolis, and spent an hour talking about those years which seemed so far away. Bradford climbed down into the boat and went back to his battery. "We'll get you out of there, all right," Cushing called across the widening space of water. Otey Bradford smiled and waved his hand.

It was great fun now to trade shots with the battery— "Shoot as carefully as possible," Cushing ordered. "We don't want those rebels to think we can't handle our guns." It would be more fun still to take the place by storm. He would capture Bradford and keep him for a week for old times' sake, and then send him to prison for rebelling against the Union. Fifteen sailors and a howitzer were loaned to a Rhode

Island regiment, which attempted a probing attack, but at the first enemy fire the troops ran, leaving the sailors to fight their way back alone. "Hereafter I shall only aid them by water," Cushing wrote Lee, furious. "I should not feel justified in risking men or guns ashore . . . with such troops." Eventually he succeeded in making the battery withdraw from its position. It was, he said, one of his most satisfying achievements of the war.

After May 4 the Confederates retired from the area and the Suffolk operation was finished for the navy. It is hard to say who was victorious in the entire campaign; hard because no one is quite sure what Longstreet wished to do. If he intended to take Suffolk, then the Union gunboats prevented it. If, as he preferred to think in later years, he intended only a successful supply-gathering expedition, then the supplies were gathered at what might have been a terrible price. With Longstreet absent with more than a quarter of Lee's troops, Hooker crossed the river and fought at Chancellorsville. Lee had to overcome odds of more than two to one. That he did so does not diminish the price he might have paid.

Lamson and Cushing were heaped with praise for their exploits. Admiral Lee reported to Gideon Welles that the two young men had "exhibited remarkable zeal, courage, and discretion." Welles wrote a letter of commendation to Cushing in which he praised his "gallantry and meritorious services." Even General Peck, whom Cushing then and later claimed had acted with so much deliberation as to allow Longstreet to escape unscathed when he might have been trapped, reported that Cushing and Lamson were "gallant spirits" and spoke of "their untiring energy, unfailing resources, and excellent judgment." "The past two months have been marked ones," the young man wrote his cousin, "even in my eventful life. First came the service on the Nansemond River, when the rebel Longstreet was trying hard to surround our forces at Suffolk. I was sent there to take charge of the naval force, whose duty it was to keep the enemy from crossing the river. Well, we did it, after some hard fighting, but not without the loss of a quarter of our men. The enemy fought with determined pluck, but as I had made up my mind not to be beaten, and as one side or the other always *is* beaten, the rebels concluded to make a 'strategic movement' and 'change of base.' I was three weeks in the river, and had a fight great or small nearly every day. I have since received some very handsome letters from the Secretary of the Navy, and the admiral, in acknowledgment of my services. I am in high favor with the department."

When the *Commodore Barney* was withdrawn from duty in the Nansemond River it was so cut up by artillery and small-arms fire that it had to be sent to Baltimore for repairs. Cushing took the vessel to the navy yard and then reported to the Navy Department in Washington. He visited Welles, and they had a pleasant chat. When Welles was finished he cleared his throat and asked the young officer, "Would you like to be presented to the President? I have spoken to him about the good work you and Lieutenant Lamson have done for us and I think that he would be pleased to meet you."

Cushing could not think of anything to say, but his eyes must have indicated his eagerness, for an appointment was arranged for the following week. He spent a sleepless night before the morning when he would see the President in an attempt to learn by heart a speech which would express his admiration and his intention of giving his all, not excluding his life, for the Union cause. But the President was not eager to hear the speech delivered. Cushing was "privately presented" to the President and "enjoyed keenly an hour's conversation with him." Lincoln had once taken a flatboat down the Mississippi from Illinois to New Orleans, and perhaps they talked about that. "The President was pleased to compliment me on my success," Cushing said. "He seemed rather subdued and sad—and did not talk about the war. It is said that Chancellorsville was a blow to everyone here, and that the

President was very depressed by it."

Cushing spent three weeks in Washington, going to the theater with Milton and writing letters and getting over one of his colds and taking the train to Baltimore every other day to check on the progress being made on the *Barney*. The work was going slowly; when the initial three weeks was passed it was not finished, and he was given an additional three weeks' leave and, since his mother was visiting her relatives in Boston, he went there to spend the time with her. "I must say that I never have enjoyed myself before as I did there. I had a dozen different engagements a day, laughed, talked, smoked, enjoyed the society of the ladies, and had some grand rides, good fishing, and some splendid dinners on the sea beach. Don't you think I am as bad as a schoolgirl in the use of adjectives?" He wrote the letter on June 21, having returned to Baltimore to find that his ship was nearly ready. "My good time is over now, and I have hauled aboard my 'dignity tacks' and become 'Captain Cushing' instead of 'Will.' My vessel is in good repair, and my crew is replenished, my battery is heavier than before; and I am prepared to pay upon sight all that I owe the rebels in the shape of shell, grape, and canister. It is not going to be a dull summer as near as I can find out, and if I get into a good fight soon, the vessel may get cut up so as to need repairs. In that case a trip to Fredonia shall be included in my programme, and it may be a visit to the West. Have you any handsome young women in East Troy, Wisconsin? And what are the prospects of finding a sweetheart? I pause for a reply."

On June 24 Cushing and the *Barney* were sent up the York River to the junction of the Pamunkey River to assist a reconnaissance in force planned by General Dix. The idea was to send some ten thousand men to the vicinity of White House, Virginia, to test the Confederate defenses around Richmond while General Lee was up north invading Pennsylvania. The flotilla was under the command of Captain Crosby, whom Cushing transported in his ship to the rendezvous on the 25th, and consisted of the *Barney*, the *Commodore Morris*, the *Morse* and the *Western World*. On the 27th an advance cavalry force under Colonel Spear made a successful raid well within the enemy lines and captured 111 prisoners, including General William H. F. Lee, a son of General R. E. Lee, a lieutenant colonel, seven captains, and two lieutenants. The army troops having been successfully landed and the necessity for gunboat protection having consequently diminished, the *Barney* and the *Morse* were ordered to Washington on the 29th. The threat to the capital from Lee's incursions into Northern territory was of paramount importance, and Cushing was to report to headquarters for such duty as might seem most effective for the protection of the city.

VI

"Gettysburg" Cushing

THE Army of the Potomac spent the months after Fredericks-burg licking its wounds in the mud at Falmouth, and many officers and men in the regular service were given leaves during January and February. Alonzo Cushing left Washington on January 26 and arrived in Fredonia for a three-weeks visit the next day. He was tired and looked thin, but he still retained the youthful appearance, the "almost girlish look," that several of his contemporaries remembered. He was glad of the rest, and spent the first few days doing nothing in particular except sit in the warm house in a comfortable chair reading reports of the battles which he had been engaged in. He always found it strange to read about a battle he had fought in; the reporters knew so much more about it than he did himself. He had seen nothing but smoke and heard nothing but noise and everything had seemed hopelessly frantic and confused, while here an expert had figured it all out—the II Corps had advanced to here, the III to this place, the artillery had opened fire with such and such an effect, the so-and-so Massachusetts had shown extraordinary bravery in charging the rebel lines at this point and at this moment. He remembered none of it. He could not even remember being shot at, but General Couch had said he acted bravely so he must have done so. The papers made mistakes, of course—some of the things they said he knew were not true. Even his own Battery A, 4th U.S., had not fired as accurately as they said at Antietam—

certainly it had not "made every shell count," as the report said. If it had made one out of four count that would have been a good average. But it did not matter in the end, he supposed. It was better for people to believe that the shells they were paying for, and the men who were shooting them and in turn being shot and killed, were being expended for some purpose which could be measured, and which could be said to be worth the price that was being paid. He remembered how many shells had misfired and how many had been badly aimed and how many more had exploded harmlessly in the air or on the ground far from any enemy troops or even fortifications, but there was not much point in reminding people of these facts. They did not want to know about them; he had tried a few times to speak of them, but people were not interested. And he could not tell them, either, that at Fredericksburg he had simply ridden with dispatches to the places where General Couch had told him to take them, and then waited for the answers and brought them back, and started out again with new dispatches, and that though there had been rifle bullets in the air and shrapnel exploding around him at times, it had been quite impossible to think about it, or to think what would happen to his body if one of those pieces of flying steel should hit it. The mind could only concentrate on one thing at a time, particularly when the body was hurrying as fast as it had been necessary to hurry with the dispatches, many of which arrived too late or were irrelevant when they did arrive, General Couch not being any more able to see over mountains or around corners than any other man. And if he had not been able to think of the danger, then how could they say that he had been brave? Yet they did say so; General Couch had said so, and the President had sent a letter, and his name was in some of the reports he was reading. He was not displeased that it was so; he simply did not understand it.

The three weeks, spent in such leisurely amusements, were soon up, and it was time to go back to the army. It was the end of February when he returned to his battery. It was almost beginning to be spring. They would be moving, he thought, when the leaves were on the trees.

Battery A of the 4th U.S. Artillery was composed mainly of veterans—most of them Irish and Irish-Americans—and Alonzo Cushing, in the weeks between the end of February and the end of April, when the battery, attached to Hancock's 2nd Division, moved out with Couch's II Corps, spent every moment preparing for the campaign ahead. Several tentative actions prefaced the great battle which took place in the "Wilderness" on May 3, 1863, and Cushing was involved in most of them. "Fighting Joe" Hooker, new commander of the Army of the Potomac, was using Couch's II and Sickles' III Corps as bait to prepare General Lee for a main thrust, and Cushing took his battery across the Rappahannock on April 30 in line with this operation. Hooker had complete confidence in himself; after assuming command he had announced: "My plans are perfect." "May God have mercy on General Lee," he said later, "for I will have none." Lee rose to the bait at first, but the next day he saw the trick, and leaving Jubal Early on Marye's Heights to hold Sedgwick and his VI Corps, rushed back toward Chancellorsville. Hooker, becoming confused, moved like a sleepwalker. On May 1 he sent his troops out of the town to strike for more open country, but Sykes's division of regulars ran into hard fighting and General Couch with part of his corps, Hancock's second division (which included Alonzo's battery), was sent to help them. They were soon hotly engaged and were confident of success, but Hooker, losing his nerve, ordered them all back; he would set up a line of entrenchments and let the Confederates batter themselves to pieces against it. The Federal armies worked their way into position, the second division (Hancock's) of the II Corps having the position next to Meade and his V Corps on one side of the line, Slocum and his XII Corps on the other. The night of May 1 they were still confident; one more day and it would be over, and they could take Richmond and carry it

home and plant it on top of the Capitol. Instead, the next day
Stonewall Jackson came around through the Wilderness and
on the 5th of May the Union army was in full retreat to
Falmouth.

Alonzo's battery fought well on May 2, and Lincoln sent
him another letter, this one saying that he was pleased to
brevet Lieutenant A. H. Cushing major "for gallant and
meritorious services at the battle of Chancellorsville." The
new major did good service on the last day of the battle also,
though he got no more for it than the thanks of the regiments
he saved. After the defeat he and his battery helped to protect
the crossing of the Federal forces onto the northern side of
the Rappahannock, at United States Ford, and his was the last
battery to cross in the face of the advancing Confederate units.

The month of May was spent in licking more wounds.
Alonzo had lost two valuable men—wounded, however, and
not killed—and he had to train recruits to take their places.
Training with him was a serious matter, and he kept his men
at their guns all through the month, and had no time to get
up to Washington where he could have seen Will, who was
waiting for repairs on the *Commodore Barney*.

"If General Lee be in need of provisions," it is said the high
commissary wrote across his requisition, "let him seek them
in Pennsylvania." In May and June the pro-Confederate
English leaders like Roebuck were maneuvering to bring up
on the floor of the House of Commons a motion to recognize
the Confederacy. Along the Rappahannock Lee, anxious for
provisions as well as for British official recognition, turned
northward with somewhat less than eighty thousand men.
After preliminary moves as early as June 3, he slid west along
the rivers; on June 12 rebel cavalry was reported in the
Shenandoah Valley. It rode through the passes of the Blue
Ridge, and a reconnaissance showed there were still Confederates at Fredericksburg. "If the head of Lee's army is at
Martinsburg," Lincoln wrote to Hooker, still commanding
the Army of the Potomac, "and the tail of it on the Plank Road

between Fredericksburg and Chancellorsville the animal must be very slim somewhere. Could you not break him?" "Impossible," said Hooker. And the army came on.

The capital was full of strange rumors. It was very hot, and everyone was suffering from prickly heat. A spy in the streets of Chambersburg, someone said, had counted Lee's troops—more than ninety thousand men. Out on the fringe of Lee's advance the Pennsylvania roads were choked with refugees. Fourteen thousand citizens turned out to dig trenches at Pittsburgh (no one knew where Lee was heading); in Harrisburg the militia drilled in the streets with fowling pieces and scythes because there were no muskets. Business stopped in Philadelphia and veterans of the War of 1812 offered to form a regiment. On June 27 General Early, encamped around the city of York, offered to depart for $28,000 in U.S. Treasury Notes, forty thousand pounds of fresh beef, thirty thousand bushels of corn and one thousand pairs of shoes. They were supplied, along with other "sundries." That night Hooker resigned and Lincoln named George G. Meade commander of the Army of the Potomac.

There wasn't much time. Early's advance guard was planting batteries against Harrisburg and Lee's army spread in a wide circle from Chambersburg through Carlisle and York. Which would it be, the Union wondered—Baltimore or Philadelphia? Either seemed possible, but in the end, with his supply lines already longer than Lee liked (he could depend on the countryside for food but powder must come all the way from Richmond), he turned down to Gettysburg, east and south of the Cumberland chain; he could concentrate there and challenge the oncoming Union army and if attacked perhaps win a victory, or even drive through the still scattered Federal corps and besiege Washington. In the South they called it "conquering a peace."

On June 25 General Hancock, the new commander of the II Corps, had concentrated his troops at Haymarket, only a few miles from Manassas and Thoroughfare Gaps. There the

Confederate cavalry, led by Stuart, was surprised to find so
large a force and went back over the mountains—again northward, in the direction of Lee, instead of delaying the Union
army by a raid on its rear. That Hancock should parallel
Stuart's march was a matter of course, and on June 30 he was
in bivouac near Taneytown, some fifteen miles south of
Gettysburg. Alonzo Cushing had been found with his battery
in front of each successive mountain pass reached by the
invading army, and now he was prepared to stop them in their
eastward march once more, if it was possible.

Hancock's corps rested at Taneytown all day; Meade was
sure now of Lee's plans, and worked half his army into
position to stop it. At nine in the morning of the first of July
Heth's division of A. P. Hill's corps struck a Union cavalry
post west of Gettysburg. As the horsemen retreated bullets
began to fly out of a wood on the slope of a low hill behind.
"That's all right," Heth called out, "only some of that
Pennsylvania militia," and sent two brigades to clear the way
through. As they reached the wood the firing increased surprisingly. The militia were not accustomed to fight like that.
And then the first of them was seen, wearing a black hat—
the Army of the Potomac. Hill's men cried out, as indeed they
might, for it was the Iron Brigade, Solomon Meredith's 1st
Brigade of the 1st Division of John F. Reynolds' I Army
Corps. The two rebel brigades were swept back, routed,
smashed, Brigadier General Archer captured, and the battle
for America was on.

A little after noon word came to Meade that Reynolds, the
commander of his left wing, was mortally wounded, his I
Corps hard hit; there was doubt whether the position could
be held; Hill was pressing forward toward Cemetery Ridge,
and it seemed nothing could stop him. "Damn it, it must be
held!" growled Meade, and sent General Hancock to take
command. He gathered the reserve artillery and some cavalry
and went off at a trot, claiming priority over infantry on the
road because he could move faster. He needed an aide—

"Cushing!" he called out, when he saw him waiting by his guns. "Leave your battery—we haven't time to take it—we'll get guns." Alonzo mounted and rode as fast as his horse would go after his speeding general.

When the beaten troops saw the new general ride along the line their hearts lifted; they gave a yell and tightened their hold. Hancock's guns opened against the rebels. Soon Sickles and the III Corps came up, with the XII Corps right behind, and the position was saved.

Meade arrived at one in the morning, hollow-eyed from lack of sleep. Hancock reported Cemetery Hill held, and added that the young artillery officer had ridden through the storm of shot like a madman, utterly unafraid, completely oblivious of the danger. "He is," he said simply, "the bravest man I ever saw." Alonzo Cushing was presented, and General Meade breveted him lieutenant colonel on the spot.

The battle of Gettysburg was won and lost on the second day when Chief of Engineers Warren climbed Little Round Top for a better view, saw Hood's Confederates climbing through the trees to take the hill, and, recognizing the crisis, leaped his horse down the slope, on his own authority snatched two of Sykes's brigades out of formation, and took them to Little Round Top. The 20th Maine, breathless, reached the top just before the first of Hood's brigades, and plunged into hand-to-hand battle. A New York regiment joined them, then the rest of Warren's chance-met men, and a battery, dragged up the precipices by hand. The defenders lost two brigadiers and exhausted their ammunition, but continued to struggle on, stabbing, throwing stones, and growling like wolves. And they held the hill, though many Confederates felt that they had crushed the Union left flank.

In the meantime Ewell had swung round Cemetery Ridge and made ready for his blow at Culp's Hill. He got there to find a stronger position than he had expected, but many in his command felt he had turned the flank after some hard fighting, and so achieved a smashing success. The second day was over, but there was no sleep for the commanders. Alonzo had kept his guns firing when he could see movement, but the main attack had been against the flanks and he was in the center, and had not had much to do.

The Federals' best troops were now fought out, Lee explained; with their left and right dented, Meade would reinforce from the center; there would be few troops left there, mostly militia at that: batter them with artillery, then send Pickett, reinforced to a strength of fifteen thousand men, across the open space and up Cemetery Ridge, and the battle was over and won. Longstreet doubted. There was too much artillery. He did not think any fifteen thousand men could drive across that valley into it. He suggested another plan, a long flanking movement to the right. Lee came as close to anger as he ever had. The artillery could be beaten down. Longstreet, feeling such a depression as he had never known, went forth to transform the order into action.

It was a still and hazy morning, and the first rays of the sun shone brightly on the long valley, here and there faintly dotted with the bodies of the dead. The Confederate horses toiled up and down Seminary Ridge, bringing guns into position. It was noon, then one o'clock, and there was a silence in which you could have heard a whisper everywhere.

The brigades of Harrow, Webb and Hall, of Gibbon's division, Hancock's II Corps, occupied the crest of Cemetery Ridge. The men were sitting on the ground and smoking and talking; in front of them the batteries of artillery were drawn up, facing the Confederate lines. On the right side of the line "was the artillery of the II Corps, under its chief, Captain Hazard. Woodruff's battery was in front of Ziegler's Grove; on his left, in succession, Arnold's Rhode Island, Cushing's United States, Brown's Rhode Island and Rorty's New York." Between 10 and 11 A.M. Brigadier General Henry J. Hunt, Chief of Artillery of the Army of the Potomac, crossed over to Cemetery Ridge to see what might be going on in the enemy lines. "Here a magnificent display greeted my eyes," he reported. "Our whole front for two miles was covered by batteries already in line or getting into position. They stretched—apparently in one unbroken mass—from opposite the town to the Peach Orchard. . . . Never before had such a sight been witnessed on this continent. . . . What did it mean? It might possibly be to hold that line while its infantry was sent to aid Ewell, or to guard against a counterstroke from us, but it most probably meant an assault on our center, to be preceded by a cannonade in order to crush our batteries and shake our infantry; at best to cause us to exhaust our ammunition in reply, so that the assaulting troops might pass in good condition over the half mile of open ground which was beyond our effective musketry fire."

At one o'clock Longstreet sent word to his chief of artillery, signal guns were fired, and all the Confederate artillery let go with a roar. The air was filled with smoke and it was impossible to see anything clearly; it was evident, however, from the concentration of fire, that the Confederate point of attack was at the place on the ridge where Cushing, Woodruff, and Rorty were firing their guns in defiance at the enemy a mile and a half away. At one-thirty Cemetery Ridge was white with shellbursts. Many of the Confederate shells went over the line and burst harmlessly on top of the hill, but many more were accurately aimed. Three of Alonzo's limbers were blown up and changed under fire. Six wheels were shot off his guns and replaced. At one-forty a cannon ball exploded near him and a fragment tore open both his thighs, ripping the cloth and flesh as it went by. He stared down at his legs, and leaned to bind the wounds. He reported to Webb that he was wounded, but "I will stay here and fight it out." He had lost more than a dozen horses, but the infantry, lying behind stone walls and other fences along the Emmitsburg Road, which afforded them only partial cover, leaped up and helped to remove the carcasses and hitch new horses to the caissons.

"The air was all murderous iron," a soldier remembered; "it seemed as if there couldn't be room for any soldier upright and in motion." A veteran in the 1st Minnesota got the same impression, though he was farther to the left, where the fire was less intense. "It seemed that nothing four feet from the ground could live," he said. The infantry lying along the fences of the road were nearly suffocated by the clouds of choking smoke. Usually the infantry during bombardments made humorous remarks when the enemy firing seemed to be misdirected, but this was like no bombardment that they had ever seen, and they were quiet.

No one ever seemed quite sure how long the cannonade went on, and the estimates range all the way from thirty minutes to two hours; but eventually the weight of the bombardment lessened. The Federal ammunition was getting low, and the commanders agreed to cease firing, since the Confederates seemed to be ceasing also; their ammunition was probably getting low too. The guns were silent at last; they must be allowed to cool, otherwise they would shoot inaccurately. The attack would come now, in the new silence. Alonzo's remaining two guns—four had been disabled—were run forward, and loaded with canister. He hobbled with his battery. The wounds in his thighs were painful, and it was hard to walk.

The smoke lifted then, and all of the great amphitheater lay open at last, and the Union soldiers could look west all the way to the woods along the top of Seminary Ridge. They were old soldiers and had been in many battles, but what they saw then took their breath away, "and whether they had ten minutes or seventy-five years to live, they remembered it until they died." "There it was, for the last time in this war, perhaps for the last time anywhere, the grand pageantry and color of war in the old style."

The Virginians and Carolinians were massed in a little wood and they swept out from it, shoulder to shoulder, in long gray lines. General Garnett rode by. He was just out of the hospital, and had his coat buttoned to the throat on this hot day. General Armistead rode by, and General Kemper.

"Good-by, boys," the men cried to those they left behind. "See you in Washington!" Pickett rode up to General Longstreet. Will Cushing had missed him at Chuckatuck, so he was here to lead the charge. "General, shall I advance?" he asked. Longstreet looked at him. He could not bear to speak. Pickett repeated the question. Longstreet bowed and turned away, still silent. "Sir, I shall lead my division forward," Pickett said. Colonel Alexander came up to report that his ammunition was so low that he could not support the charge properly. Longstreet ordered him to stop Pickett until the ammunition could be replenished. "There is no ammunition to replenish," was the reply. By this time Pickett was gone, and could not be stopped anyway.

"As he passed me," Longstreet wrote afterward, "he rode gracefully, with his jaunty cap raked well over his right ear and his long auburn locks, nicely dressed, hanging almost to his shoulders. He seemed rather a holiday soldier than a general at the head of a column which was about to make one of the grandest, most desperate assaults recorded in the annals of war."

"Here they come! Here comes the infantry!" The cry rang out all along the Union line as the Confederate advance line appeared in front of the woods, dressed right on Pickett's division, marching steadily; then, as they came nearer, breaking into a run. This was the moment General Hunt had been waiting for, and all along the left of the Union line the guns opened fire and began to hit those neat ranks, tearing ragged holes in them. Along Hancock's line, to the right of the clump of trees, the guns were silent, for they had nothing left but canister and would have to wait for pointblank range. Alonzo Cushing stood leaning against his cannon, sucking at his thumb. He had been serving vent without a thumb pad, and it was burned to the bone. Soon little puffs of smoke issued from the advancing line as it came dashing forward, firing in reply to Union skirmishers in the valley below. In the intervals of artillery firing the silence was broken by this faint crackle of musketry, in contrast to the terrible clangs of the exploding shells a few minutes before.

Never hesitating for an instant, driving the Union men before it or knocking them over by a biting fire as they rose up to run in, the Confederate skirmish line reached the fences on the other side of the Emmitsburg road. Cushing had brought his guns down to the fence on this side of the road; he was firing now, double charges of canister, at four hundred, three hundred, two hundred yards' range. A bullet from a musket passed through his shoulder and he stumbled, but leaned on his gun. It was his last cannon. The others were lying in wreckage all about him, the ground covered with wounded and dying men and horses, pieces of limbers and wheels of caissons and broken ammunition boxes. It had been impossible to remove the wounded, and they lay there amid the carnage. "One gunner, dreadfully cut by a shell fragment, had been seen to draw a revolver and put himself out of his pain by shooting himself through the head."

Lieutenant Milne, commanding the other half of Alonzo's battery, was struck by a shell fragment and fell, killed instantly. The orders of the officers commanding the infantry regiments drawn up and waiting could be heard distinctly in the intervals of silence: "Steady, men, steady! Don't fire!" The main line of the Confederate advance veered to the left, toward the clump of trees, as the fire from Woodruff's and Rorty's batteries was particularly heavy. Alonzo leaned against his cannon, First Sergeant Frederick Fuger helping to hold him erect and to pass his orders on to the gunners. He was calling for triple charges of canister now. By an undulation of the ground to the left of the clump of trees the rapid advance of Confederates was lost to view; "an instant after they seemed to rise out of the earth, so near that the expression on their faces was clearly seen." A bullet struck Alonzo in the stomach, and he fell into Fuger's arms. "You must go to the rear," the sergeant said. "There's no time, Fuger. I stay right here and fight it out, or die in the attempt." Dimly the men behind the wall could see the Confederates coming in over the fences, brigade lines disordered, "the spearhead of the charge a great mass of men sweeping over the fences and up the last of the slope like an irresistible stream flowing uphill."

The enemy were within a hundred yards, and were almost within the angle in the stone wall behind which Cushing's last gun had been drawn up. General Webb was standing nearby, his figure almost obscured by smoke. Fuger reported that only one triple charge of canister remained. "I'll give them one more shot, Webb," Alonzo cried, his voice rising almost to a scream. He stood as straight as he was able, and cried to Webb, "Good-by!" A bullet struck him in the mouth and passed downward through his throat and out the back of his head, and he fell again into Fuger's arms, killed instantly. The last shot was fired by the sergeant, and it tore a wide hole in the advancing enemy, who were within the angle now and among the remains of the battery. General Armistead had climbed the fence, bringing with him a hundred men, and he reached forward to touch the cannon beside which Alonzo lay, and then fell himself, mortally wounded.

Fuger called for bayonets, and the cannoneers and drivers, fighting with bayonets and pistols, sabers, handpikes and rammers and whatever else they could find, fought hand to hand with what remained of Armistead's men. Behind the Union gunners the infantry was firing now, the constant musketry a crackling roar. The charge stopped, hesitated, and was broken; the gray coats were turning now, leaving their muskets and their ammunition behind them. They were struck as they climbed the wall again; a few of them got away and back to their own lines, more were taken prisoner, more still were lying on the field. General Kemper had fallen in the concentration for the final assault, and Garnett was down as they got in among the first line of guns. Armistead was dead, lying by Cushing's last cannon, which was also disabled, the battery thus utterly destroyed. He had fallen twenty feet from the spot where Alonzo lay, their hands outstretched in death toward one another.

Now the counter charge thundered over the stone wall, Harrow and Hall leading their infantry with blades and heads low. The artillery from the flanks, from Little Round Top and other elevations, never stopped shooting the rebels down— and the high tide ebbed and flowed backward, ebbing backward to the sound of General Lee's terrible words to General Longstreet: "It was all my fault; get together, and do the best we can toward saving that which is left to us."

Losses in all the batteries of the II Corps were heavy. Rorty and Woodruff were killed as well as Alonzo Cushing and Milne; Sheldon was severely wounded. In Alonzo's battery alone seven enlisted men were killed and thirty-eight wounded, out of ninety on duty at the beginning of the fight. Not an uninjured wheel remained, and nine ammunition chests were blow up. Out of ninety horses taken into action eighty-three were killed. The battery was now under Fuger's command. He assigned Corporal Thomas Moon to guard the area. "All we had to guard was a few dead men," he said. "We took Lieutenant Cushing and three or four men off the field. It rained all night." It was quiet on the field that night, and the men of both sides sat silently, remembering the strangest fact about the battle: during the hottest part of the fighting in the "angle," there had been a sound which none of the oldest veterans had ever heard before—"strange and terrible," one soldier said, "a sound that came from thousands of human throats, yet was not a commingling of shouts and yells but rather like a vast mournful roar." Another observer called it "a moan" which "went up from the field, distinctly to be heard amid the roar of battle." No one who was at Gettysburg seems ever to have forgotten the sound.

The next day the papers were full of the victory. Lee was in full retreat for Virginia, and the bells tolled for it in Baltimore and Philadelphia and Washington. It was Independence Day, and to heighten the celebration an aide had ridden into Holly Springs, plastered with mud and almost incoherent with excitement, to say that Grant was in Vicksburg, the Confederate army of the west cut off. Howard Cushing was there, in Blair's command. Howard was as yet only a private, so there is no record of what he did there.

In August, 1863, Captain Hazard, commanding the Artillery Brigade of Hancock's II Corps, wrote an official report to Colonel Morgan. Alonzo Cushing, he said, "especially distinguished himself for his extreme gallantry and bravery, his courage and ability, and his love for his profession. His untimely death and the loss of such a promise as his youth cherished are sincerely mourned." Alonzo was twenty-two when he died. Secretary of War Stanton said later that if he had not been killed on that third day at Gettysburg he would have been twice brevetted, to the rank of brigadier general. It is doubtful that anyone in the Union army with the exception of George Custer, who was Cushing's classmate at West Point but a year older, was promoted so quickly at such an age. Mrs. Cushing had placed all her hopes in Alonzo, believing him to be the most likely to be able to support her declining years. She received a pension from the government of seventeen dollars a month until 1891, the year of her death, when it was raised to fifty dollars a month.

Gettysburg is now a quiet park with smooth fields and little wooded hills where the battle once took place, and everywhere the tourist goes he finds monuments rising out of the grass, and markers to say that here this brigade took a stand, here that regiment made a desperate charge. At the "angle" and at the "clump of trees" Alonzo Cushing is remembered. A large marker at the angle says that his Battery A of the 4th U.S. Artillery stood there, and that he was killed repulsing the charge on the third day. There is a flagpole, for this position is the very center of the field, and in its shadow is a small stone erected, the inscription reads, in memory of Lt. A. H. Cushing by Col. R. Penn Smith and his 71st Penn. Vols. They were among the infantry detachments that repulsed the charge, and without Cushing and his battery, the stone indicates, they would have been overrun. Twenty feet away is a sloping stone which marks the place where Armistead fell. Standing there in the afternoon the sun is in your eyes, but if you shade them you can see, against the dark line of trees which marks Seminary Ridge, the white statue of General Lee; and the fields and fences between, with the Emmitsburg Road a dividing line, are hardly changed from the way they were on the afternoon of July 3, 1863.

Will Cushing was in Washington during the battle, waiting for news and for orders should the Confederates break through. It was vaguely supposed that the *Commodore Barney* might help to defend the Potomac in the last emergency. On the evening of July 3 he went up to Gettysburg. He told Captain Hazard that he wanted to take over his brother's guns, and to command his battery. Captain Hazard explained that there was hardly anything left of the battery; in fact Cushing's and Woodruff's United States, and Brown's and Arnold's Rhode Island batteries had been consolidated to form two barely serviceable ones. Will's next wish was that he might take his brother's body home, but again he was disappointed. The body had been placed on a train, under guard of two wounded corporals, and was on its way to West Point. It is buried there, surrounded by the graves of famous Union generals: Sykes, Gregg, Kilpatrick, Buford. "The wounds were not alone for those who fell upon the field," Will wrote to his mother. "There is suffering greater than the dying know, the prolonged anguish of those left behind to mourn them." It is likely that she agreed.

A year before he had written to his cousin sentiments that were his feeling now. "I don't know but [what] I may resign before long and go into the land service. I have no doubt but that I can procure a captain's berth in the volunteers. I so long to be near Allie. It seems as if I might be some protection to him in the hour of action. If the rebels should kill him I don't think that I would be a man any longer. I should become a fiend. I love that boy better than I do my own life, and I would not live without my brother."

He went back to Washington the same night, arriving very late. He looked older. His cheeks were pale, and his eyes had sunk deep into his head. He spent the following days with Milton. In the middle of July he was relieved of the command of the *Barney* when she was again withdrawn from service, and spent several weeks waiting for reassignment. By August 9, when he was given a new ship, the U.S.S. *Shokokon*, he had learned to live with his irreparable loss. He had even remembered how to be gay once more, though he never referred to Alonzo without a shake of his head and a mournful look. The *Shokokon* was nothing but "a large and fast ferryboat with the hull built out," he wrote his cousin. It was believed that the vessel, being of so shallow a draft, could be used to advantage in the shoals off Wilmington Harbor. Admiral Lee doubted whether it could survive the strong gales and nasty weather encountered along that section of the North Carolina coast, but it was worth trying, he said. Would Lieutenant Cushing make the attempt? The young officer agreed that the *Shokokon* was probably not seaworthy, but it was a challenge of the type he could not ignore. He consoled himself, he wrote, "with the philosophy of Bryan Bolin, 'That there's ground at the bottom.' "

He joined the blockade off New Inlet, reporting to Captain A. Ludlow Case, who ordered him to a position on the extreme southern end of the line. He was to watch Smith's Island and the surrounding waters, which were often used by blockade runners on their way in and out of Wilmington.

He did not have to watch long. On August 18, the blockader *Niphon* sighted the *Hebe* attempting to reach Wilmington via the New Inlet Channel and drove her aground at Federal Point. By the time the *Shokokon* reached the scene the *Niphon* had sent off boatloads of boarders, and the crew of the *Hebe* had fled; it seemed that it would be easy to capture the grounded vessel and either move or destroy her. The seas were heavy, but one of the *Niphon*'s boats succeeded in getting alongside; however, the boat was stove, leaving the crew marooned on the deck of the prize, and in desperate straits, since they had already set her afire. The Union sailors extinguished the blaze and signaled for help; at this moment a party of fifty or sixty Confederate riflemen, with some cavalry and two heavy fieldpieces, opened fire from the sand hills along the shore.

Acting Ensign Breck of the *Niphon* sent two additional boats to help the stranded sailors, and Cushing sent off a boat also. A strong wind from the northeast had made the beach a lee shore, and progress in the surf was difficult; the *Shokokon*'s boat and one of the *Niphon*'s succeeded in taking off two or three sailors, but the *Niphon*'s other boat was driven upon the beach and its crew made prisoners by the Confederate cavalry. The surviving boat from the *Niphon* was sent in again but it capsized and its crew was also taken.

Cushing and Breck agreed that further attempts at rescue would be fruitless. They carefully fired wide of the *Hebe* until the stranded Union sailors aboard her realized what was intended and made their way to the shore and surrendered. Then shell fire from both blockaders was poured into the *Hebe*, twice setting her afire only to have the sea extinguish the flames; the third time a large fire was started which engulfed her and destroyed her. The attack was pressed closely, the two vessels steaming to within one hundred yards at times in their attempts to destroy the *Hebe*. The Confederate artillery fire was ineffectual and a hit from the big guns was never scored on either of the Union vessels, and although both were somewhat marked by rifle fire, they suffered no casualties. The *Hebe* was a serious loss: she was carrying "a full cargo of coffee, drugs and medicines, clothing, and a few bales of silk."

Cushing was furious at the frustrating loss of boats and crew, and when it was learned that night by means of a small-boat reconnaissance that a schooner was moored in New Topsail Inlet he determined to destroy it before it could get out into open water. The small boats had been driven off by artillery fire, and he proposed a plan to Captain Ludlow for cutting the schooner out, which was, in the manner of most of his proposals, turned down. He went ahead without orders and had the dubious satisfaction of hearing Admiral Lee, after it was successful, say that he had previously cleared the attempt.

It was six miles up the inlet to the place where the schooner was moored at a wharf, and Cushing's superiors felt it was impossible to destroy the ship. To Cushing it was only apparent that more than the usual degree of "strategy" was needed. He anchored his ship on the evening of August 22 some five miles from the mouth of the sound and sent ashore two boatloads of men who shouldered the dinghy and carried it across the narrow neck of land which divided the sea from the sound. The task was a difficult one, for while the distance was not above half a mile, the neck at that point was covered with heavy brush. When his men reached the water inside they were in the rear of the artillery posted to command the mouth of the sound; the *Shokokon* was out of range and served to divert the attention of the batteries. Acting Ensign Joseph S. Cony started down the sound with six men in the dinghy to do what damage he could. The *Shokokon*'s smokestack had been spotted by the schooner's lookouts, and a sharp watch was ordered toward the south where the mouth of the inlet lay. With every Confederate eye straining in the wrong direction, the dinghy landed fifty yards from the wharf. Robert Clifford, the master at arms, was sent to spy out the strength of the enemy and reported that there were about twenty men against them. Ensign Cony had been to school with Cushing, and knew exactly what to do. He ordered an advance, and the seven men, shouting at the top of their voices, charged the bewildered Confederates, who broke and ran. Twelve prisoners were taken, including a captain and a lieutenant, along with a twelve-pound howitzer, eighteen horses (the horses were shot and the howitzer spiked) and some salt works, and the schooner, which was called the *Alexander Cooper*, was now Union property.

It was long after dark and the prisoners did not realize the slenderness of the force that held them. Ensign Cony, again applying Cushing principles, used various ruses to convince the rebels that he and his six men were part of a large attacking party. Orders were shouted to imaginary boats out in the sound, and the men talked loudly among themselves of the large force which was preparing for an invasion. Two men were sent out as pickets, two guarded the prisoners, and the remaining two, with the help of some courageous slaves, fired the schooner and the salt works. After accomplishing all this destruction Ensign Cony decided that a quick retreat was the better part of valor. The question was what to do with the prisoners, since the dinghy would not take them all. The answer was simple—take only the officers. But which were the officers? It was known that there were two, but all the prisoners were dressed alike and none would admit to bearing rank. Cony settled the matter "by picking out the three best-looking ones, who all turned out to be privates. So the officers owed their safety to their lack of physique, a new feature in military strategy." To confuse the nine prisoners for whom there was no room they were ordered to go a quarter of a mile up the bank to report to a mythical Lieutenant Jones. Cony and his sailors then made their way up the sound and rejoined the rest of the *Shokokon*'s men, who had been doing picket duty along the inland shore and had successfully repulsed, without loss to themselves, a Confederate scouting party which had discovered them. All made their way safely back to the ship. Much damage had been done to the enemy without the loss of a Union sailor.

A great alarm was raised on shore. The Confederates were certain that a large force had been landed, and as a result the only available regiment, the 50th North Carolina, was marched off from Fort Fisher across country to New Topsail Inlet. The walk was wasted, however; Cushing and the *Shokokon* were already steaming to join the main blockading force off the Cape Fear River.

Cushing was lavish in his praise and Clifford and Cony were promoted. Cushing's official report of the exploit was widely published in the Northern press, which was anxious to acclaim such heroics. He could not resist, however, in his report of the affair to the Fredonia *Censor*, putting himself ashore with the landing party. It was an adventure, he told Mary Smith, that he had fiendishly hated to miss.

When Cushing reached the main force, the squadron, led by the old *Minnesota*, decided to investigate the wreck of the *Hebe* to see if any salvage could be effected. The squadron ran in close and a boat was sent out to investigate. The boat was fired on from shore, the squadron replied in kind, and a fierce cannonade ensued. It occurred to Cushing, who could not bear to remain on the water for very long, that it would be interesting to try to land a party to take the rebel guns. He communicated this design to the admiral, who turned the idea down, but the young lieutenant went ahead anyway, lowering two boats and with about twenty men making his way around the stern of his vessel to the beach. The Confederates, seeing the landing party and being out of ammunition, abandoned their guns and fled to Fort Fisher. No aid could be sent them, as all spare troops were at New Topsail Inlet looking for the *Shokokon*. Cushing seized the guns and awaited the official landing party, led by his old commander, Captain Pierce Crosby. But official reports do not mention Cushing's part in this affair. "I never was credited officially with this," he wrote, "perhaps because I disobeyed orders, or, maybe, for the reason that the great fish present could not surrender so dainty a morsel to a youngster."

He did not have long to brood. Three days later a gale blew in from the northeast, and all the Union ships ran out to sea. It appeared to Cushing that the only chance of saving the fragile *Shokokon* lay in running under the shelter of a shoal on the lee side of Smith's Island. He raced the storm and just succeeded in getting his ship anchored in the lee of Frying Pan Shoals; if he had had ten miles farther to go, he thought, he would never have made it. Even so, when struck by the wind and the high seas the *Shokokon* "seemed to give and bend like india rubber." "Sponsons [were] torn off or crushed, forward decks started and seams opened, forward ports carried away, and sternpost split. [Also the] wood ends opened about half an inch," and she was leaking water at the rate of "450 gallons a minute." When the *Minnesota* returned to her position in the blockade line Admiral Lee was astonished to discover the *Shokokon* still afloat, being under the impression that she must have foundered. He was quite ready to accept Cushing's report that he did not "deem [the vessel] fit for blockading service."

She was sent to Hampton Roads for repairs, and Cushing was given dispatches to take to the Navy Department at Washington. One of them called him a "zealous and able young officer," and expressed the hope that the department would give him a new command and reassign him for duty with the blockading squadron. Things had changed since the time when he had had to beg the navy for a job. Assistant Secretary Fox ordered him to take command of the *Monticello*, then undergoing a thorough overhaul at Philadelphia. "You are ordered to this command for distinguished services rendered," he said.

The *Monticello* was a far different proposition from the ships Cushing had commanded heretofore. She was a real war vessel, extremely seaworthy, and with a good armament. She was a ship of trim lines, lying low in the water, and capable of well over twelve knots under a full head of steam and canvas. She had one funnel amidships and two masts; the rear was gaff-rigged while the foremast carried two square sails. She could fly at least two jibs, and had been known to rig a starsail. She was painted black, but alongside her bows was an intricate curling decoration in gold paint with the letters of her name picked out in gold. Lieutenant Cushing thought she was the most beautiful ship in the navy.

He was able to get home to Fredonia for a week in September. His mother seemed very old (she was hardly sixty) and her sadness depressed him; he did not know how to bear the burden of it, on top of his own. Allie, he thought, would have done better at it if it had been he, Will, that had been killed. He was pleased to discover that his adventures were well known in the town, that the paper reported his arrival on its front page, and that all the little boys hung on his every word when they could get him to describe his exploits—and not only the little boys; everyone seemed appreciative. Two or three other men from the town had been killed in various battles, so the town understood, too, about Alonzo. But Will did not remain long. He was very restless, he found, without a ship to command, without a gun to aim and fire; his fingers itched for the feel of a carbine. He could not tell his mother this; her mute request was impossible, she knew, but still heartfelt: her eyes asked him not to return to the war, yet she was aware that he would go. Nothing, it seemed, had been heard of Howard for more than a month. It was known only that his Illinois regiment was in the west, probably with Grant in Tennessee. Was there anything Will might do to find out about the boy? she wondered. He would do what he could. Each night before she went to bed she asked him to kneel with her and pray, and he did so, but with misgivings. He could not honestly forgive his enemies, and it pained him to say that he did. He would do anything to please her, though; so it had always been, if she would not ask impossible things.

One morning he took the train back to Washington, and from there went to Philadelphia to oversee the repairs on the *Monticello*. They went slowly, and he was angry at the delays and continuing delays. While he had been at home a great battle had been fought on Chickamauga Creek on the Georgia-Tennessee line. Howard might have been there, Will thought (in fact he was not), and he read as much about the battle as he could. On November 19 he journeyed up to Gettysburg once again, this time to the cemetery which was to be dedicated—already Gettysburg was the most famous battle of the war. Edward Everett was to give the oration, and the President was to say a few words. Everett spoke for two hours, and then stepped back, "his white hair shining like the snow on a mountain peak," while the audience pattered applause. People whispered and stirred, there was even a slight titter as the President began to speak in the thin, high-pitched voice. Will could not hear a word. He was far in the rear, and had even had difficulty making out Everett's speech, though the old man was one of the great orators of the day, and had a voice like Stentor. Will returned to Washington, disappointed, and read the President's speech the next day. "The world will little note nor long remember what we say here, but it can never forget what they did here." He at least, he knew, would never forget what they had done there.

He had been involved in an action earlier in November, but it was not something he could be proud of. Pennsylvania was deep in a gubernatorial election, and feeling ran high. There were charges and countercharges, and as was to be expected the opposition party catered to those individuals who thought the war a failure, and nourished their discontent. In this time of excitement several Democrats insulted Cushing (at least he felt so) "because he was a naval officer." It was a challenge he could not ignore. The affair ended when he thrashed the "Copperheads," but was apprehended by the local police, who threw him into jail for a night. He was disgusted and ashamed, for he had seemed to insult, rather than glorify, as he had intended to do, his brother's memory, and he longed to put to sea again. But the *Monticello* was still not ready, the delays went on and on. And then a disastrous fire broke out in the yard, and the repairs were put back a month or two at least.

At the end of November came news of the battle at Chattanooga, even better news a week later: Howard was alive and well, had been promoted to second lieutenant (he had served eighteen months as a private, which was enough for any man, too much for any Cushing), might be getting to Washington soon—at least he had applied for duty in the 4th U.S., Alonzo's old battery, and thought the chances were good for the transfer to go through; had written Mother, Will need not do so. Will knew the feeling; he knew the pride that had kept his brother from writing through the long months when he could recount no successes. He felt closer to Howard than he ever had before. The boy (but he was twenty-five now, more than four years older than Will) was a fighter, a brave lad with the wild streak in him that Will loved—Milton he loved, but for other things: a certain solidity, temperateness, calm. They were good in their place, of course. And with Allie gone, they must all come closer together. He wrote Howard a long letter, full of gossip and news. But the melancholy showed through. If he could only get to sea again!

The weeks wore on, and turned into months. At Christmas Mary Smith was in Washington with her father, and Will spent the day with them. There was much gaiety, but it was not too easy to join in. After New Year's he was back in Philadelphia, waiting. It was a bitter cold winter. There was a shortage of coal, not due to a lack of fuel but to an administrative mixup, and tempers were short. And the time went on.

Everything, though, comes to an end, and in January the last touches were being put on the *Monticello*. She was beautiful, her captain thought: sleek and long and shiny black, with her guns oiled and ready for carnage, her engines in perfect order, her sails new and clean. He spent a week assembling his crew; he meant to have the best the navy could give him, and picked and chose as much as they would let him. He met Ensign Howorth for the first time, and took him on sight; he tried to get some of the men who had served with him on the *Ellis* and the *Barney*, but most were at sea, on other ships. He was particularly sorry not to have the services of Mr.

Valentine, but that worthy old sailor was in the Gulf with Farragut, and busy. By the first week in February his crew was complete. The *Monticello* slid down the ways on the seventh of the month, and sailed from Philadelphia on the 9th. It was with a light heart that her commander saw the land fall beneath the horizon as he set his helm for the south. Up the Roanoke River they were putting the last rivets into the iron sides of the *Albemarle*.

VII

Albemarle

~~~~~~

THE *Albemarle* was conceived in the mind of Gilbert Elliott, engineer and inventor. The Confederate States Navy signed a contract with him, as agent for J. G. Martin of Elizabeth City, North Carolina, on January 13, 1862, for three vessels to be built in the North Carolina sounds. But as a result of the victory by Lieutenant Cushing and others at Fort Hatteras, New Bern fell to the Union, as did Plymouth, six miles up the Roanoke River, along with most of the inland waters. The plans had to be changed. On April 16, 1862, a new contract was signed giving the contractors a free hand in selecting a place to build an ironclad vessel. The battle situation was stabilized in the next few months, and in September more definite contracts were let with two firms, superseding the April agreement, specifying sites of construction for two vessels. Completion dates were set for the following March.

It was slow going. All manner of delays and disappointments occurred, and some despaired that the ironclads would ever be finished. They had a point; construction was not even begun until January, 1863. To expedite matters John L. Porter, who had built the iron superstructure of the *Merrimac,* was sent to supervise the work. When he arrived at the "shipyard," which was up the Roanoke River near Halifax, North Carolina, at a place called Edwards Ferry, he found it to be no more than a cornfield. None of the usual facilities were available. There were no engines, no derricks and pulleys, no power tools—nothing but men, who were willing enough, and saws and hammers. But in spite of the primitive working conditions construction was begun. It proceeded slowly for a year, at the end of which time little had been accomplished. One of the troubles, the authorities felt, was the agreement Porter had made with Elliott: Elliott employed his force by the day, and hence there was little incentive to hurry, rather more incentive to prolong matters. Commander James W. Cooke was sent to replace Porter, and brought with him additional tools and facilities and men. Meanwhile in Richmond, far from the shipyard, the guns to form the battery of the ram were being cast and bored and readied.

Cooke had better success than Porter. He was a veteran of thirty-three years service in the regular navy who had resigned at the outbreak of hostilities and been commissioned in the Confederate Navy, and he wanted the vessel finished with all his heart. He was told there was a shortage of iron, and that it was causing most of the delay; he attacked the problem as he had attacked the enemy, sending raiding parties to all the farms in the neighborhood to gather scrap and bolts and bars —no particle of iron was too small to escape his ruthless conscription—and he made such a fuss in his importunate demands of the Tredegar Works at Richmond and the Clarendon Foundry at Wilmington that they nicknamed him the "Ironmonger Captain." When the iron became available, the problem of transporting it to Edwards Ferry was as great as its original procurement, but Cooke solved that too. He believed in the new ram, which he had christened, as soon as there was a shape that could be seen, the *Albemarle*, after the part of the sounds she would be used to liberate.

News of the *Albemarle* was brought by a man called Michael Cohen, a one-time plumber and gas fitter, who had converted his distillery, situated along the shore of the sound, into a grist mill with which he supplied the Confederate forces in the area; this, incidentally, exempting him from military service. A Union raid burned his mill and his regret was multiplied by the knowledge that he was now liable to be conscripted, and he took to his heels. Charles Flusser received him when he heard the man had information, though much of it was in fact inaccurate. One thing was now clear; the Confederates were building a ship which could clear the Union navy out of the sounds.

The news worried Flusser. Other spies and runaways added what information they could obtain. A floating battery was also being built at Edwards Ferry, for example—it could do a lot of damage if it could be brought to play on the defenses of Plymouth. When Flusser learned that iron was actually being put upon the *Albemarle* in June and July he began to worry seriously, since it seemed the ram would soon be ready for action. If it was not destroyed, it would "give trouble yet." It seemed to him that a relatively small force would be sufficient to do the job, estimating five hundred cavalrymen to be ample. But his request to the army was held up for two weeks—a question of channels.

In August, 1863, Flusser was instructed by Admiral Lee to contact the army generals in the area. It was necessary to depend upon the army, the admiral felt, because Edwards Ferry was so far up the river, above Rainbow Bluff: fortifications on this bluff, together with the low level of water in the river, made any naval attack out of the question. Flusser sent a full report to the army, and Gideon Welles wrote to Secretary of War Stanton: if the Confederates were allowed to finish their ram unmolested it presaged a powerful land and water attack on Plymouth, and the navy could bring nothing but wooden ships to oppose the ironclad, since the Union ironclads drew too much water to enter the sounds.

By the fall of 1863 the navy was thoroughly alarmed, and had strengthened the blockading squadron off Plymouth. Torpedoes (i.e., mines) were laid at the mouth of the Roanoke River and obstructions were sunk in the channel. But the army was not impressed by the danger. General Peck reported to General Butler, commanding the department of

North Carolina, that the alarm was exaggerated. The ram was still without plating or guns, he said; it would be months before it was ready. General Butler wrote to Admiral Lee: "I do not much believe in the ram." And a flood of contrary reports continued to pour down the river to the Union fleet from deserters and runaway slaves. Statements about the time the ram would be ready, along with its dimensions and armaments, varied widely.

In the spring the work was nearly complete, and despite Butler's lack of belief, the *Albemarle* was a formidable foe. She boasted a power plant consisting of two engines of two hundred horsepower each. They had been built out of odds and ends, but they would work. She was 158 feet long, 35 feet 3 inches in the beam, and 8 feet 2 inches in depth; her frame was of solid yellow pine timbers, 8 by 10 inches thick, dovetailed together and fastened with iron and treenails; her sheathing was also of yellow pine, 4 inches thick. Her octagonal shield was 60 feet long and covered by two layers of iron plating, each two inches in thickness. The prow, which was to be used as a ram, was plated with two-inch-thick iron and tapered to a sharp edge.

Toward the end of March the water in the river began to fall, and though the vessel was not quite completed it was thought expedient to send her down the river twenty miles to the town of Hamilton, where the finishing touches were applied. On April 16 General Robert F. Hoke, commander of the Confederate land forces in the area, paid a visit to the *Albemarle* where she lay moored in the river off Hamilton. He urged that the vessel be made ready at once to join in an attack upon Plymouth, and advised that Cooke had been appointed to command her. Hoke's division was in a position to attack the city and was ready to launch an assault the moment the *Albemarle* cleared the river front of Union gunboats.

On the 17th the vessel cast off and started slowly down the river. As it splashed its way workmen still swarmed over it, hammering the last rivets into place. A small flat boat bearing a portable forge was towed behind; its services were soon needed, for the ram's machinery failed a mile or so after it had started, and six hours were lost repairing a coupling in the main shaft. When this task was completed the rudder head broke, causing an additional four hours' delay. When it could move again Commander Cooke turned his ship's stern down the river, since the current was strong and the stern offered more resistance; he dragged chains from the bow, further to slow his vessel and render it easier to control. Finally it came to anchor three miles above Plymouth, near Thoroughfare Gap, where mines, sunken vessels and other obstructions had been placed by the Union forces. A preliminary expedition was sent out under one of the lieutenants. He returned after two hours to report that the obstructions were impassable. Cooke ordered the fires banked, and all hands except the watch turned in for a night's sleep.

Gilbert Elliott, the architect of the vessel, who had come along as a volunteer in order to keep track of his offspring, could not sleep. If the *Albemarle* could not pass the obstructions that night, he thought, it never could with falling water in the morning. He asked Cooke to let him make a personal inspection, and started off with three men in a small boat. He discovered ten feet of water over the obstructions, the result of a "remarkable freshet" then prevailing, and returned to his vessel after penetrating almost to Plymouth. If the ram stayed in the middle of the channel it could surely pass, he reported to Commander Cooke. The vessel got under way as soon as possible, even slipping its cables to gain time.

A Union fort at Warren's Neck opened fire near the mouth of the river, but the ram disdained to answer. "Protected by the ironclad shell, to those on board the noise made by the shot and shell as they struck the boat sounded no louder than pebbles thrown against an empty barrel." At Boyle's Mill, lower down, a fort mounting a very heavy gun opened fire, but with similar lack of success. The ram passed the fort and the obstructions without difficulty, but then, looming out of the darkness, suddenly spied two Union steamers coming up the river.

They were the *Miami*, a heavily armed gunboat under Flusser's command, and the *Southfield*, a converted ferryboat, also with a heavy armament. The two ships "were lashed together with long spars, and with chains festooned between them"; the design was to trap the ram, and while holding it fast batter it to pieces with gunfire at close range. It was not too difficult to divine the plan, and Commander Cooke ran his vessel in close to the south shore, suddenly turned into the middle of the stream, and steamed at full speed directly toward his entangled enemies. He struck the *Miami* a glancing blow and bounced off, but plunged his beak ten feet deep into the *Southfield*'s side. He reversed engines immediately, but the chain plates of the ram's forward deck had fouled in the frame of the sinking Union ship, and the ram's bow was pulled down until water poured in torrents into the portholes. It seemed likely that the victor would be destroyed with her victim, but the *Southfield* touched bottom in the shallow river and turned over on her side, releasing the ram, which bobbed to an even keel once more.

The pressure of the *Albemarle* between the two side-wheel steamers had partly broken the fastenings which bound them together, and the *Miami* swung round near the disabled ship and a number of the *Southfield*'s officers and men leaped across the space to safety, including Lieutenant Charles A. French, commanding. At the same time the *Miami* was firing away so furiously at its tormentor that Captain Cooke later reported that it carried thirteen guns (the number was eight). But his confusion was as nothing compared to the frustration of the Union gunners, who were scoring hit after hit with their heavy guns only to see the shots ricochet harmlessly off the Confederate man-of-war. Commander Flusser steered his ship as close as he could and then leaped to take personal command of one of his forward guns. On the third round of fire Flusser himself pulled the lanyard, sending a nine-inch shell with a ten-second fuse against the side of the ram, now at point-blank range. The shell rebounded and landed on the *Miami*'s deck near the place where her commander stood, the lanyard still in his hand, and exploded, tearing him almost to pieces and killing him instantly, and wounding several of his crew.

The *Albemarle's* broadside could not be swung round to hit the *Miami*, so Cooke ordered the crew on the top deck to engage the Union vessel with small-arms fire. At the same moment part of the crew of the *Miami* were gathering on their own top deck, preparatory to board; as many of them as could crowd into the small space available were keeping up a hot fire. On the ram the men who could not climb up to the deck loaded muskets and handed them up to their more fortunate comrades. The Confederate fire held the boarders at bay until the opportunity was lost when the ram wrenched free.

Lieutenant French, who was now in command of the *Miami*, determined to retreat rather than lose his vessel, as seemed likely if he remained within range of the ram's big guns, and he turned and fled. The slower *Albemarle* lobbed two more rounds after the speeding vessels (two or three smaller boats had accompanied the Union flotilla, but were not engaged), and then gave up the chase. She came about and rescued eight crew members of the *Southfield*, who were helplessly swimming about in the cold water—they were the only Union seamen left alive anywhere in the Roanoke River or the adjacent waters of Batchelor's Bay. Naval supremacy having been achieved, Commander Cooke acquainted General Hoke of the fact, and received instructions concerning the operation against Plymouth. Some of the Union strong points had been taken by assault, but others near the water front were still holding out. The ram drove in close to shore and began steadily and slowly to pour its fire into the fortifications, absolutely impervious to the rattle of Union artillery against its iron sides. All day the Federal troops held out, but the following morning their position seemed hopeless, and they surrendered. In all the Confederates had taken sixteen hundred prisoners and twenty-five pieces of artillery, immense quantities of commissary and other stores, and above two hundred tons of anthracite coal, and they had regained free access to two of the richest counties in North Carolina.

To add to this, the *Southfield* was lost with part of her crew, the *Miami* damaged, and Flusser killed—all with the loss of only one rebel sailor, who had stuck his head out of one of the ram's portholes and been shot through the brain by a musket ball. The ram itself had been only slightly damaged; only nine iron bars had been broken during the engagement. She was repaired, other finishing touches were applied, and she was ready for further adventures. The Confederates now possessed control of the interior sounds west of Roanoke Island, and meant to keep it.

It might have been better if they had not killed Charles Flusser. William Cushing had not forgotten *Naval Enterprise, Illustrative of Heroism, Courage and Duty*, nor had he forgotten that Flusser had encouraged him when he needed it most, nor that the man had been his closest friend after his brother. "I shall never rest until I have avenged his death," he said grimly when he heard the news.

His time was not yet. On April 29 the *Albemarle* was still queen of the surrounding waters, and she set out from Plymouth to convoy a steamer, which had been captured from the Union army on the Alligator River, back to Plymouth. On the way to pick up the steamer the ram chased a Union gunboat out of its path, which was gall and wormwood to the vessels which had so long controlled these waters. Having pursued the fleeing vessel as long as she chose, she put into the Alligator River and picked up her charge. With it and several corn barges the ram steamed majestically back to Plymouth, while the vessels of the Union fleet huddled miles away in the shelter of Roanoke Island, impotent to intercept their awesome foe.

Unable to discover any means of dealing with the ram,

the army and navy fell to blaming each other. Butler had a plan. Send a few small army gunboats; he was sure they would "run her down." The arrival of the boats contributed nothing except to create confusion over whether or not the navy had or should have jurisdiction over the army craft. The army, in a pique, refused to give the naval commander sufficient coal to keep a vessel under steam for a reasonable period of time (the navy had lost its coal at Plymouth; they should replenish there). Many army officers could not conceal their glee at the rough handling the navy had suffered. Butler, adding fuel to the fire, reported that the navy was entirely to blame for the disaster. Admiral Lee challenged the assertion, and a full-blown squabble was in the making. Butler was concerned with keeping his reputation intact; it looked very much as if the Republicans might drop Lincoln as their standard bearer in the fall campaign, and Butler was an ambitious man. He asked the Assistant Secretary of the Navy to come down with Lincoln to see him, and Fox was willing to come, assuming that Butler was anxious about the *Albemarle*. In fact the "intrepid" general had a wild plan for a combined land and sea attack upon Richmond that would make him a military hero of the first magnitude, and the visit never took place.

Late in April, Admiral Lee sent Captain Melancton Smith to see what he could do about the ram. Smith had fought the ram *Manassas* in the New Orleans campaign, and Lee felt he was qualified to lead the expedition the admiral was preparing. Smith was given detailed instructions: from close quarters, with guns loaded with extra-heavy charges, he was to pour a hot fire onto the ram's ports, stern, and roof (they were considered its weak points); if possible a shell was to be dropped down the smokestack; during the broadside the crews of the Union vessels were to lie flat on the decks, in order to avoid repeating the kind of tragic accident that had killed Commander Flusser; in the last resort they were to ram the ram.

The Confederates had plans of their own. Sixty miles south, on the Neuse River, was the great port of New Bern. The Southerners hoped to seize it as they had Plymouth. General Beauregard suggested to General Hoke that an assault could be made, but that it was essential that the *Albemarle* be present, since the ironclad on the Neuse River was aground and could not be refloated in time. Commander Cooke, convinced that he had a better vessel than he had anticipated, agreed to take part, although the route he would have to follow—across Albemarle Sound, through Croatan Sound off Roanoke Island, across Pamlico Sound to the mouth of the Neuse—was a great deal farther than the sixty miles across country to New Bern, and was also lined with Union fortifications. But a great deal, he admitted, was at stake.

Late in the afternoon of May 5 the *Albemarle* weighed anchor and set off on her hazardous journey, with a captured Union steamer and a floating battery puffing along behind her. With her two consorts the ram advanced about ten miles toward the sound, when she was attacked by the entire Union fleet under Captain Smith. It was quite a surprise to Commander Cooke; only a few days before he had seen the enemy gunboats turn and flee when he showed himself in these waters, and now they looked like a fight. He sent the steamer and the battery back to Plymouth, and prepared for battle. The little steamer did not receive the order until too late, and was soon captured by the Union force.

The Union battle plan had been worked out days before. It called for seven vessels to be formed into two lines, the first line to be led by the *Mattabesett*, followed by the *Sassacus*, *Wyalusing* and *Whitehead*, the second to be led by Flusser's old command, the *Miami*, followed by the *Ceres* and the *Commodore Hull*. The *Ceres* and the *Whitehead* were small gunboats, the *Hull* a converted ferry (with, as usual, a very heavy armament), and the others double-enders, side-wheel ships able to steam in either direction. The larger vessels were to pass as close as possible to the ram without endangering their paddle wheels, firing and then coming around after reloading for a second volley: "a terrific grand waltz," the Confederates were to call it. They were to concentrate their fire on the stern of the ram, and, of course, to try not to hit their sister ships. The *Miami* was specially equipped with a torpedo on a boom, which she was supposed to use at the best opportunity. All the vessels carried lines and nets with which to foul the *Albemarle*'s propellers. Ramming was optional with the commander of each attacking ship.

The *Albemarle*, as was fitting, perhaps, considering the odds against her, opened the action at 4:40 P.M. Her second shot carried away some of the *Mattabesett*'s rigging, and she followed up her cannon by steaming directly for the Union flagship, the *Miami*, her iron prow eager for destruction. The *Mattabesett* and the *Sassacus*, following closely, eluded the ram and poured their fire into her sides and roof. This time the shots were more effective. Although the ram's iron plating still presented a hide tougher than the fire of the Union fleet, she suffered a minor disaster when a shot tore off some twenty inches of one of her two great guns. Though the cannon was badly damaged, the Southerners continued to work it throughout the action.

The *Sassacus* was now occupied in capturing the *Bombshell*, the little steamer which had not retired in time to escape its fate; the activity had taken the big Union vessel some distance away from the *Albemarle*. Her captain, Commander Roe, considered this a good opportunity to ram the ironclad. His ship had acquired a distance from the Confederate vessel of about four hundred yards and the latter, to evade the *Mattabesett*, had sheered off a little and turned her broadside to him. The Union ships were now on both sides of the ram, with engines stopped. Commander Roe cried to the engineer, "Crowd waste and oil in the fires and back slowly! Give her all the steam she can carry!" To acting Master Boutelle he said, "Lay her course for the juncture of the casemate and the hull!" Then came four bells, and with full steam and open throttle the *Sassacus* "sprang forward like a living thing." The guns ceased firing, and the smoke lifted from the ram as every effort was made to repel the attack. Aboard the ram it seemed that the *Sassacus* must be attempting a torpedo attack. All hands were ordered to stand by to repel boarders, but many of the Confederate crewmen edged close to ports and hatches in case they should be struck by a torpedo. With a crash that shook the *Sassacus* like an earthquake, she struck full and square on the iron hull, careening over it and tearing away her bows, ripping and straining her timbers at the water-line. The *Albemarle* heeled over, and some water poured over the shield. Her crew milled about, not knowing whether the ship was fatally wounded or not. The coolness of her subordinate officers was remarkable, and the men manned their stations after the momentary confusion. "Stand at your guns!" shouted Cooke. "If we must sink, let us perform our duty and go down like brave men." (One of his crew later reported that his commander looked "kinder scared like," which emotion might have been perfectly consonant with his words.)

The *Sassacus* had quivered for a moment after contact and now was stuck fast. The Confederate gun crews, stripped to the waist and blackened with powder, fired a shot at ten-foot range which plunged through the Union vessel "from the starboard bow to port side on the berth deck." For ten minutes or so the Union sailors did their best to throw grenades into the portholes of the ram and powder down her smokestack, but without great success. Then the *Albemarle* sent a second hundred-pound rifle shot through the *Sassacus'* starboard boiler and into the wardroom. Escaping steam soon filled every part of the ship from hurricane deck to fire room. The cries and moans of scalded men mingled with the terrible roar of the guns and the crackling of musket and pistol fire. It appeared that the ram would try to board, and Commander Roe ordered his signal books thrown into the water, but the attempt was beaten off. When the steam cleared it was evident that the *Sassacus* was free of her adversary; she continued to fire at the *Albemarle* until she drifted helplessly out of range.

The ramming might have been more successful if the other Union ships had closed in while the two vessels were engaged. Commander Roe, in fact, was afterward bitter about the lack of support. Undoubtedly it was from fear of destroying his ship and her crew that the *Mattabesett* and the others held off, however; for as soon as the ram was free again they brought every gun to bear on their foe. The *Albemarle*'s colors were shot away, and it seemed possible that she might be about to surrender, but her continued firing disabused those who held the notion. But she was up against more than she could handle; the only fact in her favor was that the smaller Union vessels, against instructions and even disobeying frantic signals from the *Miami*, continued to lay down a barrage of fire which was more dangerous to the large Union ships in close than to the ram itself, which lay between them. An attempt was made to foul the ram's rudder with a seine, but to no avail. The *Miami* exploded its torpedo, but did no damage.

The steering mechanism of the *Albemarle* had by this time been damaged, and she became hard to manage. She was having great difficulty in making steam; her smokestack had been literally riddled with shot, and it was impossible to keep up pressure in the boiler. It was apparent that she was in no condition to continue the trip to New Bern, and with some difficulty she turned and made her way back to Plymouth. In an effort to raise steam, butter, lard and bacon, as well as part of the ship's bulkheads, were thrown into the boilers.

The engagement was broken off at 7:30 P.M. Smith did not try to follow his adversary into her lair. He had seen what had happened to the *Sassacus*; the *Wyalusing* was signaling, through an error, that she was sinking; he could not afford to lose still another vessel. He was content to follow the ram at a safe distance, having compelled her to retire. But the results of the battle were not exactly encouraging to the Union navy. They had forced the *Albemarle* into port, and

as a consequence the Confederate attack on New Bern collapsed. And the *Bombshell* had been retaken with over thirty
prisoners and many supplies. But in the matter of casualties
and damage inflicted the Federal forces had suffered heavily.
Three men were injured aboard the ram, but on the *Mattabesett* two men were killed and six wounded, one was killed
on the *Wyalusing*, and the *Sassacus* had suffered one killed and
nineteen injured, most of them badly burned; four of these
wounded later died. And the *Sassacus* itself was so badly disabled that it had to return to base for extensive repairs to
its boiler and hull, and the six other Union vessels suffered
varying amounts of damage, which while not disabling required serious repairs. On the other hand, though Captain
Smith had counted fifty-four solid shots which had struck the
iron sides of the ram, the only damage which had been inflicted
by this hail of metal was "two timbers broken, the port
shutters damaged or carried away, one gun disabled . . . some
plating knocked off the ends and sides, and the stack riddled."
One of the crew later recounted about the same amount of
damage, adding that the steering mechanism had been im-
paired; some twenty-five shots, he thought, had caused breaks
in the iron, and two had actually penetrated the wood beneath.
Most important, after the action, he remembered, there was
"no leak more than ordinary." No one felt more deeply the
strength of the ram than Commander Roe, who had beaten his
Sassacus to death against her sides. When solid shot split and
flew back upon his decks after striking the *Albemarle*, it
showed her to be "more formidable than the *Atlanta* or the
Merrimac." A final pessimistic word: "She is too strong
for us."

This then was the Goliath.

The *Albemarle*, Admiral Lee asserted, and everyone agreed,
must be destroyed. This even though the Confederates, unhappy that the last engagement had not proved a clear-cut
victory for the ram, had resolved that the vessel should never
again be risked in a pitched battle if they could prevent it.

Captain Cooke had retired; the strain of the two battles had been great, and he was relieved at his own request by Commander Maffitt in June. But Maffitt was not to be allowed to fight the ram. General Baker to Commander Maffitt: "I beg leave to remind you of the importance to the Confederacy of the country opened to us by the taking of Plymouth, to suggest that its recapture now engages the serious attention of the U. S. Government, and that the loss of the gunboat which you command would be irreparable and productive of ruin to the interests of the Government, particularly in this State and district, and indeed would be a heavy blow to the whole country." Not content with this, Baker, fearful that Maffitt might go off on some mad scheme of his own, protested to the army department; the protest was forwarded by General Beauregard to the Secretary of War in Richmond, who sent it on for appropriate comment to Mallory, the Secretary of the Navy. Mallory argued that the *Albemarle* was not a floating battery and thus could not have its movements dictated by army commanders, but the influence of army opinion was strong enough to keep the vessel from being used pending the projected completion of additional fleet units to aid her.

There was no doubt about it, the ram must be destroyed. If nothing else, a strong force of Union ships had to be kept from other tasks to guard against its reappearance.

But how was it to be done? Admiral Lee was against sending any more wooden ships against the *Albemarle;* he did not have any more wooden ships to lose. Gustavus Fox sent a telegram to Captain Ericsson, inventor of the *Monitor:* could any arrangement be worked out whereby one of the navy's newer monitors might be floated over the bar and into Albemarle Sound? Ericsson thought not; they all drew much too much water. Melancton Smith proposed that a tug might go in and torpedo the monster in her lair. How to get the tug near enough, though? The suggestion seemed impractical. No, there was only one possibility: send a small-boat raid, either to cut the vessel out and capture her, or blow her up with powder; the only trouble here was that the men would not return alive.

Another difficulty: the navy was not sure exactly where the vessel was, so patiently, over a month, the Navy Department built up, by the use of spies and painstaking observations, all the pertinent data on the *Albemarle*'s location and situation. When the charts were deemed reasonably complete the department cast about for one of its senior officers to lead the expedition. Welles and Fox drew up a list of names; that of Commander Stephen Clegg Rowan headed the list. Commander Rowan had helped seize Alexandria in the early months of 1861, when the Confederates were on Washington's doorstep. He had commanded various blockading vessels, and had climaxed his services by commanding the powerful ironclad *New Ironsides* in the attacks upon the Charleston harbor fortifications. He was offered the command of the expedition but he did not think the plan would work; "with the conviction begotten of long experience he declined."

Welles and Fox went down the list, checking off names: this man was in New Orleans, he could not be spared; that one was in hospital, after being wounded three times at Charleston; this one again was doing valuable work in the blockade of the Gulf ports; that one again did not function well with small boats, he was better at a broadside. Was there no one in the navy to do this task? Not, they agreed, among the senior officers, at least; those who could be spared could not do it, and those who could, could not be spared.

It was the beginning of July; Admiral Lee sat in his cabin on the *Minnesota* reading the report of Cushing's extraordinary reconnaissance in the Cape Fear River. Three days behind enemy lines, a mailbag captured, many prisoners taken, the cutter had escaped the clutches of ten times its number of men and boats—the admiral laid the paper down and sat, softly humming to himself, smoking a big cigar. He rapped on the table, and an aide appeared. "Get Lieutenant Cushing.

Bring him to me as quick as you can." "Lieutenant Cushing?" "The young officer in command of the *Monticello*. I've got some work for him."

Cushing was standing in the cabin five days later. He was smiling; the admiral had proposed that he lead an expedition against the *Albemarle*. "I had thought of it, sir. My friend, Commander Flusser . . ." "Yes, I know." "I shall lead a flotilla of gunboats against the ram?" "We have decided," the admiral said, "not to risk any more wooden ships." "Then an expedition—I will need eighty men." The admiral sighed. "You shall have them, Mr. Cushing." He leaned forward, and began to sketch his plan. A torpedo attack might be made either with an India-rubber boat, which could be transported through the swamp and launched at a point across from the ram's berth at Plymouth, or by "light-draft, rifle-proof, swift steam barge, fitted with a torpedo." The admiral ordered the lieutenant to draw up his "mature views" on the subject, and return with them in a day or two. Cushing stated formally in a letter to Lee that he believed it was feasible to destroy the *Albemarle*, that from his knowledge of the Roanoke River and Albemarle Sound he believed himself qualified to attempt it, and that he would be willing to lead either kind of expedition. If tugs were to be used he thought at least one of them should be armed with a torpedo, and three should have "light howitzers." This was, he said, his favorite plan: the boat with the torpedo should dash in for the attack, while the other or others fired canister to disconcert the defenders, and stood by to pick up survivors of the first launch if it was disabled. And he requested that he be detailed for the work of preparing his boats if it was decided that he should make the attempt.

Admiral Lee read the letter. He agreed to send the young adventurer to Washington with dispatches—such an expedition must not be undertaken without the personal go-ahead of the department. A replacement for the *Monticello* was requested, but was tardy in arriving. Cushing found it difficult to wait. A report was received that the Confederate cruiser

Florida was nearby, and off he dashed in his sleek black ship to intercept her. The pursuit was fruitless. When he returned Lee ordered him to Washington, where he arrived on July 27, 1864.

Gustavus Fox was not enthusiastic. The work was extremely dangerous, he said soberly; it was unlikely that the lieutenant would return alive; it was equally unlikely that he would be successful. Fox outlined the situation fully, returning always to the same fundamental fact: the *Albemarle* must, despite the difficulties, in some way be destroyed. He could not dampen Will Cushing's ardor. The young man turned to him, his eyes beaming. "I'll try it, sir; I'll do my best." Fox wrote the order: Cushing would report to Admiral Gregory at New York, where he would, with Gregory's assistance, purchase "a suitable tug and India-rubber boat." A salute, and he was gone. Fox sat drumming on the table with his fingers. He wrote a note to Welles: the attempt would be made. The David had been found.

In the navy yard in Brooklyn Cushing found several boats being built for picket duty, and, unable to discover a suitable India-rubber boat, selected two "open launches about thirty feet in length with small engines and propelled by a screw." Each vessel was fitted with a twelve-pound howitzer and, with the help of Assistant Engineer George W. Melville, with a complicated torpedo device. The device was the invention of Engineer John L. Lay; Cushing later remarked laconically that it "had many defects and I would not again attempt its use." He tested it, however, exploding several torpedoes in the Hudson River, and found that it could be made to work if one had enough leisure to make sure that the lanyard and trigger line were pulled at exactly the right moments. But he was not overly concerned with the difficulties; there still lingered in his mind the idea that he might be able to surprise the *Albemarle* and take her by boarding, cutting her out from under the Confederate guns.

Some time after the middle of September the boats were

ready, and Cushing, wishing to spend a last few days at home, asked permission of the department to send the boats down the canal route to Chesapeake Bay in charge of his junior officers, and to join them there "by the usual route." Fox replied in a telegram (he was not unaware that the "usual route" would be via Fredonia, but he was sending a young man to his death, he believed): "Send the boats on. You can come yourself by rail." Cushing went off to the west and his two small vessels started from New York on September 22, Picket Boat Number One in charge of Ensign Howorth, Number Two under the command of Ensign Andrew Stockholm.

Howorth and Stockholm were brave men and worthy companions, but they were not experienced seamen, and they had a good deal of trouble with their little craft. By September 25 they were at New Brunswick, at the entrance to the Delaware and Raritan Canal, but both boats were in need of repair. Number One had been on the rocks for one tide near Bergen Point, New Jersey, and Stockholm had spent two days on a sand spit near the same place. Captain Charles Boggs was at home in New Brunswick, and, being a navy man, the arrival of the two launches was reported to him. He had them raised out of the water and inspected their hulls; he found that the coppering of both was damaged, and that Number One had a hole in the bottom and a damaged keel. They were quickly repaired and about six in the evening of the 25th, Captain Boggs having obtained a pilot, they left for the Delaware River.

They puffed their way to Baltimore, via the Chesapeake and Delaware Canal, without further mishap, but on the way south to Annapolis Number One's engine broke down and Stockholm had to take it in tow. In this fashion they reached Annapolis, on October 5, and remained overnight. They set out the next morning, with Number One still in tow, but a southeast wind, which had sprung up at dawn, grew stronger as they progressed, and they were forced to take refuge in a harbor on the Eastern Shore. The time was used to get

Howorth's engines working again, and in the afternoon the wind switched to the southwest and the boats were forced to run across into the West River, where they spent the night.

They reached Point Lookout, the southern tip of Maryland, by nightfall of the next day, but at this point Stockholm's engine began to cause trouble. Howorth, believing that too much time had already been lost, did not wait for the necessary repairs to be finished but pushed off at once for Fortress Monroe. Stockholm put to sea as soon as possible the next day. Once more faced with an unfavorable wind, and with his engine acting up again, he put into the mouth of Reason Creek, in the Great Wicomico Bay. The repairs were almost completed when a roving home guard unit, seventy-five or eighty men under a Captain Covington, appeared from the surrounding woods and opened fire. Stockholm slipped his cable and attempted to escape, but the launch ran aground on a sandbar and lay helpless under the Confederate fire. The crew fought back until its ammunition was exhausted and then, having destroyed everything they thought would be of value, surrendered. The Confederates then burned the boat to the water line. Stockholm was later exchanged, and asked why he had dared put into a cove on the Virginia coast. He replied that he thought he was in the Patuxent River where, indeed, he would have been perfectly safe, but his ignorance of the geography of Chesapeake Bay would seem to justify Cushing's angry judgment that the loss of his "best picket boat" was "stupid."

The summer of 1864 was, for the Union, almost the darkest period of the war. The country was tired and there were many in the North who no longer believed that it was possible, even desirable, to "win" the conflict. Grant had been named commander of all the United States forces and was personally conducting the Army of the Potomac in its penultimate campaign, but between May 4, the first day at the Wilderness, and June 3, at Cold Harbor, the army lost fifty-five thousand men. The Army of Northern Virginia had lost about twenty-five thousand men itself, and that loss was terrible because in large part it could not be made up, but the price that the North had paid was almost too much for the country to stand.

"Looking backwards," D. S. Freeman said in his *R. E. Lee*, "it is obvious, of course, that the reduction of the food supply, the death of Jackson, the defeat at Gettysburg, the virtual starvation of the horses in the winter of 1863-64, the inability of Lee to force Grant back across the Rappahannock after the battle of the Wilderness, and the failure of the conscription in the summer of 1864 marked definite stages in the approach of defeat that may have been inevitable from the first. None of this was plain at the time, and even if it had been apparent to the rest of the world, it would not have been admitted by the majority of Southerners. Lee saw clearly and without illusion, but most men hoped that the experience of Washington's continentals would be repeated and that a final Yorktown would redeem disaster."

After Cold Harbor the Army of the Potomac was shaken, and though not in as hopeless case as after the defeats in the earlier years of the war due to Grant's rocklike determination not to retire from Virginia, it returned to its almost helpless inability to do the one thing that would end the war with victory—destroy Lee's army. Grant settled down outside Petersburg, only twenty-five miles from Richmond but still a long way from his ultimate goal, and the Confederates dug in for a last stand that might, as far as anybody could tell, last almost indefinitely. Early in the morning of July 30 the famous Petersburg mine was exploded, resulting in one of the grand fiascoes of a war noted for its fiascoes. The men were exhausted on both sides after two months of continuous fighting, and with the failure of the attempt to blow the Confederate lines into the sky and thus break through to Richmond and victory the Army of the Potomac settled back to rest for a while.

The politicians were not resting. On August 23 Lincoln somewhat mysteriously asked members of his cabinet to sign a paper folded in such a way that they could not see what was written upon it, and then tucked it away in his desk. In Lincoln's handwriting the paper contained this statement:

"This morning, as for some days past, it seems exceedingly probable that this administration will not be re-elected. Then it will be my duty to so co-operate with the President elect as to save the Union between the election and the inauguration; as he will have secured his election on such ground that he cannot possibly save it afterwards."

Lincoln was not the only pessimist. "Mr. Lincoln is already beaten," Horace Greeley had recently written. "He cannot be re-elected." With other prominent Republicans, Greeley had been working at a scheme to hold a convention of radical members of his party at the end of September so as to concentrate support "on some candidate who commands the confidence of the country, even by a new nomination if necessary."

In Chicago on August 29 the national convention of the Democratic party met to choose a candidate to run against Lincoln. Broadly speaking, this convention brought together almost everybody who disliked the way the war was being conducted with the single exception of the dissident Republicans, who thought that Lincoln was not tough enough. The convention adopted a platform deploring the "failure" of the war and calling for "immediate efforts" to end all hostilities. Having adopted this peace plank to pull in all of the people who were tired of the war or had not believed in the war in the first place, the Democrats hedged their bet by nominating a soldier for their candidate—George B. McClellan, the enduring hero of the enlisted men in the Army of the Potomac and a leader whom the Democrats considered a military genius who had been unfairly treated by the Washington politicos.

That week in Chicago was probably the high point of antiwar feeling in the north. The tide began to ebb very quickly after the first of September, when Sherman wired Lincoln: "Atlanta is ours, and fairly won." On reflection McClellan found the peace plank rather too much to swallow, and interpreted it as a mandate to see the war through to victory, remarking that to do anything less would be to betray the soldiers he had led. On top of all this, Sheridan had been ordered to the Shenandoah Valley with an army to "eat out Virginia clear and clean as far as they go, so that crows flying over it for the balance of the season will have to carry their own provender with them," as Grant put it. In the middle of September Grant went up to the valley and had a talk with Sheridan, ordering him to follow Early and destroy his army as well as to continue scorching the earth of Richmond's bread basket. On September 19 at Winchester Sheridan obeyed his orders, following up his victory over Early three days later at Fisher's Hill. "Since spring the Confederacy's one hope had been that the people of the North would get tired and quit," says Bruce Cotton. "After Winchester that hope no longer had any roots."

The *Albemarle*, at least, remained. Its retaking of Plymouth and the freeing of the northeastern part of North Carolina were one of the significant Confederate victories of 1864. No one in the Union navy, least of all Will Cushing, was unaware of the political as well as military importance of sinking the ram. No doubt he exaggerated this importance, but it seems to have been his belief that if he could destroy the *Albemarle* before November the re-election of Lincoln, which with Grant and indeed most members of the armed services he considered essential to the Union cause, would be practically assured.

Western New York had never looked so beautiful, Cushing said, as when he took that trip home at the end of September to see his mother for what might be the last time. He was nervous and seemed, as several people remembered it, to be "on to something big." He was as youthfully obstreperous as ever and went to call on the Whites, his mother's cousins, and rode into their kitchen on his horse. "There was a great and sudden racket," Belle White described it, "and the screams of a servant, and all the frightened family congregated toward the sound, and there was Will, cap in hand, saying 'I've come to call.'" He also visited the offices of the Fredonia *Censor* again, and though no doubt he would very much have liked to tell the editor about the *Albemarle* he was able to hold his tongue. (The editor was one of those who remembered that he had suspected Cushing was up to something.) Will did describe his adventures in the Cape Fear River, however, and an account of them was published during his stay.

Cushing had known a number of girls—at Annapolis, in Boston, Washington, New York and Baltimore, and in Fredonia—but he seems never, up to this time, to have enjoyed a serious relationship with one of them unless it was with a certain Carrie Stevens of Jamestown, New York, a close friend of his cousin Mary Edwards. He was still extremely young, and it might be said that he had had little time to devote to love affairs. It may have been in some sense a family trait. Will's half sisters and half brothers had married early, but in the fall of 1864 Milton was twenty-seven and Howard twenty-six yet neither had married, and Alonzo had died without having been engaged, at least formally. The children took the straitened circumstances of the family very much to heart, and this may have kept the boys from undertaking permanent responsibilities. And of course the war had changed everything.

But Will appears to have enjoyed an active flirtation during this last visit home before going after the *Albemarle*. The girl was named Mary Colman, and though nothing ultimately came of it—she married someone else a year or two later—he saw her often during his stay. One night there was a party at her house, and Cushing went. Mr. Colman was a veteran of the Mexican War and wanted to talk about military subjects even more than Will could stand. When it came time to leave Will kissed Mary's hand gallantly, explaining that "it was a custom of the old navy," and then announced loudly "that he needed a talisman." The room was silent. He had noticed a gold chain with a curious little gold pendant about Mary's neck, and he reached behind her and undid the clasp and held the chain out. The little gold links winked in the light. "You don't mind?" he asked Mary. She looked a little astonished. He clasped the chain around his own neck—later it was sewn underneath the collar of his officer's jacket—and accompanied his mother home.

The next morning was clear and cold. Will got up early but he ate very little; he seemed restless, and his mother observed him silently with misgivings. In the afternoon he came to her suddenly and said that he must tell her something. He would take her for a ride away from the town where it would be impossible for anyone to overhear them. She was frightened by the urgency in his voice but she went with him to the barn. He harnessed the horse and drove out of town, along the winding dirt road to the Arkwright Hills. When he reached the highest turning of the road he seemed satisfied and helped her down and sat her under a tree, being careful to see that she was comfortable. He knelt before her, his back achingly straight as ever, and told her his plan. He spoke at length, describing the *Albemarle* in detail, her great strength, the necessity that she be destroyed, his proposed method of doing it, leaving out nothing, including Gustavus Fox's belief that the undertaking was, at the least, extremely hazardous. She was silent for a long time after he was finished. Finally she spoke, but her voice was harsh.

"I don't understand all this. I don't see how you can succeed. If this ship is so strong that a thousand men and nine ships could not destroy it, how can they expect one man to do it with two little wooden boats?"

"I will succeed, Mama," he said gently, "or you will not have any Will Cushing."

He put out his hand and rested it on her arm. "But I don't

understand," she went on, "why you . . ."

"There's no one else, Mama," he said. "And if . . . well, it's in a good cause. I would want to do it for the country."

"The country," she said. She did not look at him, but continued to stare into the distance.

"I hoped you would pray with me, Mama," he said. She rose to her knees and he knelt beside her. "God, have mercy on my son," she said. "And let the war cease." She repeated the Lord's Prayer, and he said the words with her.

He took the train back to New York the following day. It rained hard through the last half of the trip, and the sky was gray, with grayer clouds driven across it by a strong wind. The train was more than two hours late. He walked for a long time in the rain, hardly aware of where he was going. Finally he realized that he was wet to the skin. He hailed a horse cab and gave the driver the address of his cousin George White, who was working as a procurement officer in the city. White was glad to see him, and put him up for the night. In the morning Cushing took the train for Baltimore. White wrote Mrs. Cushing some months later that, before he left, Will said to him: "Cousin George, I am going to have a vote of thanks from Congress, or six feet of pine box by the time you hear from me again."

On October 10 he arrived in Hampton Roads to find that one picket boat had made the trip successfully, but that there was no word of the other craft. He spent two days waiting impatiently for the appearance of Stockholm and his crew. On the 12th Admiral Lee was relieved, and Admiral David D. Porter took his place as commander of the North Atlantic Blockading Squadron. Porter, who, unlike Lee, had no high opinion of Cushing but thought of him as a daredevil with more luck than ability, sent the young officer, weak and worn from exposure and lack of sleep, out in an army tug to find his second boat. The search was fruitless, of course, and only after the Admiral had sent one of his own vessels to aid the tug did he reluctantly listen to Cushing's plea that he be allowed to proceed with one launch.

Cushing had only recently received the reprimand from the Navy Department concerning the affair of the *Hound*, the British ship which he had treated with such disrespect early in the summer, and Porter suggested later that Cushing's willingness to proceed with only one picket boat was because of his desire to overcome the disfavor which he had fallen into with the department. Cushing himself never hinted that this was even a possible reason. Porter ultimately came to have a grudging but almost uncomprehending respect for Cushing. "Cushing's hazardous undertakings were sometimes criticized as useless," he wrote after the war, "but there was more method in them than appeared on the surface, and important information was sometimes obtained, to say nothing of the brilliant example of courage and enterprise which they afforded to others." "The fearless fellow never stopped to consider whether he was charging fifty men or a thousand," Porter said of one of Cushing's exploits near Wilmington. "It seemed immaterial to him, when his blood was up, how many of the enemy faced him." At still another time he said, "He would undertake the most desperate adventures where it seemed impossible for him to escape death or capture, yet he almost always managed to get off with credit to himself and with loss to the enemy."

Feeling, despite his misgivings, that he had no alternative since time was slipping quickly by, Porter sent the lieutenant off with a dispatch to W. H. Macomb, commanding the squadron in the North Carolina sounds, asking that Cushing be given the additional men he required to carry out his mission. "I have no great confidence in his success," he wrote. "but you will afford him all the assistance in your power, and keep boats ready to pick him up in case of failure." If the *Albemarle* should appear again in the waters around Plymouth, Macomb should attack it boldly and keep attacking it, even if "half your vessels are sunk."

Cushing set out from Norfolk on October 20 by way of

the Chesapeake and Albemarle Canal, with five men beside Howorth and himself: William Stotesbury, his engineer, Samuel Higgins, fireman, and landsmen Lorenzo Deming, Henry Wilkes and Robert King. Halfway down the canal Cushing discovered that it had been filled in, for strategic purposes. The little craft chugged back up the canal two or three miles until a small creek was discovered that seemed, by the map, to empty into the canal below the obstruction. The launch puffed and clanked along the stream until Wilkes, sitting in the bow, signaled wildly to his captain that the boat could go no farther, for a mill dam was in the way. A tide mark along the bank indicated that the water would rise, and at dusk Cushing took the vessel over the dam with only a few scrapes and bruises. In the darkness, however, he ran aground. The men slept on the deck and in the morning, having procured a flatboat at rifle point, they took off the howitzer and the coal; thus lightened the picket boat was again afloat. They were soon back in the canal, and reached the sounds in two days. Cushing was rewarded when the first officer he met told him, astounded, that it had been madness to try this route, as thirty miles of the canal were unprotected by any Union guard, and all the farmers were of Confederate sympathies. Cushing laughed and turned to Howorth. "I thought that man who 'gave' us his flatboat didn't seem too pleased!"

On the afternoon of the 23rd he arrived finally at Roanoke Island, the great Union strong point, where he was confronted with two bits of information of the most serious character. He was shown a newspaper in which the plan for the destruction of the ram had been printed, though incorrectly—but the Confederates could not have missed this warning; and he was told of the attempt (he had not known of it till now), five months before, by five volunteers, all enlisted men, to blow up the *Albemarle* with torpedoes. A coal heaver named Charles Baldwin, with four companions, had carried two one-hundred-pound torpedoes on stretchers across the swamp be-

hind Plymouth until they reached the bank of the Roanoke
River opposite the point where the *Albemarle* was moored,
from which vantage point Baldwin and another had swum
across the river to a place on the bank upstream from the
vessel. Baldwin then connected the two torpedoes together by
a cable and swam down the current, intending to place the
charges on either side of the ship's bow, where they could be
exploded from the other side of the river. Baldwin was seen,
however, while he was in the water, and the five men had to
retreat under a hail of small-arms fire. (They eventually all
regained the fleet.) Because of this, the officer asserted, the
Confederates would have such a close guard about the ram
that Cushing should not look forward to getting anywhere
near the vessel, much less to destroying her. He shrugged,
though he was angry about the fact that the newspapers had
got hold of the story; but it was a common thing in the war,
and did not surprise him.

He told the army commanders that he would push off for
Beaufort in the morning, and even made arrangements to take
on two passengers for the trip—if there were any Confederate
spies in the establishment they would certainly report this as
soon as possible—and slipped away quietly in the night and
steamed up the sound, rather than down, the fifty miles to
where the Union fleet stood outside of Plymouth, blockading
—but rather fearfully—the *Albemarle* in her lair. He reported
to Macomb, then on board the *Shamrock*, the largest ship in
the fleet. Macomb read the dispatches presented to him, and
nodded thoughtfully when Cushing entered the cabin. He
would need a few more men, he thought; Macomb said he
would procure them. Quietly, he sent to the commanders of
the other ships: without stating the duty, ask the various crews
for volunteers for an extremely hazardous undertaking, and
pick your best men. In the afternoon the chosen few reported
to Cushing on the *Shamrock*: they were Acting Master's Mate
John Woodman, of the *Commodore Hull*; another engineer
to assist Stotesbury, Charles L. Steever of the *Otsego*; Richard

Hamilton, coal heaver, of the *Shamrock*; William Smith, Barnard Harley and Edward J. Houghton, ordinary seamen from the *Chicopee*. They had been picked from a much larger number, they said, and some of their comrades had even offered an entire month's pay to "be allowed to go along." None had taken the opportunity to refuse the duty, however; the word had got about that it was Lieutenant Cushing who would lead the expedition, and no one would want to miss going with him.

Cushing called his crew together on the afterdeck and explained what it was that they were going to do; he had told no one except Howorth until now, believing that it was the best way to maintain secrecy. "Not only must you not expect," he finished grimly, "but you must not hope to return. I can promise you nothing but glory, death or, possibly, promotion. We will have the satisfaction of getting in a good lick at the rebels, that is all." Without a word the twelve men stepped forward. "I am not surprised," Cushing said. "We will have a day or so to go over every detail of the matter."

Requesting Ensign Howorth to explain the expedition fully to his crew, Cushing retired to Macomb's cabin for a conference with Ensign Rudolph Sommers, of the *Otsego*. Sommers had completed a series of small-boat reconnaissances of the *Albemarle*; he had returned from the last of them only the night before, completely exhausted, for his boat had been detected, part of his crew had been captured, and he had spent four hours in the water under fire. The ram was moored along the water front of Plymouth, he explained—Plymouth was eight miles up the river. The average width of the river at that point was from 150 to 200 yards—plenty of room to maneuver, at least, Cushing said. He was not sure of the number, Sommers went on, but several thousand soldiers— perhaps four thousand, perhaps fewer—were on the river-banks and in the town. And finally, about a mile below the ram lay the wreck of the steamer *Southfield*, which had been sunk in combat with the *Albemarle* the previous April. "She was sunk in the battle in which Commander Flusser died," Macomb put in. Cushing nodded. Although submerged to the hurricane deck, Sommers explained, she seemed to have a picket guard on board, although he was not sure. One of his men had thought he had seen it as they slipped quietly past in the darkness. The three officers talked for two hours, and Cushing finally stated that he was ready. Sommers then requested that he be allowed to go along. "But you can't even walk!" Cushing said. Sommers smiled ruefully. "If I *could* walk I'd like to go."

The sun set behind thick clouds on the night of October 26, and Cushing decided that it would be dark enough for success. At about nine in the evening he ran his launch alongside the *Otsego* to pick up the men from that vessel who were to go along. As they were descending the ladder a young, eager face appeared at the taffrail. "Lieutenant Cushing!" the young officer called in a stage whisper. "I'll pay you ten thousand dollars if you'll let me go along!" Cushing laughed. "You haven't got it," he called. "But I'd give it to you if I did," came the answer. "Who is that—is that Ensign Gay?" asked Cushing. "If it is, you're on—I need another madman on this expedition." Gay swung down the ladder, laughing. "Acting Ensign Thomas S. Gay reporting, sir," he said. "The only ten-thousand-dollar ensign in the fleet."

It was a mile or so from the place where the *Otsego* was moored to the mouth of the river, and the launch cut across the open water, her engines chugging in the night. Luck was not with them. They had misjudged the tide, and at the entrance to the river they ran aground. Cushing swore loudly, but soon swallowed his anger and set about trying to get the boat off the bar. But the tide was ebbing—they had started too late; he had thought it was so, but Macomb had disagreed with him. It was two in the morning before the boat was free, and he hesitated to continue at this late hour, but decided that having to wait another day would be good for no one's nerves, and so set off up the stream. Within five hundred yards a sharp hail rang across the water, and the dim shadow of a picket launch loomed out of the darkness. "Who goes there!" came the peremptory demand. "My God," Cushing muttered, "the Johnnies can't be down this far, can they?" Woodman plucked at his sleeve. "Army picket boat, sir," he said. "Better answer."

Cushing stood up in the launch. "Lieutenant Cushing and crew, of the U.S.S. *Monticello*," he called. "How do we know that?" was the answer from the tug, which was pointing its howitzer menacingly. "Come aboard and see, damn it," Lieutenant Cushing answered. The tug drew alongside and two men jumped onto the launch's deck, the howitzer covering them. They carried a lantern, which they flashed in Cushing's face, and then swung round to illumine the rest of the crew. "Tom Gay!" said the man with the lantern. Gay stepped forward. "It's Lieutenant Wilson, sir," he said to Cushing. He explained their mission briefly to the inspecting officer, who seemed satisfied. "Got to be careful, sir," Wilson said, and swung back onto his craft, which chugged away in the darkness.

Cushing looked at his watch; it was three in the morning. "Back we go," he said to Howorth. "It's too late now." The launch swung around and started toward the fleet once more. On the way Cushing explained to Howorth and Gay that if the launch's motor made enough noise to be detected by the picket boat, it would surely be heard by the Confederates when it was still far from its objective. The engine could be boxed in by the fleet's carpenters, he thought. In any case, they would try again the next night. Howorth and Gay agreed.

At noon three escaped slaves were picked up in the water, swimming out to the fleet. When it was discovered that they had information about the *Albemarle* they were brought to the *Shamrock*, where Cushing and Howorth interrogated them for an hour. It was true, they said, that a picket guard was on the half-submerged wreck of the *Southfield*; moreover, the

Confederates had a schooner anchored near the wreck on which were a lieutenant and twenty-five men, an artillery piece, and rockets to signal the ram. Cushing looked at Howorth; Howorth looked at Cushing. The Negroes were put to bed for the first time in forty-eight hours, they said, and the two officers joined Macomb and Lieutenant Duer, executive officer of the *Shamrock*, for a conference. They discussed various possibilities, and finally Cushing suggested that they tow a cutter behind the launch with twelve or fifteen men; they could cast off at the place where the schooner was moored and capture the guard; at the worst they would divert the attention of the ram's defenders. "Maybe," said Commander Macomb, but Duer was enthusiastic, and Macomb finally concurred.

The crew of the *Shamrock* was lined up in the waist of the vessel and addressed by Lieutenant Duer. "I want eleven men and two officers to accompany Lieutenant Cushing on a dangerous expedition, from which probably none will return. None but young men without encumbrances will be accepted. Those who wish to volunteer will step over to this side." The entire company of the *Shamrock*, two hundred and seventy-five men, moved over. "I thought so," Commander Macomb said. "Pick your men." Duer chose the best and bravest of his crew, and appointed Acting Gunner William Peterkin and Acting Master's Mate Wilson D. Burlingame to lead them. They were armed and given instructions, but it was not until the cutter had been attached to the launch, at 8:30 in the evening, that they were told, out of earshot of the rest of the ship's company, what exactly it was that they were to do.

The night of October 27 was cloudy with some occasional spits of chilly rain, with a light wind blowing from the south; the temperature was about 65 degrees, in the water about 55 degrees. At 11:28 the launch, with the cutter in tow, reached the mouth of the Roanoke and started up the river. It was raining harder, and the men shivered in silence—they had been warned not to talk, not even to whisper, lest a

sentry on the bank hear them and give the alarm. The engine
had been boxed in during the day, and a tarpaulin was tucked
around it for further muffling. The launch puffed, and moved
slowly upstream—it would take more than two hours to
reach the *Albemarle* at the speed they were making. It was
hard not to be able to talk. Once one of the seamen had a
coughing spell, but Howorth leaped to his side and muffled
him in his coat; when he returned to Cushing's side the latter
was smiling. "Good for you, Mr. Howorth," he whispered.
"I'll muffle you up, sir," said Howorth, "if you say another
word." Cushing continued to smile, but was silent. He was
standing, with most of the officers, in the forward half of the
vessel. On the deck at the bow was Ensign Gay. He would
handle the boom, swung round to the stern now, on which the
torpedo was fixed; around his wrist was a line which Cushing
held in his hand; the boom was to be moved forward when
he pulled the line. Another line was attached to Engineer
Stotesbury's ankle; a pull on it would increase the speed,
two pulls would stop the engines altogether. Still another
line was attached to the howitzer; if it became necessary to
shoot it, Howorth would man the gun, and receive firing
orders by means of the line, which he would attach to his
person at the last moment. Lieutenant Cushing held these
three lines in his right hand; in his left he held the two lines
which controlled the torpedo. He had worked out the manner
in which he would, in an emergency, distinguish between the
five different lines, and had no doubt that his mind would,
at the last moment, be absolutely clear.

He was, in fact, happy to discover that he was completely
calm. He was aware that the success of the expedition de-
pended entirely on his keeping his head. There would not be
much time to think, he knew, when the *Albemarle* was
within striking distance; he was doing his thinking now,
while there *was* time. But his thought was all to the purpose;
it was as though the future did not exist any more, and he
did not waste a valuable moment in considering the possibility

that he might be dead in an hour or so. He did not expend any thought on the past either; what was done was done, there was no changing it now; he could not remember that there was anything to regret. He concentrated on the *Albemarle*, on the launch, on the torpedo, hanging ominously at the stern. Once or twice memories of Alonzo obtruded on his consciousness, but he put them aside as quickly as they came. They were likely to bring anger with them, and he could not afford anger any more than regret or fear.

For the first two or three miles the river ran between wide low banks, but soon the stream narrowed; on the banks great trees grew almost to the edge of the water, and their low-hanging branches obscured the sky and doubled the darkness. Even with his eyes accustomed to the night Cushing could hardly see to the rear of the launch, but he knew, from the constant twitching in his hand, that Stotesbury was moving around in the stern, tending to the engine and doing other necessary tasks. (He worried about Stotesbury, for he had never been under fire before, but he was acting well.) On Cushing's left stood Howorth, his hand on the breech of the howitzer. Cushing could just make out the peak of his cap and the heavy line of his jaw. Between them sat Woodman, close to the wheel of the vessel, where his knowledge of the river could be put to use. Behind Cushing stood Assistant Paymaster Francis H. Swan. He had also talked himself aboard at the last moment, claiming as his reason that "he had never been in a fight." He had served with Cushing on the *Minnesota*, and the latter knew him as a capable officer and a brave man, and so took him along, telling him, however, that it was a poor time for a start. Higgins was the best steersman, beside Cushing, in the boat, and he was at the wheel. The other seamen were arranged at battle stations. A pair of firemen were in the stern, ready to clear the tiller ropes in case of an accident in that quarter.

Two o'clock: they had come, Cushing thought, about six miles; the *Southfield* would soon be visible. He took a hand-

kerchief out of his pocket and waved it; at the signal the
men in the cutter took their places by the oarlocks, their oars
poised and ready should the pickets sing out a challenge.
Cushing was worried for a moment lest the cutter's crew be
unable to see even the whiteness of the handkerchief in the
gloom, but he was relieved when he heard faint sounds of
movement from the craft in the rear.

There was a sudden jerk on one of the right-hand lines.
Cushing looked down; it was the one that led to Ensign Gay.
He must have seen the schooner ahead; yes, there it was, a
darker shadow in the darkness. They were headed directly
for it, and Cushing leaned down and gave the wheel a quarter
turn with his finger. Now everyone in the launch had seen it;
they were standing, looking toward the bow; even in the
darkness their tenseness was perceptible. Slowly the launch
puffed, its muffled engine almost inaudible in the stillness.
Slowly they drew near; they would pass within twenty yards
of the schooner, but the wreck of the *Southfield* was visible
now, they could not turn without coming even closer to it;
in any case there was not much room between either of the
vessels and the bank. There was the sudden soft sound of voices
in the night, and then the quick light of a match which
flickered and was gone. Fifteen men in the launch and thirteen
in the cutter did not draw a breath for a minute, and then
they were through, they had passed between the two enemy
vessels and had not been seen. Another minute passed, and
then another; the launch pushed on; it seemed impossible that
the gurgle of water around its bows had not been heard, and
yet there was no sharp hail behind them. In another minute
they were around a bend in the river, and safe. Twenty-eight
men drew a deep breath; twenty-eight men wanted to cry out
in triumph, but did not. Cushing turned to look forward once
more. It would not be long now.

His mind was working fast. He had not supposed that he
would pass the pickets without being discovered, but he had
considered the possibility. From the beginning he had had a

project in the back of his mind: land at a wharf downstream from the ram; lead his crew, which was heavily armed, in a surprise attack on the vessel from the shore; cut the hawsers and push off from the bank—the ironclad ram was invulnerable to any guns the Confederates would have to guard her with, either at Plymouth or on the way downstream; cut their throats or otherwise deal with whatever skeleton crew might be aboard (he had twenty-seven men and it would be at least a fair fight); float down the river, with all the time in the world to start the engines and steam majestically out into the bay with the Union flag at the masthead (he had brought one along just in case). It would be an unspeakable triumph and in the end probably safer, for if the ram was blown up it was likely that most, if not all, of the attackers would die or be captured in the action. Therefore he did not give the three sharp pulls on the line tied to Stotesbury's ankle that would have directed the engineer to cast off the cutter, but instead stood without moving, his eyes staring into the darkness. If the men in the cutter were wondering what had changed the plan they would just have to wonder. A word at the moment of landing would be sufficient; they would follow him, he knew.

Five minutes passed, then ten. Any time now the ram should appear. He wondered what she would look like; would there be enough light to see by, for instance? And then, suddenly, as they swept around a bend, there she was, looming darkly in the distance, visible only by the squareness of her silhouette against the faint light in the sky. They had not yet been seen; his heart leaped; the plan would work. He turned the wheel sharply and headed in toward the bank, and then saw, about a hundred yards below the huge mass of the *Albemarle*, a wharf jutting out into the water. He headed for it, every muscle tight. Howorth looked at him, and then nodded. Good for Howorth! So he had understood.

Rome was saved by some frightened geese, which cackled and squawked on the Capitol two thousand years ago; the

Confederate Navy was saved from the final ignominy of losing its *Albemarle* in this humiliating way by a quick-witted dog, whose short, sharp bark woke a nodding sentinel on the great dim bulk of the ram just as the launch was shearing in toward the wharf. "Who's there?" came the voice across the water, and then, when the hail was not answered, "Who's there, who goes there?" urgently, anxiously. Cushing realized at once that the time for boarding was passed, and without a moment's hesitation thrust the plan from his mind. He gave a hard pull on the engineer's line, but there was no need for concealment any longer: "Ahead fast!" he cried, his voice shattering the stillness, and in almost the same breath, turning to the cutter: "Cast off, Peterkin, and go down and get those pickets on the schooner!" The launch leaped forward in the water, her engines throbbing—Stotesbury was handling the steam perfectly—when the drag of the cutter fell away. Straight for the great "dark mountain of iron" they sprang, under a full head of steam; on the *Albemarle* the defenders sprung their rattle, an angry sound like the screeching of birds; around them in the water the bullets started to splash, first one, then ten, then the sound of firing was almost constant. "Who's there? Who's there?" came the cry from the ram, in the interval between the popping and crackling of muskets. The defenders, Cushing had a short moment to think, seemed much confused.

When he was within fifty yards he began to worry about the darkness, but his prayer was immediately answered, for the Confederates had prepared a large bonfire for just such an emergency, and it now blazed up, throwing gigantic leaping shadows on the hulk of the ship which loomed ahead. By its light Cushing could see, when he was within twenty yards, that a semicircle of logs, their tops showing above the surface, ringed the vessel—express defense against a torpedo attack, he knew. (They had been placed there the day before, and Sommers had had no chance to see them; the captain of the *Albemarle*, hearing of the arrival of a steam launch at Roanoke

Island, had divined its purpose; in fact he had feared this dark, rainy night and had placed a double guard on board his vessel.) Entirely oblivious of the bullets which whistled around him and splashed in the water, Cushing ran in close to the circle of logs and examined them coolly. He spun the wheel and the launch shot away. He looked up to see Howorth's white face, staring at him in disbelief. "Full speed!" Cushing shouted. He sped across the river, turning in a great circle. Once over the boom of logs he would never get out again, he knew; but he had not come here to get away again. He was perfectly cool, as he had hoped to be; he had dropped three of the lines and now held in his right hand the one which released the torpedo, the trigger line in his left. As the launch completed her turn a charge of buckshot tore the entire back out of his coat; if he had not been standing perfectly straight, he said, it would have taken his back with it, but in fact he was not touched by one of the pellets, though they ripped his shirt. At almost the same moment a rifle bullet carried away the sole of his left shoe. He felt the tug at his foot but there was no time to look down. The launch was speeding toward the logs; in the fantastic light of the fire the crew saw men leaping and shouting and kneeling to shoot. Ahead loomed the ram, the firelight flickering on its sleek black sides.

There was a momentary lull in the firing, and the only sound was the pounding of the launch's engines as it sped nearer and nearer. It was within twenty yards when across the narrowing gap of water came the cry of the *Albemarle*'s captain: "What boat is that?" The men in the launch "were relieved by the question" and Cushing shouted: "We'll soon let you know!" Several other members of the crew "added humorous remarks of their own."

Cushing ordered Gay to swing the boom around, and the ensign did do. As if in reply to the desperate question from the ram Cushing pulled the lanyard of the howitzer, and a double dose of canister buzzed and sang against the iron sides of the

Albemarle and spattered into the "mass of men standing fire-lit upon the shore."

There was a tearing, grinding wrench—the launch had hit the boom. The bows rose, and then the boat's headway was lost, and it hung there, quivering. Cushing stumbled but quickly regained his footing. Behind him he could hear the hiss of escaping steam. This, then, was where the launch would stay. He quickly judged the distance—it seemed about right to him, though it was hard to see anything since they were in the shadow of the ram.

The boom was in place now; the grinding of the winch in the bottom of the boat was clearly audible as the torpedo was lowered below the surface of the water. For a moment Cushing looked up, and then shuddered. Ten feet away was the muzzle of one of the ram's eight-inch guns. Every word of command aboard the *Albermarle* was audible. They would fire, Cushing estimated, within twenty seconds or so.

Twenty seconds was time enough to do what he had to do. The torpedo was completely submerged now, the boom angled into the water. Slowly, for he could not jerk it or he might break the pin, he pulled the right-hand line. He counted slowly to five, to allow the torpedo to rise under the hull of the *Albemarle*. A bullet tore at his collar, then another ripped his sleeve, then two more plowed through his clothing. Slowly, for he could not jerk it or he might break the slender cord, he pulled at the firing line. The ball dropped on the pin, and the roar of the explosion filled his ears.

At the same time the *Albemarle* fired its eight-inch gun. The gun could not be depressed far enough, and most of the charge passed over and out into the river. But the immense body of water thrown up by the explosion of the torpedo dashed into the frail picket boat and it seemed "to flatten out like a pasteboard box on the logs." If there was a chance that it could have been extricated it was gone now.

In the silence after the gun was fired cries from the ram and from the shore were heard by the men in the launch: "Surrender or we will blow you out of the water!" The firing started again, and the launch was blanketed with bullets. Cushing looked down at his left hand, which had pulled the trigger line. It was bleeding freely; it must have been struck by a bullet just as he fired the torpedo, but he had not noticed until now. "Surrender!" came the cry again, and Cushing shouted back, "Never! I'll be damned first!" He threw off his sword, his revolver and his coat, knelt and tore off his shoes. "Men, save yourselves," he shouted, and dived into the cold water of the river.

Several of the crew dived in with him, but he was soon separated from them. He was a strong swimmer, and he struck out toward the opposite shore, within a matter of seconds being beyond the circle of light thrown by the fire. But he was not yet safe; a boat put out from the bank with torches, and fired on anything seen moving in the water. Otherwise the shooting had stopped. He assumed that the rest of his crew must have surrendered. He held his breath and sank beneath the surface; the boat was coming toward him, but swerved away at the last moment, and he was not seen. Again he struck out for the dark line of the opposite bank. It soon occurred to him that they would be watching the shore there, and then he saw, ahead of him, down by the edge of the water, a group of men with torches, and he turned and started to swim down the river. At this moment he heard a swimmer not far away in the water splashing and yelling; there was a gurgling yell, and then silence as the man went down for the last time. It was Samuel Higgins, fireman first class. The Confederate boats had heard the sound, and set out toward the spot. Cushing sank again below the surface and waited until he could hold his breath no longer. When he rose the boat was far behind him, having misjudged the direction of the noise. He heard them call in the darkness: "Cushing! Cushing!" He was beginning to be tired, and the water seemed icy cold. But he was not safe yet, he knew, and he continued to swim down the current.

At last he decided that he was far enough downstream and turned out of the current, with some difficulty, for he was very tired, to attempt a landing on the dark, forbidding bank of the river. He had heard no sound for minutes now, but suddenly a groan came from close by in the water. It took no more than a moment to decide that he must help his comrade in this desperate business, and though his wounded hand was beginning to throb painfully, he struck out once more into the middle of the river. He heard splashing close by, and a few rapid strokes brought him up to the man. It was John Woodman, gasping, "Cushing! For God's sake help me! I can't swim any more." Instantly Cushing was at his side, and with his uninjured right arm was sustaining the exhausted officer. For ten long minutes he swam with one arm, straining every muscle to reach the shore, but the current tugged irresistibly at his body. For five minutes more he held his friend, no longer able to swim, but floating with the river; then Woodman slipped silently from his grasp and sank beneath the surface.

Cushing was shaken by the immediate presence of death, and he was tiring very fast. His clothes now were like iron chains dragging him down, and little waves "splashed with a choking persistence" into his mouth and nose. But he would not give up; swimming mechanically now, his body and mind almost numb, his weary arms rose and fell. At last his feet touched soft mud, and the gentle touch roused him for one last effort. Delirious with the realization that he had not lost the battle he stood erect, but toppled forward after one step and lay, up to his knees in the water, face down on the muddy shore.

Other men saw the attack; John C. Howard, for example, who was in the *Shamrock*'s cutter. "I was sitting in a boat," he wrote, "only a few feet away, with nothing to do but look, and with a bright light from the shore to enable me to see clearly.

"The launch never went over the boom. At the first attack she did not have speed enough to either push the boom out of place or to ride over it. On the second trial the boat's bow struck the boom with such force that it was forced in the water and the boat overlapped it two or three feet. The launch's bow was thus suspended in the air, and her stern was well set in the water. Cushing finding his boat useless, promptly launched and exploded his torpedo. Almost at the same instant that the torpedo exploded, the ram fired her gun. The shot passed directly over the launch, and the air pressure was such as to force the launch, boom and all under water. Cushing, thinking that his boat was struck, threw off his overcoat and shouted: 'Every man save himself,' and jumped overboard at the same time. Three men followed him. Two of them were drowned, and the other reached the fleet three days after.

"The air pressure was so great that if it had been maintained a few seconds longer, the boat would have filled and gone to the bottom, but as it lasted only the tenth part of a second, no great amount of water came over the gunwales, and the boat came up to her bearings faster than she went down, and slid off from the logs uninjured, and the men in her were taken prisoners. The launch carried the Confederate flag the next morning and was used against us for months. Although she occasioned us much anxiety, she fortunately never did any harm. When the waters of North Carolina were cleared of the enemy the old boat fell into our hands and was sent to the Norfolk Navy Yard. [She was used for instruction at the Naval Academy for many years after the war.]

"It must be remembered that the troops and the artillery began firing into the bosom of the river immediately after the explosion of the torpedo. The balls pattered on the water like a shower of hail, consequently it was dangerous to venture out into the river, and the launch was safe from harm as she had the *Albemarle* for protector. We, in the *Shamrock's* cutter, however, pulled into the heaviest of the shower, and, strange to say, not a bullet or a shot struck us or the boat.

"Our capture of the pickets on the *Southfield* was quite easily accomplished. After the torpedo had been exploded, a battery of artillery and two companies of infantry, who were stationed on the shore, began firing indiscriminately, and at they knew not what. The pickets hearing the uproar, and thinking the town was being attacked and possibly captured, were paralyzed as to their patriotic ardor, upon our sudden appearance over their ship's side and surrendered without a protest. In fact, they were too terrified to offer any opposition. If they had preserved a particle of pluck, they could have murdered all of us, as we were not in a position to defend ourselves.

"The object in taking the *Shamrock*'s cutter on the expedition was to capture the pickets on the *Southfield*, on our way up, so they could not give the alarm, but we missed her on the way up and it was more by accident than design, we ran across her, on the way down, so we boarded her then and captured the pickets, thus performing the duty we were sent for, although not in the way it was intended to be done."

Captain A. F. Warley, of the *Albemarle*, was unstinting in his praise for the way the task was performed. He had heard, he said, that a steam launch had been seen in the river, and had taken extra precautions. "Yet on the night of the 27th of October Cushing's steam-launch ran alongside the schooner unobserved by the picket, without a sound or signal, and then steamed up to the *Albemarle*.

"It was about 3 A.M. The night was dark and slightly rainy, and the launch was close to us when we hailed and the alarm was given—so close that the gun could not be depressed enough to reach her; so the crew were sent in the shield with muskets, and kept up a heavy fire on the launch as she slowly forced her way over the chain of logs and ranged by us within a few feet. As she reached the bow of the *Albemarle* I heard a report as of an unshotted gun, and a piece of wood fell at my feet. Calling the carpenter, I told him a torpedo had been exploded, and ordered him to examine and report to me, saying nothing to any one else. He soon reported 'a hole in her bottom big enough to drive a wagon in.' By this time I heard voices from the launch: 'We surrender,' etc., etc., etc. I stopped our fire and sent out Mr. Long, who brought back all those who had been in the launch except the gallant captain and three of her crew, all of whom took to the water. Having seen to their safety, I turned my attention to the *Albemarle* and found her resting on the bottom in eight feet of water, her upper works above water.

"That is the way the *Albemarle* was destroyed, and a more gallant thing was not done during the war."

James R. Soley, naval historian and later Assistant Secretary of the Navy, had a word to say: "In considering the merits of Cushing's success with [the torpedo], it must be remembered that nothing short of the utmost care in preparation could keep its mechanism in working order; that in making ready to use it, it was necessary to keep the end of the spar elevated until the boat had surmounted the boom of logs, and to judge accurately the distance in order to stop the boat's headway at the right point; that the spar had then to be lowered with the same precision of judgment; that the detaching lanyard had then to be pulled firmly, but without a jerk; that, finally, the position of the torpedo under the knuckle of the ram had to be calculated to a nicety, and that by a very gentle strain on a line some twenty-five or thirty feet long the trigger-pin had to be withdrawn. When it is reflected that Cushing had attached to his person four separate lines, viz., the detaching lanyard, the trigger-line, and two lines to direct the movement of the boat, one of which was fastened to the wrist and the other to the ankle of the engineer; that he was also directing the adjustment of the spar by the halyard; that the management of all these lines, requiring as much exactness and delicacy of touch as a surgical operation, where a single error in their employment, even a pull too much or too little, would render the whole expedition abortive, was carried out directly in front of the muzzle of a 100-pounder rifle, under a fire of

musketry so hot that several bullets passed through his clothing, and carried out with perfect success, it is safe to say that
the naval history of the world affords no other example of
such marvelous coolness and professional skill as were shown
by Cushing in the destruction of the *Albemarle*." Soley differs
from Cushing's account in a few details, but it is impossible,
one feels, to miss his point.

How long Will Cushing lay on the muddy bank of the
Roanoke River "unable even to crawl on hands and knees,
nearly frozen, with my brain in a whirl, but with one thing
strong in me—the fixed determination to escape," he never
knew. When he awoke the eastern sky was light; within an
hour the rays of the sun were strong enough to warm him
and to give him back a portion of the strength which he had
lost. Looking about him, he discovered that he must have misjudged his position during the night, and was in fact on the
Plymouth side of the river, in a point of the swamp that
entered the outskirts of the town. The sun's light "showed
me the town swarming with soldiers and sailors, who moved
about excitedly, as if angry at some sudden shock. It was a
source of satisfaction to me to know that I had pulled the
wire that set all these figures moving, but as I had no desire
of being discovered my first object was to get into a dry fringe
of rushes that edged the swamp; but to do this required me to
pass over thirty or forty feet of open ground, right under the
eye of a sentinel who walked the parapet."

He lay on the bank, his feet out of the water now, his body
soaking up the heat of the sun, hoping that the sentry would
be relieved or perhaps sit down for a smoke. But he began to
realize that the camp was full of dogs, and knew that he could
lie exposed no longer. The sentry was walking up and down
with his musket relaxedly on his shoulder. Waiting until the
man turned for a moment, Cushing leaped to his feet and
started to dash across the open space. The sentry had completed only half his tour when he turned again, seeming to

have noticed a noise in the distance, and the Union officer had to drop to the ground and crouch there, between two paths through the swamp and almost entirely unshielded. When the sentry turned again Cushing flopped over onto his back and lay there, his face in the sun. The mud that covered his clothes and body blended with his surroundings and made him invisible to the sentry, who continued to walk his rounds, unaware that the very man for whom thousands were searching was almost at his feet.

Cushing lay waiting. His legs were so sore that he did not think it would be a good idea to make another dash across the open space. He began to feel desperate; there seemed no way to escape. "Soon a party of four men came down the path at my right, two of them being officers, and passed so close to me as almost to tread upon my arm. They were conversing upon the events of the previous night, and were wondering 'how it was done,' entirely unaware of the presence of one who could give them the information." They spoke some more, but were gone without the answer to the question that was beginning to torture him: had he sunk the *Albemarle*, after all? For there would be the same commotion in the camp if he had not.

He determined that he must remove himself from his precarious position, and decided that it would be safer to try to regain the swamp he had just left. He sunk his heels and elbows into the soft ground and inched his way slowly along, stopping absolutely still when the sentry was turned toward him. He was close enough to see the color of the man's eyes: they were brown, he remembered, and the soldier needed a shave. For an hour he crept slowly along the ten feet that separated him from the high rushes along the bank of the river, and then when he reached them safely, spent four hours more crawling and sliding through the dirty water and foul-smelling vegetation of the swamp. He finally discovered a clear place where he could rest upon solid ground. The cypress swamp was a network of thorns and briers that cut into his bare flesh like knives (he had thrown off his shoes when he dived into the river, and had no hat or gloves); frequently, when the soft mire would not bear his weight, he had been forced to throw his body upon it at length and haul himself along with his arms. For a delicious ten minutes he lay on the solid ground he had attained; then, having to force his bleeding hands and feet, which were nearly raw, into activity, he started forward again. But his difficulties had only begun. As soon as he raised his head he saw, ahead of him— he could not understand why they had not observed him—a working party of enemy soldiers engaged in sinking some schooners in the river to obstruct the channel. He slithered around and back into the edge of the swamp, where he found a corn furrow which he followed around the clearing, passing the soldiers only twenty yards in their rear, and gained a little patch of woods below. He lay quiet again, breathing hard. He glanced up at the sun. It must be about noon. His eyes closed and he jerked them open again. He must not sleep.

He was fully wakened by the crackling of twigs nearby, and before he had a chance to move a tall thin Negro with rheumy eyes, dressed in an old blue shirt and pair of pants, was upon him. The man stood still, surprised to see the muddy apparition in front of him, while Cushing got laboriously to his knees and crouched, ready to spring. The look in his eyes had frightened braver men, and the Negro trembled. "I'm a Union officer," Cushing said, slowly and distinctly, "and if you let out a sound Abraham Lincoln will come down here and skin you alive." The Negro by signs gave Cushing to believe that he would not open his mouth for forty thousand devils. The lieutenant relaxed, and sat back against the tree, reaching in his pocket for his billfold. From it he extracted twenty dollars in muddy, sodden greenbacks and some texts of Scripture ("two powerful arguments with an old darkey"), and handed them to the man. "Go into town and find out what happened to the *Albemarle*," he commanded. "The *Albemarle*?" "The big ship that was moored to the wharf.

And don't say a word about me being here." The Negro took the proffered money and nodded, and then stamped off through the underbrush. Cushing lay back against the tree. It was taking a chance, but he had to know.

The man was back within an hour, his eyes big with his news. "She is dead gone sunk, and they will hang you, massa, if they catch you," he breathed in admiration. "You didn't tell them I was here?" Cushing asked threateningly. The Negro wagged his head violently. The officer rose to his feet, exhilarated at his success. He patted the Negro on the back and started off down the stream. He was soon back in the swamp; it was now so thick that he could hardly see ten feet ahead, and could only tell his direction by using the sun as a guide. About two in the afternoon, as near as he could judge the time, he emerged upon the bank of one of the many deep, narrow streams that filter through the region. Right opposite was the only road in the vicinity. "It seemed providential, for, thirty yards above or below, I never should have seen the road, and might have struggled on until, worn out and starved, I should find a never-to-be-discovered grave. As it was, my fortune had led me to where a picket party of seven soldiers were posted, having a little flat-bottomed, square-ended skiff toggled to the root of a cypress-tree that squirmed like a snake in the inky water. Watching them until they went back a few yards to eat, I crept into the stream and swam over, keeping the big tree between myself and them, and making for the skiff. Gaining the bank, I quietly cast loose the boat and floated behind it some thirty yards around the first bend, where I got in and paddled away as only a man could whose liberty was at stake.

"Hour after hour I paddled, never ceasing for a moment, first on one side, then on the other, while sunshine passed into twilight and that was swallowed up in thick darkness only relieved by the few faint star rays that penetrated the heavy swamp curtain on either side. At last I reached the mouth of the Roanoke, and found the open sound before me. My frail boat could not have lived in the ordinary sea there, but it chanced to be very calm, leaving only a slight swell, which was, however, sufficient to influence my boat, so that I was forced to paddle all upon one side to keep her on the intended course.

"After steering by a star for perhaps two hours for where I thought the fleet might be, I at length discovered one of the vessels, and after a long time got within hail. My 'Ship ahoy!' was given with the last of my strength, and I fell powerless, with a splash, into the water in the bottom of my boat, and awaited results. I had paddled every minute for ten successive hours, and for four my body had been 'asleep,' with the exception of my arms and brain."

The gunboat was the *Valley City;* the only word it had received of Cushing's fate had been brought by the *Shamrock's* cutter, which had regained the fleet early in the morning. They had heard firing, they reported, and did not know whether the attack had been successful; they supposed that Lieutenant Cushing was dead. Therefore, when at 10:15 in the evening of the next day the officers of the *Valley City* heard a hail from a small boat they assumed that it must be a torpedo attack by the Confederates, in retaliation for the attack of the night before, and the ship's cable was slipped and general quarters sounded. When no attack developed an armed boat in charge of Acting Ensign Milton Webster was lowered and sent to investigate.

The boat approached Cushing's little skiff and discovered a man lying in the bottom half unconscious. Webster, who did not know him, took Cushing into his boat and brought him aboard the gunboat, swinging his body up the ladder as though it were a sack of meal, and laid it on the deck. Lieutenant Cushing opened his eyes. Acting Master J. A. J. Brooks, commanding officer of the *Valley City,* came closer. "My God, Cushing," he said, "is this you?"

Will Cushing smiled weakly. "It is I."

"Is it done?"

"It is done." He was carefully attended, given a little brandy and water, and afterward a crumb or two of bread. Within an hour he was on his way to the flagship to report to Commander Macomb. "As soon as it became known that I had returned, rockets were thrown up and all hands were called to cheer ship. . . ." Peal on peal of cheering rang out over the water as Cushing sat on the deck of the *Shamrock* watching the arching rockets as they flew over the gathered ships.

"In the morning," Cushing wrote, "I was well again in every way, with the exception of hands and feet, and had the pleasure of exchanging shots with the batteries that I had inspected the day before." . . . At 11:15 A.M. Commander Macomb got under way, and his fleet proceeded up the Roanoke River. Upon arrival of the fleet at the wreck of the *Southfield*, after exchanging shots with the lower batteries, Macomb discovered that the Confederates had effectually obstructed the channel by sinking schooners alongside the wreck, and the expedition was compelled to return. The next day an alternative route was found, through the Middle River; the fleet "threaded the channel, shelling Plymouth across the woods on the intervening neck of land on its way up, until it reached the head of the Middle River and passed into the Roanoke, where it lay all night. At 9:30 in the morning of the 31st . . . the line was formed, the *Commodore Hull* being placed in advance, as her ferry-boat construction allowed her to fire ahead. . . . Signal was made to 'Go ahead fast,' and soon after 11 the fleet was hotly engaged with the batteries on shore, which were supported by musketry from rifle-pits and houses. After a spirited action of an hour at short range . . . the *Shamrock* planted a shell in the enemy's magazine, which blew up, whereupon the Confederates hastily abandoned the works. In a short time Plymouth was again . . . in possession of the Union," along with the torn and beaten wreck of the *Albemarle*.

In the town's post office a letter was found by Union sailors from a certain "E.L.K.," probably an officer on the *Albemarle*.

"Esteemed Friend," it began: "I received your kind epistle of the 20th instant, finding me lingering under a severe attack of fever. I am now up and about again, nearly as well as ever. They are sending out expeditions every now and then. We captured a Yankee yawl boat. It is supposed we killed nearly all of her crew, consisting of about eight men. But the most awful thing of all (perhaps you will hear of it before this reaches you) is that a Yankee torpedo boat steamed up the river Thursday night, and about 3 o'clock Friday morning ran into the *Albemarle.* The torpedo burst and blew a great hole in her some 6 feet long, sinking her almost instantly. She is now lying at the bottom of the Roanoke River. The crew lost everything they had, bed clothing and everything. Some lost their hats and shoes, and some even came out in their shirts and drawers, barefooted. We are in an awful condition. I believe they are going to hold the place to the bitter end. Captain Warley says he intends to fight as long as there is a man left (this is all gas). I never did witness such an uproar before in my life. Troops were hurrying to and fro, expecting every moment to meet in battle dread."

Most of the men who had been in the launch with Cushing were captured. Ensign Gay, for example, dived into the water after Cushing. "I had not proceeded far from the boat," he wrote, "when I fell in with Acting Ensign William L. Howorth on a log, unable to proceed farther without assistance. Having a life preserver with me, I gave it to him and returned to the boat to procure another, not knowing how far I might have to swim, and at the same time I destroyed two boxes of ammunition and several carbines. I had not gone far the second time when I found myself chilled, and after a severe struggle I regained the circle of logs, where I found several of the crew, with a boat from the ram in charge of Lieutenant Roberts. We were all taken on shore and marched to the prison, where we remained until our gunboats made their approach up the river. We were then marched to Tarboro, N. C., a distance of sixty miles, [at] which place we arrived on the 2d of November, being very tired and feet badly swollen. On the 3d we were sent to Salisbury, where we arrived on the 5th. After marching about 2 miles we arrived at the stockade, where we were enclosed with some 10,000 prisoners. Here we suffered immensely for the want of shelter from the inclemency of the weather and also for provisions, as our fare was very poor, being one-half pint of meal per day, which was very inconvenient on account of having no cooking utensils. On the 13th we were sent to Danville, where [we] arrived on the 14th. Here we were placed in a brick building with about 500 army officers. This place we found to be more comfortable, as we were sheltered from the weather, but still not having a blanket or cover of any kind, which made it very severe for us. Our ration here was a piece of corn bread, 4 inches long, 2 wide, and 1½ thick; this consisted of our day's ration. On the 11th of December we were sent to Richmond, Va., and confined in Libby Prison. There we found the treatment much the same as at Danville. On the 21st of February, 1865, we were paroled, and arrived at Cox's landing the same afternoon and repaired on board the flag-of-truce steamer *New York,* where we received a bountiful supply [of] edibles."

Cushing was not there to see the fall of Plymouth. On October 30 the *Valley City* left the fleet and steamed northward to Hampton Roads, carrying him for a personal report of his success to Admiral Porter. The admiral had already heard the news, and had telegraphed to Washington, where the papers had it in their headlines. It was not known that Cushing was alive. In Washington his brother Howard waited anxiously until news came that Will was at Hampton Roads, and that he was safe and sound. Howard sent a telegram to his mother which was followed by one from Will himself on the 3rd of November. "Mrs. Cushing," it said: "Have destroyed the rebel ram *Albemarle.* Am all right. Thanks of Congress, promotion and fifty thousand (50,000) prize money. W. B. Cushing, U.S.N."

There were other messages to write and to read. There had been his own report to Admiral Porter, written in Albemarle Sound on October 30, as the *Valley City* steamed northward. "Sir: I have the honor to report that the rebel ironclad *Albemarle* is at the bottom of the Roanoke River." There was the letter from Commander Macomb to Admiral Porter: "From circumstances which have since occurred and which I will explain in a detailed report by the first opportunity, I am able to inform you that the ram was sunk." There was Porter's note to Gideon Welles: "Sir: I have the honor to inclose herewith copies of the reports of Commander Macomb, dated October 29, 1864, and of Lieutenant Cushing, dated October 30, 1864, of the destruction of the ram *Albemarle*, at Plymouth, North Carolina, on the night of October 27th ultimo, by the steam torpedo launch under command of Lieutenant Cushing."

Welles's answer made pleasant reading. "Navy Department," it said, "Nov. 9, 1864. Sir: Your report of October 30 has been received announcing the destruction of the rebel ironclad steamer *Albemarle*, on the night of the 27th ultimo, at Plymouth, N. C.

"When last summer the department selected you for this important and perilous undertaking, and sent you to Rear-Admiral Gregory at New York to make the necessary preparations, it left the details with you to perfect. To you and your brave comrades, therefore, belongs the exclusive credit which attaches to this daring achievement. The destruction of so formidable a vessel, which had resisted the continued attack of a number of our steamers, is an important event touching our future naval and military operations. The judgment as well as the daring courage displayed would do honor to any officer, and redounds to the credit of one of 21 years of age.

"On four previous occasions the department has had the

gratification of expressing its approbation of your conduct in the face of the enemy, and in each instance there was manifested by you the same heroic daring and innate love of perilous adventure—a mind determined to succeed, and not to be deterred by any apprehensions of defeat.

"The department has presented your name to the President for a vote of thanks, that you may be promoted one grade, and your comrades also receive recognition.

"It gives me pleasure to recall the assurance you gave me at the commencement of your active professional career that you would prove yourself worthy of the confidence reposed in you, and of the service to which you were appointed. I trust you may be preserved through further trials, and it is for yourself to determine whether, after entering upon so auspicious a career, you shall by careful study and self-discipline be prepared for a wider sphere of usefulness on the call of your country. Very respectfully, Gideon Welles, Secretary of the Navy."

The best of all was still to come: "December 8, 1864. Referred to the Committee on Naval Affairs and ordered to be printed.

"To the Senate and the House of Representatives: In conformity to the law of 16th July 1862, I most cordially recommend that Lieutenant William B. Cushing, U. S. N., receive a vote of thanks from Congress for his important, gallant, and perilous achievement in destroying the rebel ironclad steamer *Albemarle* on the night of the 27th October, 1864, at Plymouth, N. C.

"The destruction of so formidable a vessel, which had resisted the continued attacks of a number of our vessels on former occasions, is an important event touching our future naval and military operations, and would reflect honor on any officer, and redounds to the credit of this young officer, and the few brave comrades who assisted in this successful and daring undertaking.

"This recommendation is specially made in order to comply

with the requirements of the ninth section of the aforesaid act, which is in the following words, viz: 'That any line officer of the Navy or Marine Corps may be advanced one grade if upon recommendation of the President by name he receives the thanks of Congress for highly distinguished conduct in conflict with the enemy, or for extraordinary heroism in the line of his profession. Abraham Lincoln, Washington, December 5, 1864.'

Honors poured upon Will Cushing. Admiral Porter, in General Orders No. 34, read to the officers and crew assembled on the quarter-deck of every ship in the squadron, said that it gave him "pleasure to inform the officers and men of the squadron under my command that the rebel ram *Albemarle* . . . has been destroyed by Lieutenant William B. Cushing, who, in this hazardous enterprise, has displayed a heroic enterprise seldom equalled and never excelled. . . . To say nothing of the moral effect of this gallant affair, the loss of this vessel to the rebels cannot be estimated. It leaves open to us all the Albemarle Sound and tributaries, and gives us a number of vessels for employment elsewhere. . . . The gallant exploits of Lieutenant Cushing previous to this affair will form a bright page in the history of the war, but they have all been eclipsed by the destruction of the *Albemarle*. The spirit evinced by this officer is what I wish to see pervading this squadron. He has shown an absolute disregard of death or danger. . . ." Porter announced at the same time that he wanted twenty volunteers for especially hazardous duty, as he had in mind projects similar to Cushing's. So infectious was Will's example that seventy-seven officers and a hundred and forty-nine enlisted men responded, plus the entire complement of the *Tuscarora*. Cushing's old comrade, Lieutenant Lamson, offered to take a torpedo boat like his friend's and go in to destroy two Confederate steamers lurking near Wilmington.

Early in November Cushing started home. (He arrived in time to cast his first vote in a Presidential election, for Abraham Lincoln.) The news had spread quickly in Fredonia concerning his daring exploits and miraculous escape, but word preceded him that he was being stopped so frequently on his journey by grateful Northern citizens that it was not certain when he would arrive. A war meeting, one of a series, was in progress the evening he reached Fredonia. The Concert Hall was packed, and he entered alone and walked up the center aisle. As soon as he opened the door he was recognized, and a ripple of excitement passed over the assemblage, and by the time he had gone halfway up the aisle the entire audience had risen and cheer after cheer rang in the auditorium. The president of the meeting descended to meet him, and from every side the people crowded around him and carried him to the platform, where he made a brief speech. Then the cheers rang out again, and everyone crowded forward to shake his hand and embrace him. The meeting was adjourned in his honor.

He remained at home for a week, sleeping late in the mornings and spending the evenings making speeches at various gatherings. The practice the Lawrence Literary Society had given him was valuable now. The local Union (Republican) Club wrote him an open letter of praise. His selfless courage, they declared, reminded them "of the spirit that animated . . . Decatur and Perry."

In New York City on November 19 there was a meeting of the Union League Club. One of the members described the occasion: "According to our abominable national usage, somebody had to make a 'few remarks' . . . and John Jay was happy to make them and belabored this modest, boyish-looking young hero with ten minutes of eulogy. He blushed and looked uncomfortable, but made his inevitable reply, simply and briefly, and passed this ordeal as creditably as the other, which I dare say he found hardly . . . trying. He seems a most charming young fellow; handsome, intelligent, and dignified in his bearing, though very young (twenty-two) and looking much younger."

On November 20 he took part in the serenade to honor the Republican governor-elect, Reuben Fenton. After a number of speeches, both political and heroic, Cushing was introduced by the governor of Wisconsin. He "must have been almost stunned," reported the New York *Herald*, "by the thundering cheers which greeted him as he hesitatingly took the stand." His speech was simple; he accepted the applause, he said, as a "compliment intended for the United States Navy." The Union League of Philadelphia gave him an engraved letter "to transmit to you the accompanying Silver Medal as a mark of the RESPECT and a testimonial of the APPRECIATION of your GALLANTRY AND DISTINGUISHED SERVICES to our Country in the most perilous days of her history." His popularity was universal among the people of the North. There was a craze to get his portrait, and to meet the demand thousands of "cheap oval cuts and lithographic portraits" were turned out, and were hung in as many parlors, alongside pictures of President Lincoln, and Generals Grant, Sherman and Sheridan. His own account of the destruction of the ram was published in almost every newspaper, and long interpretations were written and published in periodicals. He was even given a nickname, and was known everywhere, and for years afterward in the navy, as "Albemarle" Cushing.

Congress passed the requested resolution of thanks on December 20, 1864, and Cushing was promoted to lieutenant commander as of October 27, 1864, the youngest of that rank in the navy. Yet in some respects the government was niggardly in its reward. The promotion which Cushing received advanced him approximately fifteen numbers in rank and fifteen months in date. Richmond Hobson, for gallantly failing to sink a collier across the escape channel of the Spanish fleet in the harbor of Santiago, was promoted four grades and thirteen years in date. Stephen Decatur, for the burning of the frigate *Philadelphia* in the war with the Tripolitanian pirates, was advanced two grades and ten years in date. It was later believed in the navy that Cushing had been inadequately rewarded; one officer wrote, remarking on the ungenerous system of promotion, "and even the wonderful Cushing, whose exploits were said to have spoiled romance, never complained of [his] meager recognition by an advance of one grade."

Even the matter of prize money was, at least at first, disappointing. The *Albemarle* was captured at Plymouth and raised by the Union navy, and bought from a Washington prize court for $79,944. Using this as a basis the Navy Department ordered prize money apportioned among the seamen and officers of the launch, as well as among several commanding officers who had not accompanied the expedition. The method was complicated. Ordinarily Cushing, as commanding officer of the launch, would have gotten a straight one-tenth share; however, it was decided to pay him on the basis partly of his salary as a lieutenant and partly on that of lieutenant commander. In 1865 he was, therefore, awarded a sum of just under eighteen thousand dollars. If it be thought that this was a handsome amount, it must be remembered that Admiral Porter, who risked nothing, received almost four thousand dollars; Ensign Howorth, one is glad to hear, received over eleven thousand. Cushing's disappointment (he had hoped for fifty thousand for himself alone) was alleviated when Congress reopened the question, and in 1873 it was determined that over two hundred thousand dollars' worth of property had fallen into the government's hands as a result of the sinking of the *Albemarle*. Further apportionment of prize money was voted, and as a result of this readjustment Cushing received an additional award of thirty-eight thousand dollars, bringing his share to fifty-six thousand dollars in all.

The first installment of the money reached Cushing in the spring of 1865, just before he was to leave on a new assignment. "I was visiting him at the Astor House," his sister wrote, "to see him off for the Pacific. He placed the check of six thousand dollars in my hands, saying: 'I intended to make it ten thousand dollars, but give this to little ma for me.' "

One more detail is worthy of record. When the great gun of the *Albemarle* fired into the launch, Cushing threw off his coat, removed his shoes, and leaped into the water. The coat was a frock coat, with the insignia of a lieutenant upon it, and was worn over his service jacket. When Cushing had disappeared in the dark waters of the river, Paymaster Frank Swan picked it up and threw it over his arm just before he surrendered (he had been painfully wounded in the leg—his first action was not an auspicious one). Knowing that it would be taken from him by his captors, he entrusted it to one of them, a Confederate naval lieutenant, for safekeeping. When the town of Plymouth was captured three days afterward, the Confederates left in such a hurry that the coat, along with a great deal of plunder and war matériel, was left behind, and was captured by the naval force. The recovery of the coat came to Commander Macomb's attention, and he had it forwarded to Cushing, who was in Washington, toward the end of December. It was in no condition to be worn again since the back was out of it and half of one sleeve was gone; it was torn and ripped by bullets in half a dozen other places. But underneath the collar, where his mother had sewn it in September, was Mary Colman's gold chain and pendant, unharmed by the vicissitudes the coat had undergone.

VIII

Fort Fisher

~~~~~~~~~~~~~~~~~~~~~~~~~~~~~~~~~~~~~

HERMAN MELVILLE was, as an American, deeply involved in the war; as an artist he was fascinated by it (as all artists were, and still are; it was, somehow, "the last war in which Providence seems to have been interested"), and he wrote a series of poems, later published as *Battle-Pieces*, about many battles and incidents of the conflict. Cushing's encounter with the *Albemarle* called forth one of his strangest productions. He called the poem "At the Cannon's Mouth," and it goes like this:

> Palely intent, he urged his keel
>   Full on the guns, and touched the spring;
> Himself involved in the bolt he drove
> Timed with the armed hull's shot that stove
> His shallop—die or do!
> Into the flood his life he threw,
>   Yet lives—unscathed—a breathing thing
> To marvel at.
>
>   He has his fame;
> But that mad dash at death, how name?
>
> Had Earth no charm to stay the Boy
> From the martyr-passion? Could he dare
> Disdain the Paradise of opening joy
> Which beckons the fresh heart every where?
> Life has more lures than any girl
>   For youth and strength; puts forth a share

Of beauty, hinting of yet rarer store;
And ever with unfathomable eyes,
   Which bafflingly entice,
Still strangely does Adonis draw.
And life once over, who shall tell the rest?
Life is, of all we know, God's best.
What imps these eagles then, that they
Fling disrespect on life by that proud way
In which they soar above our lower clay.

Pretense of wonderment and doubt unblest:
   In Cushing's eager spirit was shown
   A spirit which brave poets own—
That scorn of life which earns life's crown;
   Earns, but not always wins; but *he*—
   The star ascended in his nativity.

The war was memorable for its many, many examples of extraordinary personal heroism ("what imps these eagles then"), but the great majority of them were of the sort Alonzo Cushing exhibited at Gettysburg. We should never forget what he and the others did there, and what men like him did in fifty battles and five hundred charges, both attacking and defending, but usually it is possible to understand what they did, and to feel that if we were placed in similar circumstances, with the sun shining and with fifteen thousand men marching with us or against us, we would stay for the shock of meeting, and do our duty by whatever concept of it we might have. For it was in the last analysis chance alone which determined that Alonzo should be at the very center of the charge at Gettysburg, and once there, he had no choice except to remain, being the man he was. This does not detract from his action. The rebellion came, he stayed, he fired his guns as long as he had guns or ammunition, he was killed—and the rebellion never came that way again.

But Will Cushing had, after all, much too much time to think. He had several months to acquaint himself with the power and viciousness of the ram, and there is no reason to suppose that he did not learn as much about it as he could. The skin of the ram, for instance, was of iron, and four inches thick; his own would not stop a brier's thorn. The ram had two great guns which had wreaked havoc with a whole fleet of wooden vessels; he had one small wooden launch and one torpedo which he hoped he would not have to use, since he did not entirely trust it. He could not even really suppose that his visit would be a surprise (he must have been astounded when he passed the *Southfield*'s pickets unobserved). For one thing, the history of the war abounds in unsuccessful security measures. For another, he himself could hardly keep his own secrets. His attempts at security were thus usually halfhearted, and almost always failed. In the end Captain Warley of the *Albemarle* knew that Cushing was coming, and suspected a visit on the very night when he came. Yet he still came.

Why *did* Will Cushing do what he did? What sort of man was he? Was he a madman? It is not likely, for that would imply that in some way he was not aware of the dangers he faced, and no evidence supports that. Was he simply foolhardy? The word is unsatisfactory—it leaves the question where it was. Why was he foolhardy? It was certainly not from a lack of intelligence; Cushing had a better than average mind, and could use it when he wanted to. Was he too young to know what he was doing? This hypothesis is attractive, considering that he was not yet twenty-two when the *Albemarle* was destroyed; yet the majority of the officers of the war were young, and pictures taken of Cushing as early as the age of fourteen show that he was more than ordinarily mature, even for his time—by the time he was twenty-one he had the sagacity of a man of thirty-five. Was he ambitious? Certainly he hoped for fame, riches, promotion. Among other things, he remembered his promise to his mother to take care of her, and to repay her for the sacrifices she had made for her children. But there were easier ways to win fame and fortune. In any case, it seems not to have been felt in the navy that he was any more ambitious than he ought to have been. Finally, was he deficient in feeling? Did he enjoy some mysterious physical faculty which allowed his nerves to react in the presence of danger as if there were no danger at all? He *was* able to act with all circumspection on a moment's notice, and he *was* able to ignore the death that awaited any false step. But to say that he was in some way different from other men is no more illuminating than to say that he was "foolhardy," or, simply, "brave."

In fact there appears to be no easy answer to Melville's question. Perhaps, finally, we are left with nothing but this: Cushing was a hero. Was he intended for a hero from the very beginning? Would he have been nothing without the war, and did the war make him what he could be only in its terrible, fecund soil? If this was true then it might be expected that he would find it hard to live in peace. And that was exactly the case.

The war was of course not yet over in December of 1864. But there no longer seemed much hope for the South; it was only, it was almost universally felt, a matter of time. Sherman, having marched across Georgia in a month, arrived in front of Savannah on the 10th, and the city fell by Christmas. Thomas destroyed the remaining Confederate forces in the west of Nashville, on December 15 and 16. The Confederacy was surrounded now, and no one doubted that the noose would be drawn tighter and tighter with the approach of spring. There was still General Lee, waiting in Virginia; but Grant had twice as many men, and his army was growing, while Lee's was diminishing day by day. And Abraham Lincoln was President for four more years. As a strategist he may have had faults, but as a moral force, as a rallying point for all Northern patriotic ardor, he was essential.

It was important to take Fort Fisher, which defended the entrance to the Cape Fear River and thus the city of Wilmington, the last great Confederate port; Lee said he could not hold Richmond if he lost Wilmington. On December 2 Cushing was named commander of the *Malvern*, Admiral Porter's flagship for the combined operation now being planned against the fort. On December 13 the *Malvern* left Hampton Roads and reached Beaufort two days later, where Porter conferred with General Butler. Three days later the vessel, along with most of the mighty fleet off North Carolina, sailed south to the attack.

The operation was interrupted by a storm which scattered the vessels, driving the troop transports to the shelter of the land, and Porter determined on a naval attack. (He did not like the idea of having to co-operate with Butler; few men did.) A powder vessel had been prepared; the idea was to float it as close to the fort as possible and then blow it up, along with a good part of the fortifications. The *Louisiana* exploded with the loudest bang ever heard, before or since, in that vicinity, but with absolutely no effect on Fort Fisher. The noise bothered the sea gulls. More prosaic methods would have to be tried.

Fort Fisher was a noble work—its walls were twenty-five feet thick in spots—but it had its weaknesses. It was not well protected on the land side, for instance; it also lacked a sufficient supply of ammunition for a long siege (a common Confederate difficulty at the end of the war), and had only fourteen hundred or so troops, many of them boys and old men, to serve its powerful battery. It had one advantage, however: it was fully expecting just such an attack as was finally made. One of the surest guarantees, the Southerners felt, was the mere presence of Will Cushing. He was beginning to be a bogey with which to scare Confederate children. As an example of the power of Cushing's name, while awaiting the Union attack, early in December, the garrisons of the forts had little to do, and a Captain Chapman decided to liven the dullness. He was expecting several visitors to his position one night, among them Major Venable, Assistant Adjutant and Inspector General. While Venable and his party were making their way in the darkness a group of Confederate sailors under Chapman surrounded them, saying they were Union seamen under Cushing making a raid. Venable took to his heels and made it to Fort Fisher, where a full alarm was set off, and the long roll sounded to battle stations. The Confederate general failed to see any humor in the incident and protested in the strongest terms to the Confederate Navy. The most serious result of the hoax, he declared, was "the very excited state of feeling brought about in the garrison of Confederate Point."

An unsuccessful attack on Fort Fisher was made on Christmas Eve and the next day, on the assumption that the *Louisiana* and the consequent naval barrage had done some harm to the works, but it resulted in a shamefaced withdrawal and a name-calling contest between Butler and Porter that continued sporadically for years. A typical Cushing exploit occurred that day. The channel was inaccurately marked on Union maps, and about one o'clock in the afternoon Cushing set out with a few men in a small boat to take soundings directly under the guns of the fort. He wore every bit of gold braid to which he was entitled and his boat carried the blue and white pennant of a commanding officer. He sat coolly in the stern directing the leadsman's activities. The Confederates did not fire on him for ten minutes—a newspaper reporter wrote that he felt they were "paralyzed by this audacious piece of coast surveying." They came to themselves, however, and soon made up for lost time, filling the air with shells, one of which hit an accompanying boat and sank it, though the crew was picked up. Cushing's boat drew so close to the shore that "a biscuit might be tossed from the boat to the beach"; at this point Cushing ordered his men to stop rowing and "stood up in the stern of his frail craft and took a cool and deliberate survey of the fort." In all he remained under fire for six hours; shells splashed water into his boat so often that it had to be bailed out two or three times. He returned to the *Malvern* after sundown, annoyed, he said, that the rebels had wetted his uniform. The channel, incidentally, was found to be unusable for large ships.

After Christmas Porter relieved Cushing from the onerous (or so he felt) duty of commanding the flagship, and gave him back the *Monticello* to fight with. He chased several blockade runners and destroyed one, but he was unhappy that the *Chickamauga*, a Confederate warship, would not come out and fight. It was as strong as he was, he thought, possibly stronger, and he would have enjoyed crossing swords with it. The Confederates preferred to scuttle their vessel. It was not right, he thought. She might "better have finished her career in a gallant action on the ocean." Disappointed in this, he was happy to return to the fleet, which was planning a new attack on Fort Fisher.

Butler had been relieved, for a failure which was less than ordinarily his fault, by General Alfred Terry, and preparations proceeded apace. Again they were interrupted by a storm, but on January 13 about eight thousand assault troops were landed under cover of a devastating naval bombardment, which continued all night and the next day. The fort had been weakened by the previous bombardment and by sickness among the men, and General Braxton Bragg was staging a review north of Wilmington of most of the reserve troops, but it would still not be easy to take the place, and it was decided that an assault column of sailors from the fleet should assist the army. Cushing went ashore with forty men from the *Monticello* sometime after noon of January 15 and immediately looked up two of his closest friends, Lieutenants Benjamin H. Porter of New York and Samuel W. Preston of Illinois, schoolmates at Annapolis. Ben Porter was leading a detachment of sixty men from the *Malvern*, having succeeded Cushing in command of that vessel. Preston was in charge of the "pioneers," a group made up of ten men from each ship represented in the assault, who were to go forward with shovels and throw up an intrenchment for cover six hundred yards from the fort. Later in the day they pushed their breastworks within two hundred yards. This was to be the jumping-off point for the lead elements of the assaulting column. Preston had a reputation for courage—he had been in the complement of the *Louisiana*—but when Cushing and Porter found him he looked reflective, and his long features were unusually solemn.

"Cushing," he said, "I have a prophetic feeling that I am not coming out alive."

"Nonsense," said Porter, "you bet I am."

"Cheer up, Preston," Cushing said, "and let's drink to success and little Nell." Little Nell was Ellen Grosvenor, popular with all the Cushings and their friends, and later the wife of Milton Cushing. Cushing took a bottle of beer out of his pocket, which he opened and passed around, and they all drank the toast—"Success, and little Nell."

Cushing and his sailors from the *Monticello* were to be in the last of four assaulting waves, but this was not at all to his taste, and he wangled a spot up front with the detachment from the *Malvern* led by Porter, who was carrying the blue pennant of Admiral Porter. The sailors were all "dressed as if for inspection" and the officers wore all their gold braid, Cushing, whose promotion had just come through, sporting an extra gold stripe. The sailors had been at sea for weeks, and few of them, if any, had been drilled recently in the use of the cutlass, with which they were armed. Most of them had never been in an assault force, and they looked forward to this affair lightheartedly.

The sailors were to advance across the beach and assault the fort at the northeast salient, the point of the L of the fortifications. The army was to attack the western salient at the same time. The target of the sailors, unfortunately for them, was considered by the commandant of the fort, Colonel William Lamb, to be the "vital point of the work," and he had placed a disproportionately large part of the garrison to defend it.

At three o'clock every steam whistle in the fleet was blown

as a signal for the advance. The sailors stood up and started to run across the beach. The sand was soft, and their feet often sank in to the ankle as they attempted to run forward. In the brilliant sunlight glaring down on the beach the dark blue uniforms of the sailors were excellent targets.

Porter and Cushing were in the van as the column started forward, with Preston, acting as aide for Lieutenant Commander Breese, in command of the assault, not far away. The defenders quickly found the range with cannon as well as rifles. Many of the attackers faltered and fell but the column went on, and then, fifty yards from the palisade which surrounded the outer extremity of the works, halted and milled about for a moment in confusion. Porter leaped forward, seized the flag, and waved the men on. When he reached the palisade he fell, shot in the chest. Four seamen ran to his side and he cried to them to carry him down the beach. They lifted him, but two of them fell wounded. Porter stood up unsupported and waved the other two sailors away, and then fell dead on the sand. Cushing saw this, and remembering what Preston had said, turned to see if he was all right. As he watched Preston fell dead with a bullet through his head.

There was no time for grief, as the column must be kept moving. The sailors huddled in a confused group at the foot of the palisade, a perfect target for the defenders of the fort. Cushing looked around for a way through the palisade, found it, and started through, then dropped to the sand for cover. One of his men called to him that the sailors were retreating, and he looked around to find that he was alone. The whole Union line had broken and the men were streaming toward the rear. Cushing was in a safe place, out of the Confederate fire, but he decided that his first duty was to rally his men. He sprinted across the hundred yards that separated him from them, bullets whizzing around his head and puffing in the sand about his feet. He was not hit. It was impossible to rally the column so Cushing went back with them across the beach, covered now with dead and wounded sailors.

During the next few fours Cushing was almost everywhere on the field. A half-dozen different official reports, written by officers at different places on the beach, speak of his services. Many of the officers who had led the charge remained huddled under the cover of the palisade when the men fell back, so Cushing, as far as he could see, was the senior officer present. He organized help for the wounded, seeing that those who would be drowned by the incoming tide were moved in time. Late in the afternoon General Terry saw him gathering a group of unwounded sailors for a final assault on the fort, but the general sent an orderly to stop him from what would have been a suicidal operation. Terry had taken advantage of the sailors' attack and the Confederate efforts required to repulse it to get his own army column into the fort, and he wanted to reinforce it by calling up his reserves. To replace the reserves he ordered Cushing with his sailors to hold the line of entrenchments thrown up across the narrow peninsula to ensure that General Bragg would not attack from the rear. The sailors took over the earthworks, releasing a brigade and a colored regiment for duty within the fort, and remained in the trenches all night. Bragg did not come, and in the morning the men went back to their ships.

The naval attack was a failure except as a diversion for the army attack. In all nearly four hundred sailors and marines were killed, wounded or missing, almost a fifth of the force involved. Admiral Porter and Cushing blamed the marines for what had occurred. They insisted that the failure of the marine sharpshooters to clear the wall of Confederate gunners and riflemen made the failure certain. Others suggested that Porter had been asking for a repulse when he sent badly trained sailors armed with cutlasses and pistols against the strongest point of the fortifications. Colonel Lamb, the commander of the fort, was sure that the sailors could have gained the day if the fleet had helped them with artillery fire as strongly as they helped the army later. In any case, Fort Fisher had fallen, starting a chain of events which would lead, in a month, to the capture of Wilmington.

There was still much work to be done. Cushing spent the 16th dragging the shore line for mines, and the next day Porter sent him on a scouting expedition to Smithville, where he had the great pleasure of capturing Fort Caswell, which had caused him so much trouble the previous spring, with an officer and five men in a gig. The place was deserted, and he hoisted the Union flag over the works and over Forts Shaw, Campbell and Bald Head. He then revisited Smithville, and took the town with four men, accepting the surrender of the mayor (General Hébert was again not at home when he called) with "courtesy." At the end of the main street was a cloud of dust thrown up by the hoofs of the departing Confederate cavalry. Cushing sent a man for reinforcements and on January 19 had 150 men under him and was military governor of Smithville, where he remained for a week, living in the large white house with verandas into which he had broken eight months before.

One of the first things he did was to capture the pilots who had for so long guided the blockade runners over the bar. He threatened to hang them but relented when they promised to display the usual signals off Oak Island. On the second night two ships fell into the trap, sailed into the harbor and unsuspectingly anchored next to the *Malvern.* The British captain of the *Charlotte* and his five British passengers, one an army officer, sat down to a champagne supper to celebrate their safe arrival. Union forces boarded the ship and opened the door of the wardroom. The Britishers were amazed to see a lieutenant commander of the United States Navy standing in the candlelight at the head of the table. "Steward, another case of champagne," said the officer. "Gentlemen, we will drink to the success of those who succeed." "Beastly luck!" exclaimed one of the passengers, who had come over "on a lark." "An unmitigated sell!" added one of his companions.

On the 22nd Porter ordered Cushing to search for blockade runners along the southern coast of North Carolina, but the

Confederacy was running out of ships and Cushing, bored with several days of fruitless steaming up and down, determined on another of his patented small-boat expeditions, this time up the Little River. On the night of February 4 he rowed up the river eight miles to the small town of All Saints Parish, where he landed with four boatloads of men and soon captured the town; he rounded up the mayor and other officials and demanded a warm and hearty breakfast for the morning, adding that he was the vanguard of a large invading force. The inhabitants were quick to proclaim their desire to return to the allegiance of the United States, and claimed they were only "awaiting emencipation from military rule." Cushing spent the day in town, burned $15,000 worth of cotton, ate a lunch of chicken and sweet potatoes, and departed with two flatboats loaded to the gunwales with twenty-three bales of cotton and some Negroes who wished to escape to the North. The expedition regained the *Monticello* without difficulty. A couple of days later Cushing sent another expedition which destroyed a storehouse at Shallotte Inlet, thus depriving the Confederate forces still holding out below Wilmington of a goodly amount of corn and bacon.

On February 10 the *Monticello* was in the Cape Fear River, Cushing having reported to Admiral Porter and turned over to him the prisoners he had collected in a week (they required too many men to guard them). The Confederate resistance up the river was still stubborn, the principal work being Fort Anderson, and Cushing was ordered to scout the position. He took with him four boatloads of men; with him in the lead boat was Milton Cushing, now acting paymaster, as the result of three promotions for ability. Milton was not a fighting man, but he came along on this expedition because, Will said, it would "be a lark." The men rowed stealthily past the fort and discovered a series of obstructions which could be passed at high water. They penetrated almost to Wilmington and then returned, having to lift their boats over the piles opposite the fort, the water having gone down. They returned to the fleet in safety, and Milton drew a deep breath.

Will reported to Porter, and was sent again the next night (Milton did not go along this time). He took his boats under the fort's guns and examined the obstructions carefully. There were two or three rows of piles, he found, with sand and earth filled in between them. They were too strong to be rammed; they would have to be blown up. As they came in closer to the high wall of the earthwork they heard the sound of voices, and then a cheer floating out over the night air. "What do you suppose they have to cheer about?" Cushing asked a companion. The officer shook his head. Cushing stood up in the boat and started to skip across the piles, his carbine in his hand. He went up to one of the gun ports and looked in. A band was playing "Dixie," and a crowd was gathered around a platform. The band stopped, and an officer began an oration to the soldiers, urging them to a supreme effort in the defense of the city. Cushing raised his carbine and sent a shot zinging through the crowd, and followed it by an admonition to the crowd to go "to a place warmer than Dixie." The startled defenders let fly volleys of musketry and a hail of grape and canister. Cushing bent over and ran along the piles until he had regained his boats, which beat a quick and silent retreat to the Union fleet. The Confederates believed that Cushing's shot was the harbinger of a full-scale attack and began to fire steadily at the Federal troops on the other side of the fort. The firing woke the men up from a sound sleep, and they were much annoyed, though fortunately no one was hurt.

Porter's fleet had been dispersed to other stations and he had, he felt, an insufficient force to carry out the attack on Wilmington. Commander Cushing had a suggestion: build a mock monitor to convince the rebels that a strong force was opposed to them. Porter agreed; he had done the same on the Mississippi. "Old Bogey" was constructed with much ingenuity on a flatboat, with canvas and barrel staves employed to make it as much as possible like the genuine article.

It was not possible, Cushing claimed, to tell the difference at two hundred yards.

The "monitor" was ready on February 13, but the weather was bad, and it was not until nearly a week later that the hoax could be perpetrated. On February 18 Cushing and a picked crew towed the flatboat to a position about two hundred yards below the obstructions, and there turned it loose; the tide flowed at a rate of about five knots and supplied sufficient motive power. "Old Bogey" sailed grandly past the obstructions, absorbing in its canvas and barrel staves a heavy Confederate fire (they also launched half a dozen torpedoes, all of which missed), and finally grounded on the eastern bank out of sight of the lookouts. Even Commander Cushing could not have hoped for a more dramatic success. The Confederates, fearing that the Union forces were closing in, and sure that a monitor had gotten upstream of them, decided to abandon Fort Anderson that very night. They left behind them ten unspiked heavy guns and a great quantity of ammunition when they withdrew, and "swore like pirates" when they discovered the trick.

The Confederates had other batteries between Fort Anderson and the city, but the major hurdles had now been crossed, and though the defenders spent two or three days peppering "Old Bogey" with shellfire they left Wilmington, totally demoralized, on February 22. Cushing had been withdrawn for other duty by this date, after having confidentially told a New York *Tribune* reporter that the city's fall was imminent.

Bigger game was afoot. Toward the end of January the American consul at Nantes had reported to Washington the arrival off the island of Houat of a new Confederate ram, the *Stonewall*, only lately built at Bordeaux. The ram, the Navy Department feared, was to be used to break the blockade. Porter was apprized of the danger. He alerted his vessels and sent Commander Cushing, his anti-ram weapon, to Norfolk to have a torpedo attached to the *Monticello*. Cushing left his ship in the yard and proceeded to Washington with dispatches bearing the news of the fall of Fort Anderson. Gideon Welles was on his way for a conference with the President, and he asked the young officer if he would like to come along.

The two men—the slim naval officer and the old white-bearded Yankee politician—walked to the White House, where they found General Hooker and Secretary of State Seward already with the President. Seward was "imposing," Cushing felt; Hooker he had met before, at the review of troops in the summer of 1862. "The President was cheerful," Welles wrote in his diary, "and laughed heartily over Cushing's account of the dumb monitor which he sent past Fort Anderson, causing the rebels to evacuate without stopping even to spike their guns." Lincoln also took the opportunity to compliment the young commander in person on his new rank and on his successful encounter with the *Albemarle.* Cushing left exhilarated. He yearned for more opportunities to prove his loyal affection. But the *Stonewall* never came any closer than Cuba, and on February 24 Cushing was detached from the *Monticello* to await orders.

They did not come until the war was over. Having nothing to do in Washington, Cushing went to Boston and visited friends and relatives. On March 20 he was admitted to the third degree of free masonry in the Star of Bethlehem Lodge, at Chelsea. Within a week he was home. On April 3 came the wonderful news of the fall of Richmond, and a spontaneous gathering was held at the Concert Hall. With tears running down their faces the good people of Fredonia sang hymns and patriotic songs, and heard addresses by clergymen and almost everybody else who felt he had something to say. As the meeting was breaking up the Dunkirk band came fifing and drumming into town, spirits were revived, and a procession was formed which marched to the Cushing home. Will appeared in response to the serenade and was described as being "as modest as he is brave" by the Fredonia *Censor.* He made "a few well worded and patriotic remarks" and called, at the end of his speech, "for three cheers for the old flag." After responding with three hearty whoops, the band and citizens adjourned for a late supper at Fredonia's leading hostelry, the Johnson House. Cushing, his mother and his sister joined them in the march to the hotel, where they were placed at the head table and had their healths drunk. Even Mrs. Cushing enjoyed it. Cushing had brought with him a Confederate flag, taken when he seized the abandoned Fort Caswell in January, and the "assembled company marched over it in token of their eternal hatred and detestation of traitors and their insignia." This took half the night, since there was a large number of patriots present, and it seemed hardly worth while to go to bed, so the celebration continued till dawn, when the American flag was raised over the courthouse, under it Will's captured flag flying, ignominiously, upside down.

A week later Lee surrendered his army. There was more time to plan festivities, as the word was received early in the morning, and the town let out every stop. A great celebration took place in Concert Hall, again a band was present, and the mayor, Oliver Stiles, presided. Cushing's flag hung under the Union banner at the end of the hall. The crowded schedule of events called for numerous speeches by clergymen, a concert by the band, and the firing of salutes of a twelve-pound cannon. Time was found for "an elegant tribute" to Fredonia's leading hero, and all of Will's deeds were retold. Cushing's speech in response was the event of the evening, and there were drinking and carousing until the sun was up. The hero himself spent the hours of the night walking alone on the road to and from the Arkwright Hills. The first celebration had been greatly exciting, but this one had not pleased him. He thought instead of Alonzo, lying quietly at West Point, and of Charles Flusser and Ben Porter and Sam Preston; and of the enemy soldiers who had fought him, and whom he had defeated, but whom he now found that he in some way loved. He remembered with the beginnings of revulsion the citizens of Fredonia marching up and down on his flag. He would never say anything about it, of course— he had walked on it himself—but it had not been the right thing to do.

IX

"Albemarle" Cushing

~~~~~~

"FAREWELL! Othello's occupation's gone!" said another soldier in another time and country, but the words were apt for Will Cushing in the weeks and months and years after Appomattox; the day after, in fact, when Fredonia returned to normal and seemed, by noon, to have forgotten the war, to have put away its memories and to be readying itself for the lesser conflicts of peace. His mother, he could see, was happier than she had been in years, to have him home and safe. Howard was safe too. His Battery A, 4th Artillery had fought in several small battles while attached to Sheridan's cavalry in Grant's offensive in the spring of '64; in May, at Yellow Tavern, J. E. B. Stuart had been slain in front of Howard's section of the battery, though not necessarily by his guns. As a result of the fighting the battery, for a second time, suffered so many casualties that it had to be sent to Washington to recuperate. A few months later, when Early made his raid against Washington, Howard and his guns were under fire, though no large battle resulted. He spent most of the remainder of the war guarding prisoners at Elmira, New York, where his firmness and courage in emergencies stopped more than one dangerous revolt from developing. Milton was home in May, looking older, Will thought, very much the mature man, and about to be married to Ellen Grosvenor. It was good that his mother was happy, of course, but it made it hard that he could never say to her that at the age of twenty-two his occupation was gone and that he had loved the war that had made her weep. He could not say it, either, to the Fredonians, who were already forgetting their indignation at the murder of Lincoln in their excitement that oil might have been discovered under the town—a spring which flowed through C. H. Van Wye's cellar was found to have an oily film on it, and an expert declared it to be petroleum. The *Censor* crowed that "a fountain of wealth exists beneath our feet." It was not, however, oil in sufficient quantity to make anyone a fortune. Cushing, unable to join in these festivities, spent the time sitting for his portrait, which, when it was done, the *Censor* reported to be an accurate likeness. "The design is a fine one, the expression of the countenance is spirited, and fully indicative of the earnestness and daring purpose so conspicuous in the original, while the cloudy background, formed as it were of the dun and sulphurous clouds of battle, or of smoke from a burning ship, adds materially to the effect." *Pictura poesis est.*

But it was not enough, this sitting still for art, when his blood still raced in his veins. There had never been a doubt in his mind that he would stay in the navy, and now he besieged the department with requests for new commands. They were not easy to come by. A note in the *Censor* for May 10 sent chills down his spine: "The recent orders for the reduction of expenses in the Navy Department have already effected a saving of $35,000 daily in the ocean and coast service." He wrote a letter to Welles saying that he would command a scow if it was necessary, but did not need to send it, for orders came in the middle of the month. They were not all that they might have been (they ordered him to duty at the New York Navy Yard) but they were better than nothing.

Within a month, after continuing requests, he was ordered to the Far East. He had hardly had time to say good-by when there was a change: he was made executive officer of the *Lancaster,* and would proceed with her to the Pacific station, which meant the West Coast. The duty was not arduous (though it was at first hard to serve under another man) and it was at least upon the sea. Many of his friends were having even more difficulty than he in finding berths for themselves in the regular navy. In March of 1866 Cushing had a day of glory when his vessel docked at San Francisco, where the story of his deeds had penetrated. The Board of Supervisors voted him the "freedom of the city," and he was given a welcome of appropriate proportions. Will bore his honors modestly, an observer said. He found time to call upon W. H. Parker, the same old Academy professor who had admired Cushing's report of the loss of the *Ellis*—he had resigned his commission to join the Confederate service, and had helped to set up the Confederate Naval Academy. Cushing felt no animus; if there had been no rebellion there would have been no *Albemarle*.

A year later he was in Norfolk, awaiting orders once more. He was informed that the battered hulk of the ram was moored in the harbor, and he lost no time in going to see his old adversary. She was useless, he found, for naval purposes; the torpedo had torn a great hole in her hull and the months under water had damaged her beyond repair. She was moored in a quiet spot in the harbor, "stripped," he wrote sadly, "of her iron and machinery, and . . . left to rot down. *Sic transit gloria mundi.*" It was no cause for rejoicing, he felt. He could almost wish her as she once had been.

He was home in the spring, and almost lost his life in Dunkirk Bay. Two young cousins were visiting from Boston, and he had a mind to impress them; he suggested one windy day that they all go for a sail on the lake. He was warned that the lake was treacherous in such weather, but he brushed the fainthearted citizens aside and trooped with his little party down to the dock, where a small open boat was moored. "I have not gone through all the ocean peril I have to be drowned in a mill pond," he said. The boat set out into the icy waters and for a time all went well, but just as the onlookers were about to turn away, shaking their heads, a shout went up as the little craft capsized. A rescue party was quickly organized and made its way through the floating chunks of ice to where the young people were clinging to their overturned boat. They spent the rest of the day by an open fire; the girls were not affected, but Cushing had a severe attack of pain in his hip. He had begun to have attacks only a few months after the sinking of the *Albemarle*, but this was the worst he had known, and it lasted for nearly two days. He told no one of it except his mother, who for once was not especially worried. She laid it to his ill-advised swim in Lake Erie in April, and thought no more of it.

He spent some of his leave sitting for a bust by a local sculptor, Rufus W. Lester, of which copies were made and widely distributed; Henry Wadsworth Longfellow saw one and wrote that Cushing's face had "a beauty resembling Schiller's." Whether or not this was an advantage, Katherine Louise Forbes was satisfied. Kate had become a close friend of Will's sister, Isabel, and was much in evidence during the month of May which was devoted, in the Cushing home, to preparations for Isabel's wedding. Kate's father, David S. Forbes, was a prominent Fredonian who had risen to the rank of brigadier general in the war, and had taken part in the victory celebrations with the young hero. Kate was tall and slim and held herself proudly "like a soldier," and if she was not extremely pretty she had a sparkle in her eye which Will found attractive. And she seemed to be over-whelmed by his fame, and would sit for hours, starry-eyed, while he told her of his adventures. And since she was there, and they were much together, and since he had decided, after all, to get married, and since marriage is almost an epidemic affair, he found, by the 11th of June, when Isabel became Mrs. E. F. Gayle, of Salem, Massachusetts, that he was quite in love with Katherine Forbes, and she, to his delight, with him. Toward the end of June he received new orders, and before he left, on the first day of July, he had asked Kate Forbes to marry him, and had received her consent.

They could not marry for a while. He spent the summer being shunted from one embarkation point to another, was twice reassigned, and finally, in October, received final orders to take the *Maumee* for an extended cruise to the Far East. He had a week at home, but it was best, the lovers agreed, to wait until he returned, though it would be at the least two years.

"I intend to see," he had written his cousin seven years before, "every nook and corner of this little world that is to be seen, if I live"; the *Maumee* would do as a magic carpet. The ship left Fortress Monroe on November 11 and steamed out into the Atlantic ("one of God's grand highways for all mankind," Cushing wrote in the first of a series of "travel letters" to the Fredonia *Censor*), and reached Rio de Janeiro on the day after Christmas, after forty-five days without seeing land. It was terribly hot, which seems to have surprised him, and he did not climb Sugar Loaf, but admired it from afar; it being his custom always to drive too fast, he was "fetched up and fined half a dozen times in going as many miles, for breaking the city ordinances about driving." He was impressed with the fact that "here, as everywhere, Yankee enterprise is cropping out. . . . There are American Cafes, where you get American refreshments, and drinks done up in American style. American hotels and stores abound—agents for American agricultural implements, machinery, arms, etc. On the walls you find American advertisements, such as Drake's Plantation Bitters; [and] Wheeler and Wilson's Sewing Machines. In one place I saw chalked up . . . 'Try Dr. Gifford's Soda-water you will like it!' "

Cushing was as hot-blooded as ever, and he got into difficulties in Rio which he did not mention in his letter to the *Censor*. His cousin Albert S. Barker, later an admiral, described them: "As the [South Atlantic] squadron was about to get under way for St. Catherine and Montevideo, who should arrive but Lieutenant Commander Cushing, commanding the *Maumee*, on his way to the Asiatic station. I had only a few moments to see him before we were off. Cushing was high-spirited, keenly alive to the respect due an American officer, as representing his country. In going ashore in mufti he was annoyed by a Brazilian officer in full uniform who took Cushing for a civilian. On finding that Cushing was an officer in command of an American man-of-war in port, the officer quickly apologized.

"When Captain Melancthon Wooley, the senior U. S. Naval officer of the Station, heard of the affair—for of course an incident like that soon was known to the fleet—he sent Lieutenant Commander Seely to find Cushing, to tell him to go to sea as soon as possible, adding: 'If that young man stays here, he will bring on an international war!'

"There were other incidents somewhat similar in character, which occurred at Cape Town and at Hong Kong during the same cruise, in which cases, Cushing received written apologies, for no one who knew him dared insult him."

Cushing was undoubtedly quick to see an insult, and "his reputation was so formidable that he was usually able to get a written apology," but Captain Wooley's low opinion probably went back to the affair of the English ship *Hound*, in the spring of 1864.

The *Maumee* left Rio on January 9, 1868, and went down the harbor at full steam. She steamed a thousand miles south to meet the trade winds and then turned east for Africa. An albatross was caught, pulled in with hook and line, and hauled on board. Cushing had a copper plate engraved with the name of the ship, and the latitude and longitude and date of capture, and fastened it around the bird's neck and set it free. "I presume," he wrote, "he is the envy of all the albatross in the south Atlantic by this time."

The shore of Africa was sighted on the 30th of the month, one of the quickest passages on record. "Africa is quite a tract of land," he wrote, with perhaps too heavy a humorous hand; "I could not see all of it on account of a large tree that stood directly in the way, but from the view I got I should judge it to contain 60 or 70 acres more than North America. The native African is very dark complexioned, and not very delicately perfumed, especially in hot weather. They are not at all extravagant in dress, a red handkerchief or half yard of sheeting constitutes the wardrobe of most of them. Their principal accomplishments are throwing the boomerang and eating missionaries. A well brought up African will eat his brother with the greatest nonchalance, and consider a Christian done up in a pot pie a great luxury. They do not pride themselves much on the arts, sciences or literature (which is easily accounted for from the fact of their never having seen or read the Fredonia *Censor*)." He stayed in Cape Town for nearly three weeks, and much admired Table Mountain. "It is said to be a very sightly place when you get up there, you have a bird's eye view of the world. Fredonia looks wonderfully small at that distance, and the Normal School building appears no larger than a pin's head." The letters stop with the departure from Cape Town; from there the *Maumee* sailed for Batavia, on the Island of Java, a distance of six thousand miles, which required more than two months; from Batavia to Singapore was a short hop, and thence to Hong Kong, headquarters of the Asiatic Squadron; the ship reached Hong Kong on the first of May. Cushing's arrival was a great event; many of the junior officers in the navy had heard stories of "Albemarle" Cushing, but had never had the occasion to see him before. The commanding admiral, Stephen Clegg Rowan, who had turned down the proffered chance at the ironclad as being too risky, was nevertheless generously an admirer of the man who had destroyed the *Albemarle*; the *Maumee* was the fastest vessel in Rowan's squadron, and partly because of this and partly because he liked the idea of having such an intrepid young officer near him, the admiral designated the ship as his tender. The result was that Cushing saw even more of the world than he might have, since it was necessary for the admiral to visit a number of ports along the Chinese coast that a mere lieutenant commander probably never would have seen.

Cushing's duties included, to his surprise and delight, ridding the waters of pirates, who were a great annoyance to the merchantmen, and whose depredations were sometimes so severe as to cause a marked diminution of the trade between China and Indo-China. Cushing set off in June for the island of Hainan, which was pirate quarters, with a mandarin and his retinue of servants on board. He found no pirates (the only suspicious junk turned out to be a merchantman which fled in the belief that the *Maumee* itself was a pirate), but the mere presence of a United States warship seems to have reduced their activities, at least for a time.

Though he discovered no pirates on this voyage, such was not always the case. "Fighting Bob" Evans, later a hero of the Spanish-American War, recalled, in his autobiography, some of Cushing's encounters with the pirates of the China Sea. "Cushing went after the pirates, and in a few days they began to arrive at Hong Kong by the dozen. He found, as we all suspected he would, that every Chinese junk was a pirate when it suited the owner to be so. The war junks were the worst of the lot. So Cushing ran in everything that he came across and only stopped when the authorities asked that he be recalled, as he was capturing the entire Chinese merchant fleet."

The *Maumee* spent the summer steaming about in the China Sea, and in November visited the then newly opened empire of Japan. The weather was foggy and cold, but Cushing was pleased to find that many landmarks had received American names from Commodore Perry: there were Susquehanna Bay, Perry Island, Webster Island, Cape Saratoga; "on this side of Yokohama Mississippi Bay stretches to the end of Treaty Point." The fact that the names were not used by the Japanese themselves appears to have been ignored by Cushing, who was not happy when he was out of earshot of the English language. Two other things about Japan were impressive: while the *Maumee* lay at anchor in Edo Bay, the former Confederate raider *Stonewall*, which had been taken over by the United States government at the end of the war and sold to the

Japanese in August, 1867, sent a boat asking for various supplies. Cushing remembered his tentative plans for destroying the vessel, and with the generosity of the victor gave whatever was required. He was also extremely happy to discover that his reputation had reached even to the coastal cities of Japan; curious visitants were to be expected at every port, and he always received them with the utmost civility. It was a considerable satisfaction to reflect that "Albemarle" Cushing was thus known at the antipodes.

It was not long, however, before the exoticism of the Other Side of the World began to seem pale beside the memory of Kate Forbes and Fredonia, and Will started to write fervent letters home after Christmas of 1868; he hoped and expected, he said, to return toward the end of the summer. But the *Maumee* continued to ply the waters of the far eastern Pacific until November, 1869, when Cushing was finally detached, along with his crew, from the vessel. As part of the navy's economy measures, the ship, instead of being brought home at great expense, was sold in Hong Kong, and Cushing traveled to Norfolk on another ship, his cabin piled high with curios and souvenirs; he spent the time writing his memoirs of his career in the Civil War. The writing of memoirs is not usually the task of a man of twenty-seven, but Cushing had always been precocious; indeed, he felt no longer a young man. He was to be married, he would have a family and responsibilities; and the pains in his back and hip were severe, though they seemed to come less often—he was beginning to be conscious of pain and, for the first time, of mortality. It was a new and unwelcome feeling. No doubt, though, a doctor could take care of it when he was back in the States.

The wedding of William Barker Cushing and Katherine Forbes took place on February 22, 1870. It was probably, at least according to the valiant *Censor*, the most elaborate marital ceremony which had ever been held in that part of the country. Fredonia Trinity Church was packed with friends, relatives, and curious strangers who were drawn by the groom's celebrity. The bride wore a gown of "elegant and costly Japanese crape trimmed with point lace," and Lieutenant Commander Cushing wore all his gold braid and all his medals. The Reverend Arey performed the ceremony and received the largest fee in Fredonia's history, though the amount, unfortunately, is not specified. The reception was "pleasant and brilliant," and healths could be drunk in rum that was purported to have been taken from the cellar of Miles Standish, and, for very special guests, from a bottle said to have been found in the recently opened (it was "discovered" in 1869) grave of the Cardiff Giant, and thus over four hundred years old. The Cardiff Giant was a hoax, but the liquor was certainly genuine; if not quite so ancient, it did very well for a wedding party. The groom, who was no longer required by circumstances to get up in the morning to herd Elder Kingsbury's cow before school, gave his bride a "magnificent set of fur—valued at $3000, a jeweled watch case, a sapphire ring and an emerald cross." Mrs. Mary Cushing, besides a number of practical gifts (she was a practical woman), gave the newly married couple a gift which brought tears to her son's eyes. It was a cleverly fashioned little glass cannon, complete with limber and paraphernalia for loading; inside it was a musket ball taken from Cushing's pocket after the sinking of the *Albemarle*.

The admiration for Will Cushing was not shared by everyone. There was a certain Bishop, editor of the Jamestown *Journal*; in the issue of March 11, while Cushing and his bride were honeymooning in the East, the *Journal* printed a vituperative editorial: "The Fredonia papers contain full accounts of the marriage of Lieut. Com. W. B. Cushing, U.S.N. and Miss Kate Forbes of Fredonia on the 22nd ult. The papers could be in better business than such toadying. Cushing is the most ineffable, idiotic young snob that ever trod leather. He could have secured on ten minutes notice a free ride out of F. from a delegation of his former friends and school-mates whom he has snubbed. For a little upstart like him, who by an act of insubordination in the navy blundered into notoriety, to pompously order older and better men than himself to address him as 'Lt. Com. Cushing, Sir,' is disgusting, and papers [who] toady such an egotistical ass belittle themselves beyond degree. Flunkeyism is born in a servile soul, and will show itself." To be sure that Cushing would see this attack (and perhaps to add somewhat to his circulation) Bishop sent copies of this paper to officers in the Navy Department and to prominent Fredonians.

Will had lost none of his ability, and perhaps even eagerness, to see red capes when they were waved in front of his face, and when a copy of the editorial reached him it was all that Kate could do to keep him from packing and proceeding immediately to battle. The wedded couple were back in Fredonia in April, however, and on the 21st Cushing, along with "Colonel" Forbes, his father-in-law, paid a visit to Jamestown. They strode into the office of the *Journal* about four in the afternoon, and Forbes stepped forward and graciously introduced his son-in-law to the editor. Without further ado, Will drew a rawhide whip from beneath his cloak and proceeded to lay it about the head and shoulders of the offending Bishop, who called loudly for help. Six or seven office hands came running and succeeded in getting the irate officer down the stairs; Colonel Forbes was laughing so hard that he could not take part in the encounter. Cushing was forced out into the street, and returned with his father-in-law to the Jamestown House, where they had supper, which was interrupted by the appearance of an officer who served them with warrants.

The populace of Jamestown, much surprised to find themselves living on a battlefield, took sides; most of them favored Cushing, and a goodly number of citizens and the local band marched to the hotel and serenaded their hero. In response to this demonstration Cushing made a speech, thanking the assemblage for its support, and then returned to his supper. Bishop did not push the legal action; as long as he kept the affair out of court he could go on printing his own version of the encounter (he had "whaled the tar out of the upstart and knocked out two of his front teeth," he reported). He wrote a long article about the *Albemarle* the next day, repeating his claim that it had been an act of insubordination on Cushing's part, and adding that the vessel was nothing but an "old oyster-boat." It was not likely, either, that he would have found twelve men disposed to agree with his side of the question. He had often advocated in editorials the settling of disputes by dueling pistols, but he was aware that Cushing had a pair shined and ready for use, and he was not heard to suggest such a method of adjudication in this case.

In the spring of 1870 Cushing was ordered to the Boston Navy Yard for ordnance duty. "I am enjoying my quiet married life very much," he wrote a cousin, Elliot Pillsbury, "and am completely domesticated. My bachelor habits have gone to the winds—a great saving of dollars and an improvement in health." He "made many social calls with his wife," wrote a navy biographer, "and brought some present home at every opportunity." He kept her "supplied with more hats and finery than she wanted," and insisted that she always have "a silk gown of a certain shade of blue," the same as the one she had worn in 1867, when he had seen her for the first time. While she was busy at domestic tasks he would read to her from "Thackeray, Dickens, Tennyson, and other classics and poesy." He kept a model of the torpedo which had sunk the *Albemarle* in the front parlor (it had been made and presented to him by the navy in 1865); it was mounted and inscribed, and he would show curious visitors "how the torpedo that did the work was fastened to the spar, worked by a hinge and a pulley," and explain how "an iron ball two inches in diameter inside of the tube at the base was held in its place by a trigger arrangement, attached to a lanyard held in his hand"; he invariably finished the story with a demonstration of the way he had pulled the cord, releasing the ball to fall upon the percussion cap. His eyes would gleam with memories, and his fingers would tremble with the old excitement, and he would usher the guest out proudly, limping a little as he crossed the floor.

During the next winter the Cushings spent their leave in Washington; they "had a very gay time amidst balls, parties and receptions." There was a pleasant visit with Milton, married now (they had not seen each other for five years), and Will was not displeased to find that his oldest brother could beat him at billiards. In Boston Will wrote that "the armory is turned into a ball room every Tuesday, and quite filled with the yard and city belles and beaux. The floors are waxed and the Marine Band furnishes the music." In the spring he took a house in Medford; Kate was expecting, and the previous summer had been unpleasantly hot. On the first of May the family moved to the new house. Cushing's mother had come to Boston, and was to spend several months visiting among relatives; he was happier than he had ever been, he thought; he had never known how delightful it could be to live at peace. The leaves were green, the weather had been perfect, and in the evenings he worked in the little garden behind the rented house. It was the first time he had ever had any ground of his own, and the first fruits of his efforts were wonderfully soothing. Besides this, he had not suffered the sciatic pain (a doctor in Washington said it was sciatica, at least, and had seemed to have a successful treatment) for a longer time than he had enjoyed in years.

"I was sitting at my desk one day," wrote Stanton B. Loring, a Cushing cousin and one of the bankers in the family, "when Will came into the bank and walked up to my window. As I glanced at him, I saw his face working with emotion, and his eyes filled with tears. He could scarcely command himself to speak, but he dimly muttered: 'Howard is killed.' His grief was such that I could not talk to him in the public office, and I took him into a private room, where he remained with me an hour before he was sufficiently composed to go to his home. His first thought was of vengeance, and he insisted that he should apply for leave of absence, so that he might go out to Arizona, and fight the Indians, but after we had talked a while he took a more rational view. I have been in the presence of grief many times during my life, but never have I witnessed anything like the emotion shown by this strong man. In that hour that I spent with him I got an entirely new insight into his character, and with all his impetuous bravery, I found him possessed of the tender heart of a little child."

We have had little to say of Howard Cushing; perhaps it is enough to remember only his last name. He himself was not unaware that he had two younger brothers whose deeds were known throughout the North. Certainly it was not through lack of courage that he had not gained for himself an equal name; rather, as the family itself felt (its standards were high, of course), he had been unluckily placed, and had been engaged in only half a dozen battles. He had determined to remain in the army after the war; he hoped still, it seems, to do some memorable deed, for he applied several times to be transferred to the cavalry, and was finally successful in this, being appointed second lieutenant of Troop F of the 3rd cavalry on September 7, 1867; he was promoted to first lieutenant three months later. The 3rd was sent to Texas and later Arizona, then a border territory with an Indian problem, and Howard seems to have acted practically as commanding officer of his regiment: what the troop did was credited to him, and what he did was the pride and boast of the troop. One of his junior officers, who later became a captain and who wrote a book about his experiences, *On the Border with Crook*, told one of Will Cushing's biographers that Howard was the bravest man he ever saw. "I mean just that," he repeated; "the bravest man I ever saw." "Of the distinguished services rendered to Arizona by Lieutenant Howard B. Cushing," he wrote, "a book might well be written. It is not intended to disparage anybody when I say that he performed herculean and more notable work, perhaps, than had been performed by any other officer of corresponding rank either before or since. Southern Arizona owed much to the gallant officers who wore out strength and freely risked life and limb in her defence . . . but if there were any choice among them I am sure that the verdict, if left to those officers themselves, would be in favor of Cushing."

Howard's first service was in western Texas, which he made safe for incoming settlers in 1869. The next spring, after a cruel attack by the Indians on a party of thirty men and women on their way to work at a private ranch, he was selected to head an expedition for the punishment of these murderers, which he effected after several weeks' patient stalking of their trail. Returning to Camp Grant, the troop set out on a series of fruitless expeditions, and toward the end of the summer moved their headquarters fifty-five miles west to Tucson, the new capital of Arizona and, at the time, "one of the dirtiest of little Spanish-American towns." The camp was on the eastern border of the village, and the Apaches were in the habit of coming up close to it to steal and drive away livestock. Even after the arrival of Cushing's troop, the Indians continued to harass the neighborhood, seriously wounding one of his men, and simultaneously attacking wagon trains and widely separated settlements, to confuse the calculations of the United States officers. As a crowning exploit they carried away a herd of cattle from Tucson itself, and followed that by killing a stage-mail driver and massacring a party of Mexicans on their way to Sonora.

The Apache chief was Cochise, predecessor of Geronimo, and Howard Cushing spent the summer and fall in expedition after expedition, trying to catch and capture this savage foe. With the coming of winter, Cochise came into Tucson under a flag of truce, and claimed that he wanted peace and a resting place on the reservation. He had been fighting the white invaders for fourteen years, Cushing said, and this was his best trick yet; but his protests that Cochise was simply looking for a place to spend the winter and that he would return to his depredations in the spring were overruled. In April Cochise was again on the warpath with Cushing close behind him.

On May 5, 1871, the lieutenant was at the head of a recon-
noitering party of twenty-two men at Bear Springs, in the
Whetstone Mountains, about fifty miles southeast of Tucson.
He was riding with two or three others at the head of the
column when his sergeant saw movements of some Apaches
who were trying to get to the rear of the detachment. He sent
word to the lieutenant, inducing him to fall back, although
already engaged with an ambush of Cochise's followers in
front. Cushing's little group was now surrounded, and though
they fought for half an hour they were greatly outnumbered,
and were all killed.

"There is not a hostile tribe in Arizona or New Mexico,"
wrote Sylvester Maury in a letter to the New York *Herald,*
"that will not celebrate the killing of Cushing as a great
triumph. He was a beau sabreur, an unrelenting fighter; and
although the Indians have got him at last, he sent before him
a long procession of them to open his path to the undis-
covered country. . . . He has left behind him in Arizona a
name that will not die in this generation."

The letter was published on May 15, and it was this that
William Cushing had seen on the way to the horse car, reading the terrible news in the bright morning light. He had hurried to Boston and told his mother, who was prostrated by the
news, and then walked out into the street to wander for an
hour, hardly able to see through his tears, until he noticed his
cousin's bank and entered. He stayed there all the morning
while his wife was sent for to be with his mother, and
toward noon got back enough of his strength to call for some
paper and a pen. He wished, he said, to write to Milton.

"My only and very dear brother: With a heart full of agony
I write to you of our terrible misfortune. Dear, brave Howie is
no more. I saw the news in the paper at 8 a.m. in the country
this morning, and hastened in to break the news to Mother.
Poor, dear little Ma! Her heart is almost broken. Oh! *dear*
old fellow—we are left alone now—the last of four; and let
us swear to stand by each other and our noble Mother in all

things. Let our old boyhood vows come back with full force and meaning, and let us cling together in truest and most unselfish love and friendship. I long for you, *dear* brother—for a clasp of your true, honest hand, and the comfort of one glance into your eyes. How much it would comfort Mother to see you before you go! [Milton had been ordered to the Pacific squadron.] Tomorrow I take her with me into the Country where we are living. I am in delightful quarters, and shall take good care of little Ma. God bless her! Kate is like a real daughter to her; and I thank Heaven that she was not alone.

"*Dear* old fellow—we must be doubly loving and attentive to little Ma now. Write often to her. One thing is certain of her Sons; they can not be beaten. You can kill but not conquer them. A beautiful tribute was paid to Lon by the General of his brigade at the great Army of the Potomac meeting here. He described his wonderful, superhuman bravery. How he demanded—white with loss of blood—to go again to the front. The General said, 'You have done all that mortal can do; attend now to your wounds.' Lon answered, 'No, I will fall by my guns.' He selected Allie as the only one to especially eulogize, God bless the brave boys! I can almost see their meeting—the handclasp of two who gave up life for duty; and Father joined by his noble Sons, proudly and tenderly embracing them.

"God bless you, dear brother! Don't lose love for me. We are alone now. My tears are falling so that I can scarcely see. Good bye. With all his heart your loving brother, Will."

Cushing's health did not survive this blow, and he suffered a breakdown at the end of May from which he did not recover until the middle of the summer. The symptoms were ill defined, but what started as a cold probably developed into pneumonia. (He had always had terrible colds, but this was the first one that had overwhelmed him during the warm months of the year). He was patiently and lovingly nursed by

his wife, and was back at work too soon, she felt; but he
insisted, though he did not tell her that it was necessary for
him to be busy, and that he was now unable to be too much
alone with the memories which thronged around him. At the
age of twenty-nine he had given up hope for the future,
though he still, with a hint of the old tenacity, longed for
promotion and possible action. At home he would sit and look
at the pictures of his dead brothers and his dead father and
then look across at his mother, her hair entirely gray, nodding
in her chair, and then rise and limp across the room to finger
the torpedo with which he had wrought such destruction on
his enemies. By the end of the summer he felt better, but when
the cold November days came down on Boston he was sick
again, with a cold that he could not shake off, and a cough
that racked his body, now painfully thin (though he still stood
as straight as a ramrod). On the first of December a daughter
was born; she was named Marie Louise, and she made him
cheerful when he could forget the pain that almost constantly
stalked him. Another source of satisfaction was his promotion,
on January 31, 1872, to the rank of commander; he thus became the youngest of that rank in the navy. Two weeks later
he was detached to await orders; in fact the climate of Boston
was too rigorous, the navy realized, and Cushing went south
to Washington to try to discover a station that would be more
agreeable to the state of his health; he settled on Pensacola,
and applied for a position in the navy yard there, but the
department was slow to act, and he spent the rest of the
winter in Washington and Norfolk, and was again in Fredonia
in the spring. The weeks stretched into months, and no word
came; he spent the summer seeing doctors. None of them
could make a diagnosis. The term "sciatica" was used in that
day without regard to cause for any inflammation of the sciatic
nerve, or indeed any pain in the region of the hip. Cushing
may have had a ruptured intervertebral disc—he had suffered
enough shocks to dislocate half a dozen, and with the passage
of time it would come to bear more and more heavily upon

the nerve; on the other hand he may have been suffering from tuberculosis of the hip bone, or cancer of the prostate gland. In any case there was nothing anybody could do, and he continued to suffer. In the fall he had another breakdown, and though he hoped and expected to go to Pensacola in January, and even packed his gear and sent ahead for housing for his family, it was clearly impossible, and the orders were canceled. He remained in Fredonia through the winter, spending much of the time reading the voluminous histories of the war which were already being published. "Kate could not be more perfect," he wrote to Milton; "she is never impatient with me, though I am sometimes impatient with her, but that is because I have nothing to do, and I sit around the house all the day and swear at 'dull time.' "

He had given up hope of another sea command, but early in June, 1873, came the offer to take command of the U.S.S. *Wyoming*, then in the Caribbean station. Kate read the letter first, he remembered, and handed it to him with her cheeks strangely pale, but he overruled her objections, despite the fact that she was again pregnant, and she was amazed at the rejuvenation the news brought about in him, and almost wished that the Navy Department had seen fit to administer such a cure before. A momentary setback occurred on June 21, when the order was suspended, but it was only an administrative delay, and a week later Cushing set out for his new assignment, jaunty again, and smiling (he did not tell Kate that his hip was nearly as bad as ever), leaving his wife and child to be cared for by (and to care for) his mother in a new house he had bought for them. It was not the first time, he thought, that he had left Fredonia on this twelve o'clock train that would take him, puffing steadily across the country, to the open sea that he had loved for so long, but it was almost the best. He arrived in Hampton Roads to find the *Wyoming* waiting. She was a third-rated steamer of six guns and 997 tons—not the grandest ship in the navy, but she would do. It was not until the middle of August that she was ready for an extended cruise, and Cushing spent the time impatiently in Washington and Norfolk. On August 16 the repairs were complete; a day or so was spent in filling out his crew, and then the ship steamed out of the yard into the Roads. On the 21st she was at sea, under a full head of canvas (the navy was still economical about coal).

The *Wyoming* touched at Bermuda and arrived, on September 9, at Kingston, Jamaica; after ten days' shore leave she set sail for Aspinwall, on the Isthmus of Panama, Cushing having received orders to remain there until relieved. A civil war had broken out, and the government was interestd in seeing that the isthmian railroad was not damaged in the fighting, since it was now an essential link in the travel route from the East to the West Coast. After dark on September 23 the vessel anchored off Aspinwall, and the American consul quickly came on board. The situation on shore was explosive, he said; he advised that preparations be made for any emergency. Will Cushing knew exactly what to do in an emergency, and he put his crew, most of whom were peacetime sailors who had never seen action, through its paces. Daily drill was instituted to bring the organizations—the howitzer crew, the landing crews, the gun crews—to a high pitch of efficiency. The untried men fell to with a will (they were not unaware what sort of man their commander was), and within a week Cushing was able to note with satisfaction that all his small boats could be launched and landing parties sent away within sixteen minutes after an alert. One thing gnawed at his heart: he would not, he knew, be in one of the boats if the emergency came.

It did not come, and Cushing, his health somewhat improved by the soft sea air of the Caribbean and by the excitement of possible action, was as impatient as he had ever been. On November 8 he overhauled a suspicious-looking vessel and found her to have improper papers, but that was hardly the sort of thing that would satisfy him. But a few days later his chance came. He received, within a day and a half, several

urgent telegrams from the United States consul at Santiago.
The worried official demanded the protection of a United
States warship; American lives, he said, were in danger.
Cushing, who was not so willing to disobey a direct order as
he once had been, asked for more information. The situation,
it seemed, was complicated. The Cubans, not to be outdone by
the Panamanians, were having a revolution too; it had been
going on for five years, during which time the insurgents had
tried vainly to expel the Spanish armies on the island. In 1870
the rebels had purchased an American steamer, the *Virginius*.
The vessel was used to transport irregular troops until the fall
of 1873; late in October, she left Kingston with a load of war
material as well as many passengers who intended to fight
for Cuban freedom. She was sighted by a Spanish man-of-war,
the *Tornado*, to which she had to surrender. Her captors
refused to believe that she was a neutral vessel and took her to
the harbor of Santiago, where a quick court-martial con-
demned most of her passengers to death. Between November
4 and 13 fifty-three passengers and crew were executed,
among them many Englishmen and eight Americans. As soon
as he heard this tale Cushing weighed anchor (the navy later
approved his decision) and sighted land near Santiago on the
16th, after a brief stop at Kingston in which he checked the
papers on file concerning the *Virginius* and established, to his
own satisfaction, that she was engaged in no treacherous
activity and had a right to fly the American flag.

The battery was loaded, the men were at quarters and
every precaution was taken as the ship steamed into the harbor,
but the Spanish pilots came out to meet the vessel, and guided
her through the narrow channel under the guns of Morro
Castle. Immediately after the *Wyoming* reached its anchorage
an officer came on board from the British man-of-war *Niobe*.
This vessel, commanded by Captain Lambton Lorraine, had
arrived on November 7, but Lorraine's protests to the Spanish
commandant had been unavailing, and more British subjects
had been executed since his arrival. Within an hour Vice
Consul Schmitt was also aboard. He looked harassed and un-

happy, and it was easy to believe his statement that he was overjoyed to see Commander Cushing. His earlier remonstrances to the authorities had been ignored ("Schmitt's Protests Like Water On A Duck's Back," read the headline in the New York *Herald*), and he was afraid of what might happen to the rest of the *Virginius'* crew. Cushing was genuinely indignant, and dashed off a letter: the *Virginius*, "if offending at all, was simply a neutral vessel carrying contraband of war," and was not a "pirate." He closed thus: "I question the summary trial, conviction, and execution of the captain of the *Virginius* [Joseph Fry, an American] and all the citizens of the United States who belonged to his crew. In the eye of the nations of the earth and their well-defined laws . . . such trial and execution is simply murder. I request your excellency earnestly to cease these executions, which must lead to most serious complication." He sent off the message, and wrote a report to the Secretary of the Navy, assuring him coolly that "I do not think any more of the *Virginius'* crew will be executed at present. . . ."

In order to make sure Cushing decided that a personal interview with the Spanish General Burriel was necessary. When he was met with an evasive answer, he had the *Wyoming* cleared for action, hung chains over her side to protect her boilers and other vital spots, rigged boarding nets and trained her guns on the nearest Spanish warships: "If I do not see General Burriel by the day after tomorrow, and if any more prisoners are executed, I shall open fire on the Governor's palace." He was granted the interview; "Albemarle" Cushing was not unknown in Spain. He went ashore with his executive officer, Lieutenant Hutchins. General Burriel advanced to meet him with outstretched hand, but Cushing kept his own hand tightly held behind his back. The Spaniard was ill at ease. He kept glancing furtively away, Lieutenant Hutchins said, fidgeting nervously and shaking his right leg; he wished assurances that the *Wyoming* would keep the peace. "Have I *your* assurance that no more prisoners will be executed?" asked Commander Cushing calmly. The general was not disposed to answer. "In that case, sir, I must request that all the women and children be removed from the city. I would not harm them." The general coughed. In the end he promised that the killing would stop; he would not, he said unwillingly, even remove the prisoners from Santiago unless further orders came from Havana. "It was a grand sight." Lieutenant Hutchins said, "when he stood up and looked 'The Butcher' down."

The next day, Schmitt reported, the captains of the Spanish gunboats were called to a council of war. The prisoners were a decided nuisance; could any way be found to take them to Havana? The captains, knowing "Albemarle" Cushing's reputation, were not anxious to undertake the task. Only one of them offered to undergo the risk, and that only on condition that some way be found to give him a good head start on the *Wyoming*. Burriel was angry but could see no way out of the difficulty, and left for Havana, ostensibly for consultations. (Foreign residents in the island's capital announced happily that he was afraid of Cushing.) Cushing made a trip to the spot on the outskirts of Santiago where the men had died; he was greatly affected by the plain bullet-scarred wall, and the common grave into which the bodies had been thrown. "Spain will be driven from the West Indies," he said; "the shots which killed the passengers and crew of the *Virginius* have sounded the death knell of Spanish power in the Western Hemisphere." It would be twenty-five years before the prediction would come true. In the meantime he occupied himself with plans to free the prisoners who remained alive. The *Wyoming* was close in to the city; he could shift her position so as to command the main street without arousing undue suspicion; the Governor's palace could be surrounded by a landing party; with the center of command thus neutralized, another party, armed with a spare topgallant mast for a battering ram, could break the prisoners out of their jail; the men would wear white armbands to be able to recognize each other in the darkness.

It was a fine plan, and would perhaps have worked, but it

would have meant war. Though Dan Sickles, American minister to Spain and ex-army general, was nothing loath, Hamilton Fish, the Secretary of State, did not approve of the idea (there had been enough war in his lifetime), and President Castelar of the short-lived republic then ruling Spain was fully in agreement, and was desirous only of extricating himself from an extremely dangerous international situation. In the end these calmer heads prevailed, though the New York *Herald* was mightily displeased: "And the American people are the pigmies," the editorial shouted, "who are thus metaphorically slapped in the face by the mighty Spaniard. How long shall they thus try our patience? How long shall we permit this one people of the earth, that is utterly contemptible in every respect, to play the Hector in our neighborhood?"

"For God's sake hurry on to Santiago de Cuba," telegraphed Secretary of the Navy Robeson to Cushing's senior in rank, Commander D. L. Braine, a Civil War comrade-in-arms of Cushing stationed in the New York Navy Yard. "We are afraid that Cushing will do something." On November 26 Braine steamed in the *Juniata* into the harbor, and took matters out of the younger officer's hands. Three days later an agreement was signed between the two governments which salved diplomatic consciences if not the tempers of individual citizens. Cushing's particularly—he did not have much faith in diplomacy. A French man-of-war entered the harbor and asked an interview with the authorities; it was refused, and her commander complained to Commander Cushing. "Bombard the place or go back to Martinique," was Will's simple solution. "I will let you do the bombarding, and I will return to Martinique," replied the Frenchman, and left the same day.

The affair was badly handled by the American press, which was not aware of the part Cushing had played. It seemed to them that Captain Lorraine deserved all the credit, and the citizens of Virginia City, Nevada, sent him a brick of solid silver with the inscription "Blood is thicker than water." In line with the feeling of the country a resolution was adopted in the House of Representatives tendering to the British captain the thanks of Congress. A Congressional committee looked into the matter, in order to pass on this resolution; after sifting the evidence it declared that while Lorraine had gotten to Santiago first, there was no evidence that he had interceded for the American citizens involved in any but the most general terms, and that even these had not been effective. If anyone was to be commended, the Committee concluded, it was Cushing. He "did his duty completely and gallantly in asserting the rights of the American government and its citizens," it reported, "and upholding the honor of the American flag."

The *Wyoming* spent the rest of the winter in squadron exercises. Twice her boilers broke down, and in April she was ordered to Norfolk for extensive repairs; on April 24 Cushing was detached and put on a waiting list for reassignment. He evidently believed that he would be given the *Wyoming* again when she was ready for duty, but in fact he had been ill most of the winter—the climate of the Caribbean had not been after all any more salutary than that of Boston—and the navy was not willing to entrust another ship to him. He went to Fredonia early in May to see his new daughter, Katherine Abell, who had been born the previous October. His wife was shocked by the change in his appearance. His eyes were sunk deep in his head, and the mustache that he had worn now for several years only made his face look thinner. He looked, Kate told Mrs. Cushing, like a man of sixty instead of thirty-one. The pain in his back was almost constant and, probably because of it, his friends felt that he had become irritable and short tempered. (They did not know the reason and were irritated in turn.)

Instead of a ship he was given the post of executive officer of the Washington Navy Yard. After a stay of a few days in Fredonia he went to Washington to prepare a home for his family. He rented a house and furnished it on his own, and as a surprise for Kate and the children he had dinner waiting on the table when they came. He spent the summer of 1874 pretending that he was happy in his inactive role; he played with the children and enjoyed listening to their "prattle." On August 25 he was made senior aide at the yard; in the fall he amused himself by taking an active interest in the upcoming Congressional elections. He had had a sporadic concern with politics since his days as a page boy, but the scandals of the Grant administration were almost turning him, he had to admit, into a Democrat. He was particularly displeased with Grant's Secretary of the Navy, George Robeson, whom he thought a poor replacement for his old friend Gideon Welles. He wrote Milton in November that "I am on no side at all," and wished success in the Presidential election of '76 to the party which would have the courage to face the new issues which had grown up since the war.

On Thanksgiving Day Will, Kate and his mother, who had arrived early in the fall for an extended visit, went to church in the morning. After they were settled they were surprised to see the President come in and sit down only a few pews away. Coming in late he distracted Will's attention, and the naval officer took the occasion to study the President at close range. Grant, feeling the eyes upon him, turned and looked quizzically at his observer for a few seconds as if trying to recall who the tall officer might be, but turned away without, evidently, having recognized him. The President's neck was thick and his cheeks puffed out, Will thought; he was not impressed by his commander in chief; was it possible that this was the man who was the great hero of the war? After church the trio went sightseeing in Washington for the sake of Mrs. Cushing; they spent the afternoon at the Corcoran Gallery of Art, where Cushing had never been, and he marveled at the fine works on display. Late in the afternoon they drove home, in a cold, slanting rain, to Thanksgiving dinner. That night the pain in his back was worse than it had ever been, and he could not sleep. The following Monday he dragged himself to the navy yard over his wife's protests. She sent to Lieutenant Hutchins, once of the *Wyoming* and now Cushing's aide, to see his superior home, "for he cannot last the day." Hutchins, like his colleagues at the yard, was surprised at the message. "I was with Cushing the last day that he was on duty," he wrote. "Mrs. Cushing was very much worried about him, and on his last day asked me to get him to come home. I did not realize how sick a man he was.

"He was a devoted husband and father. He loved his wife to adoration. I never knew a man so considerate of other people's feelings."

Lieutenant Hutchins remembered other of Cushing's traits. "I was on the Asiatic Station when Cushing was there and saw a good deal of him," he wrote, "and I was his navigator on the *Wyoming*. We were in the habit of calling him 'Albemarle Cushing.' Rowan, later vice-admiral, reported that the *Albemarle* had paralyzed our fleet in the sounds. Cushing sunk her with a torpedo boat of his own design—best in those days— crude in this.

"Of course, Cushing had his enemies; some from fancied ill-treatment, others from failure to understand his character, and last, but not least, enemies who were jealous of his success. He was the only junior officer that has ever received the thanks of Congress. Cushing was the soul of honor and abstemiousness to a marked degree, at all times. Nothing would give me more pleasure than to reply to all of his critics during the time that I knew him."

Cushing remained at the yard until nightfall, but went to bed when he reached his own house, and did not rise from it again. The pain was constant and terrible, and he was given injections of morphine, but they only dulled, and did not kill, his agony.

Junior officer Beardslee, a close friend and neighbor, later a rear admiral, dropped in every day to see his dying colleague. "I was not with Cushing when he died," he wrote, "but, as a near friend and nearest neighbor, was with him and his family during the greater portion of the short time in which his fatal malady apparently began, developed and ended.

"It was pitiable to see the bright young mind drift rapidly away in delirium, but I can say that through his disconnected talk and ravings there never was once to my knowledge a profane or immodest word or act, and the principal burden of his thoughts seemed to be the anger and disgust he had for conduct on the part of others which he deemed dishonorable. Cushing was a Christian hero, and only the bright episodes of his life should be placed before the world." No doubt Admiral Beardslee is correct; in any case any immoderation in Cushing's last days is not recorded. On December 8 it became impossible to care for him at home, and he was moved to the Government Hospital for the Insane. His wife and his mother visited him often, but he seldom recognized them as his life flickered away. On the 17th, early in the afternoon, he regained consciousness and reached out for his mother's hand. "Our Father who art in heaven," she began, and he repeated the words after her; "Hallowed be thy name." He closed his eyes with the amen, and lay quietly without moving. Kate rose from her knees and leaned over her husband, then put her hand on his chest, but she could not feel his heart beating. Mrs. Cushing was calm. Death was not a stranger to her.

The Secretary of the Navy had the sad duty of announcing Cushing's death to the nation, and the country's press recalled his deeds and heroism in editorials and obituaries across the land. The funeral procession started the next Sunday from the commandant's quarters in the navy yard at two in the afternoon. After the service the casket was escorted by three companies of the District of Columbia National Guard and a battalion of marines to a vault in the Congressional Cemetery, where it remained until arrangement could be made for burial at the Naval Academy. The interment took place on January 8, 1875, at Bluff Point, Naval Academy Cemetery. The grave is marked by a large monumental casket in marble, on which are raised in relief Cushing's hat, coat and sword. Along one side of the stone is cut the word ALBEMARLE, along the other the words FORT FISHER. Within two or three paces are the graves of Charles Flusser, killed in the first battle of the *Albemarle*, and Samuel Preston, killed at Cushing's side in the assault on Fort Fisher. In Memorial Hall, at the Academy, is a portrait of "Lt. W. B. Cushing" by Robert Hinckley. It shows Will in a nautical pose, sextant in hand and in full uniform. Most of the other portraits in Memorial Hall are of admirals.

In Fredonia's Forest Hill Cemetery Katherine Cushing had a monument erected to the memory of her husband and his three brothers. CUSHING is cut into the base of the stele, and above it, on four sides, are the brothers' names and dates.

Milton Cushing died on January 1, 1886, still in his forties. He had been invalided out of the navy, and spent the last year of his life in Dunkirk, three miles from his old home. His mother was with him at the end, and saw the last of her sons buried, dying herself five years later at the age of eighty-five. "My boys were all fearless," she had the satisfaction of saying before she died, "but Will was particularly daring: impatient of restraint but easily governed through his affections; very truthful, loving and sympathetic; quick to feel and prompt to act."

Kate Cushing had a strong constitution. She did not remarry, and brought up her daughters well, never letting them forget the memory of their father, as she herself did not forget him. In January, 1910, thirty-five years after his death, she wrote to a biographer in response to his queries about her husband:

"I met Mr. Cushing for the first time in the late spring of 1867—a few months before I acted as bridesmaid at his sister's wedding.

"Mr. Cushing was tall, slender, and very erect. His movements were easy and graceful, at the same time indicating force and strength. His head was well poised, his look clear, direct, and steady. His features were regular and clear cut, with a fascinating expression about the mouth when he smiled which attracted one's attention to that feature. His hair was of a medium brown, soft, fine, dark, and straight, without a suggestion of curl. His rather delicate mustache was of a lighter brown, suggestive of golden lights, never of reddish tints.

"His animation and enthusiasm in conversation lent a glow to his light, blue-gray eyes that made them seem dark. His brilliant mind was expressed in choice and facile diction—he was a fluent and charming writer. All his impulses were fine, noble. He was generous to a fault, tender and affectionate, and exemplified the sentiment,

> The bravest are the tenderest;
> The loving are the daring.

"What he achieved and lived through in the Civil War, the perilous tasks he assumed and accomplished for his country in her greatest danger, form a background from which his figure stands out in vivid relief. It beams with his indomitable courage and is gilded with his heroic character.

"I have often heard Mr. Cushing speak of his brother Alonzo, who was two years his senior and two inches taller. My husband was exactly six feet without shoes. They were as intimate and devoted as girls, and quite the opposite in manner and speech, I should say.

"Alonzo and Howard I never saw, but the picture of the former stands out in my mind as a tall, gentle, dark-haired, reticent man (he was only twenty-two when he died), as against the younger, more lively and more impressionable brother.

"Alonzo died at Gettysburg in '63, long before I knew the family. Howard was killed by the Apaches after I was married. I well remember what a shock it was to my husband, and how he grieved for him, and tried to comfort his mother, obtaining all possible details of his brilliant service and lamentable death in Arizona through correspondence with the commanding general and officers, and with the War Department in Washington."

In February, 1876, a year after Cushing died and only two years before Welles himself died, Mr. E. P. Dorr of Buffalo wrote a letter to the former Secretary of the Navy asking him for information about Cushing's life. "I am glad to learn you are preparing a letter for the Historical Society of Buffalo on the services of the late Lieut. Wm. B. Cushing," Welles answered. "You ask me to send such reminiscence as I may call to mind of that young hero which are not matters of record. His brief, adventurous and heroic achievements furnish some of the brightest pages in our naval annals, and my recollections of him are identified with them. Many who knew him not personally, and some who did, fail to appreciate his extraordinary traits of character, and impute his acts of heroic daring to wild and inconsiderate recklessness, but there was in his dashing exploits, not only audacity and intrepid courage, but wonderful sagacity and prudence. Projects which most persons deemed wild and inconsiderate will be found on investigation to have been deliberate and well planned designs, and the results, whether in overcoming or putting to flight superior numbers, naval and military, in lower Virginia, hazardous enterprises in the sounds and rivers of North Carolina, or in the destruction of the ironclad steamer *Albemarle*, demonstrate the wisdom and intelligence which prompted, no less than the courage of the young officer in every instance."

Welles recounts the story of Cushing's dismissal from the Academy, his reinstatement, and adds that "The reports and anticipations of Commodore Stringham, under whom he first served, were scarcely more favorable" than those of his Academy superiors. "The truth was," Welles says, "with his exuberant spirit he had too little to do; his restless, active mind was filled with adventure and zeal to accomplish something that would do himself credit and the country service.

"Your paper will, if I understand you, make mention of his bold, skillful and successful exploits, most of which will be found in his own reports, and the reports of his superior officers. I need not, therefore, allude to them further than to say, they were unsurpassed, I think unequaled in number, conception, plan, and courageous execution by those of any officer under our government. Our navy was filled with brave men, ready to do or die, but the youthful Cushing was personally without a rival in prolific schemes, important in their results, and in the hazardous and daring execution of which he always chose to lead. The very audacity of many of his suggestions startled and astounded those to whom they were communicated, but when accepted and accomplished, they extorted admiration.

"The official reports of his exploits are interesting, but a narrative of the details, would they be told, would be found to equal those of wild romance.

"Possessing the happy faculty of magnetizing and inspiring others, he never failed to procure an abundance of volunteers for his most hazardous expeditions. Foremost in all danger, his men were ever ready to follow, relying on his ready tact, courage, and ability. Nowithstanding his juvenile looks and manner, their confidence in him was unlimited.

"In the spring and summer of 1864 great anxiety was felt in relation to affairs on the coast and in the sounds of North Carolina. Most of the troops had been withdrawn for service elsewhere, leaving but a feeble force to retain and occupy the places in our possession. The fleet which had co-operated with the army was composed, necessarily, of light-draft vessels, for such only could enter and navigate the sounds. These seemed at the mercy of the *Albemarle*, a formidable ironclad steamer, which had been built on the upper waters of the Roanoke for their destruction. Though this powerful craft had been bravely met, and to some extent injured by our unarmored vessels, several had been sunk or disabled by her, and others remained in constant apprehension of the reappearance of their formidable antagonist.

"While the government, and especially the Navy Department, were in extreme solicitude for the welfare and safety of the force, naval and military, in that quarter, young Cushing was permitted, in July, to come to Washington and submit a proposition by which, if the Department approved, he would destroy the *Albemarle*. He was at that time only twenty-one years of age, with a youthful, almost boyish look and appearance, such as would have prevented his proposition from being entertained but for the ability he had exhibited on repeated occasions, and the reputation he had already acquired for daring and successful achievements. In fact, he came to me fresh from the execution of a remarkably bold and hazardous reconnaissance of the harbor and entrance of Wilmington. His earnestness, undoubted courage and the skill and judgment exhibited on repeated occasions inspired me with confidence in him and his project, notwithstanding his youth.

"I therefore gave him confidential orders to proceed to New York and report to Admiral Gregory, who on the 7th of August was instructed to 'fit out as early as practicable two of the picket boats for Lieut. Wm. B. Cushing.' The boats were furnished him, with torpedoes prepared by Chief Engineer Wood. With one of them he reached the sounds of North Carolina, proceeded up the river and sunk the *Albemarle* at the wharf where she was trebly guarded.

"This bold and unexampled exploit, be it remembered, was planned and executed by this young officer without adventitious aid or previous training. The government had, at that time, no torpedo stations, had not expended millions in experiments and in training its officers for torpedo service. Unsuccessful attempts, and in different ways, had been previously made to do a work which this young officer alone devised and accomplished.

"It has not been my purpose, nor does it seem the object of your enquiry, that I should specify or detail the adventures of Cushing. Circumstances connected with his entrance into the service and some of his intercourse with the Department that are not generally known, but which develop his traits, are mentioned. I may add that the great chief of the American Navy, Farragut, who was endowed with like heroism, and for whom *alone*, the office of admiral was created and its honors intended, said to me that while no navy had braver or better officers than ours, young Cushing was the hero of the War."

INDEX

Map of
THE EASTERN STATES
in
THE CIVIL WAR